8 Ball Chicks

A YEAR IN THE VIOLENT WORLD
OF GIRL GANGSTERS

8 Ball Chicks

Gini Sikes

ANCHOR BOOKS
DOUBLEDAY
NEW YORK   LONDON   TORONTO   SYDNEY   AUCKLAND

AN ANCHOR BOOK
PUBLISHED BY DOUBLEDAY
a division of Bantam Doubleday Dell Publishing Group, Inc.
1540 Broadway, New York, New York 10036

ANCHOR BOOKS, DOUBLEDAY, and the portrayal of an anchor are
trademarks of Doubleday, a division of Bantam Doubleday Dell
Publishing Group, Inc.

Book design by Brian Mulligan

Grateful acknowledgment is made to the following for permission to quote from
copyrighted material:

Lyrics from "If That's Your Boyfriend (He Wasn't Last Night)" by Me'shell Ndegeocello.
Copyright © 1993 Warner-Tamerlane Publishing Corp., Nomad Noman Music, and Revolutionary
Jazzy Giant. All Rights administered by Warner-Tamerlane Publishing Corp. All Rights Reserved.
Used by permission. Warner Bros. Publications U.S. Inc., Miami, FL 33014.

Lyrics from "KKK Bitch" by Ernie Cunnigan and Tracey Marrow.
Copyright © 1992 Polygram International Publishing Inc., Ernkneesea Music and Rhyme
Sindicate Music. Used by permission.

Library of Congress Cataloging-in-Publication Data
Sikes, Gini.
8 ball chicks: a year in the violent world of girl gangsters / by Gini Sikes.
p.   cm.
1. Delinquent girls–United States   2. Gang members–United States.   3. Gangs–United
States.   4. Juvenile delinquency–United States.   I. Title.
HV9104.S54   1997
364.3'6'082–dc20   96–23949
CIP

ISBN 0-385-47431-8
Printed in the United States of America
First Anchor Books Edition: January 1997

3   5   7   9   10   8   6   4   2

For my mother and father,
who believed daughters could do anything,
and, of course, David.

Contents

PROLOGUE   ix

WHERE THE GIRLS ARE   xv

PART I: LOS ANGELES
    "TRUST NO BITCH"   1

PART II: SAN ANTONIO
    TEXAN ROULETTE   95

PART III: MILWAUKEE
    O.G.s AND WANNA-BES IN THE HEARTLAND   175

PART IV: L.A. REDUX   231

EPILOGUE   267

AFTERWORD   269

AUTHOR'S NOTE AND ACKNOWLEDGMENTS   273

Prologue

TJ had never killed anyone before, but then who knew for sure? Sticking a pump shotgun out of a moving car and blasting into a crowd—you could never really tell which bodies fell because of you, whose life you were accountable for, the debts you'd racked up. But tonight there would be no question. Tonight's payback belonged to TJ, to own like a medal. It would be a gift for Rosa and Danny.

A few nights ago TJ's homegirl Rosa and her little brother Danny were parked in front of a local liquor store when a carload of rival gang bangers pulled alongside her truck. One of them leveled the black muzzle of a sawed-off shotgun at the truck's window. The lone blast blew Danny's head off.

Tracking down the killer had been easy. Rosa knew the guy. TJ knew him too, could recognize him on sight. The enemy partied every time one of its members murdered someone in Lennox, so TJ just had one of the prettier Lennox girls make a few calls: "What's up?" "Where's everyone gonna kick it tonight?" "Who's gonna be there?"

TJ dressed for what was ahead: baggy black dickies, black flannel shirt, baseball cap pulled down to hide identifying features. If anyone spotted their car, the most he could say was he'd seen a guy in a Raiders cap with a measly mustache—a description that fit every other Chicano gang banger in L.A.

On the way to the party, Jorge drove and TJ rode shotgun as they cruised Hawthorne Boulevard, passing grocery stores, muffler shops displaying SE HABLA ESPAÑOL signs, X-rated video stores, then the intersection near the Lennox sheriff's station, Jorge waving defiantly as they passed. At 106th Street they crossed the border between turfs. Enemy territory. TJ scanned the side streets. The houses here looked no different from those in the Lennox hood, the same small single-story bungalows with sparse yards surrounded by flimsy wire fences that kept no one out but prevented ducks or roosters from wandering into traffic. Folks lived with the same deafening roar of planes landing at LAX, while their children took advantage of the noise to fire their guns without getting caught. TJ and Jorge watched a plane flying so low it looked as if it would take out the telephone poles. They could see the wheels, the headlights, the name of the airline on the side. Nothing was different here, except the lurid scrawling on walls that declared their rivals' reign, words that meant nothing to outsiders but triggered gut-wrenching rage in TJ.

No one in the car spoke. TJ was thankful for the silence, necessary to reach the place deep within where hatred burned. The flier soliciting donations for Danny's funeral, along with his photograph, was folded in the glove compartment, but TJ didn't need to look at it. Picturing the kid was easy: a big puppyish twelve-year-old, feet permanently fixed to a skateboard, too happy-go-lucky to die. Unlike most of the neighborhood kids, Danny stubbornly clung to childhood, refusing to give it up early.

Until three nights ago, when he took the bullet intended for Rosa. Or was it? When the gunman told Rosa, "This is for you" as he thrust the weapon inside her open window, maybe he knew she would suffer more watching him fire into her baby brother's head, seeing Danny's brains spray against the windshield. TJ glanced in the backseat. Rosa stared straight ahead, eyes focused on some distant unseen point. Feeling nausea well up, TJ turned back around and concentrated on the image of Danny's shattered body.

The Chevy Impala ducked down a side street. Cars jam-parked in front of the house, the blaring rap music—there might as well have been neon signs blinking SHOOT HERE. TJ wished they hadn't taken a white car, too easily spotted and remembered, and told Jorge to cut the lights, then reached beneath the seat, pulled out the gun, and cocked it.

Shit, they'd have to double-park. The Chevy crept forward until the passenger door was positioned between two parked cars. "Here," TJ ordered. "Stop."

And then TJ was outside, charging toward the front door, on automatic pilot. In the street-lit darkness of the yard, a guy nuzzled a girl, grabbing at her waist as she laughed and turned her face away. She caught sight of the dark figure rapidly approaching, her eyes running down from the cap to the loose black clothing to the glint of metal; in seconds she registered danger. Her boyfriend, feeling her stiffen, looked too. Instinctively they backed away, then ran.

TJ kept moving, fixed on the screen door. What if I trip? These stupid shoes are too big, TJ thought. What if the girls fucked up—what if he isn't here? But there he was, slouched in an overstuffed chair just inside the door, rolling a joint. The enemy didn't even glance up until TJ was inside the living room, willing the gun upward.

In the moment before it went off, TJ sensed the boy's panic. A familiar expression of dread and expectation crossed his face, a face so much like TJ's that each of them could have been staring into a mirror. The kid jerked himself up from the chair, spilling the bag of weed onto the carpet. TJ heard his sharp intake of breath.

Here's the payback from Lennox!

TJ wanted to say the words out loud but was scared they would crumble and everything would fall apart. In the end the gun spoke for itself. It sounded like someone slammed two pots together; the ringing made the room bizarrely quiet. TJ watched a pantomime of people gaping in shock at the figure writhing on the floor. Ears still ringing, TJ turned away and in a moment was back in the car.

"Go!" TJ screamed.

"Motherfucking *Lennox* style!" Jorge cried out.

"Was it him?" Rosa's voice was nearly a screech. "Was it him?"

"Fuck yeah." TJ's hands scrambled beneath the front seat, yanked out the purse, and, dumping out its contents, groped in the dark for the bottle of baby oil and a wad of Kleenex. Pouring oil on the tissue, TJ hurriedly wiped at the mustache in the rearview mirror until it melted into an oily brown mess. "Give me my shoes!" TJ leaned against the door, pulling off one baggy pant leg, then the other, then wrestled out of the flannel shirt. Rosa grabbed the clothes, shoving them under the backseat. Now dressed in tight blue jeans and a lacy white tank top, TJ snatched off the baseball cap, pulling away the elastic rubber band. Long chestnut curls cascaded down her back.

"Shotgun's shoes are too big for me," she said. "Next time we borrow some other homey's." But no one was listening. Jorge kept shouting, "Motherfucking Lennox style!"

They pulled up near TJ's house and she climbed out, the Chevy making a U-turn behind her. Not looking back, TJ started down the sidewalk, just another neighborhood girl on her way home from a party.

TJ told me the story of this shooting more than half a dozen times. I kept trying to trip her up on details because I had difficulty believing it. Gang members often distort the truth, making a claim to achievement or to a crime—often the same thing in their world—as a way of inflating their importance or solidifying as fact what they wish had happened. It was this last reason that I felt might motivate TJ to lie, if she were lying; in her self-mythologizing, she could envision herself an avenging angel—or demon—in order to make sense of Danny's death. Each version changed slightly in the retelling. And though I could corroborate certain details surrounding Danny's murder, one that I could not was whether TJ actually shot Danny's gunman or a convenient substitute.

The last time we discussed the shooting we met in a church near her mother's house, one of the neighborhood's few sanctuaries from gunfire. She showed up in high heels and a black suit, dressed for Sunday service, but the new outfit would double for her job. Nineteen years old, TJ worked part-time, illustrating children's books, creating scenes she herself never experienced of yellow-haired girls cradling rabbits on lawns with white picket fences. "I'm an all-American girl," she said and I noticed she'd bleached her dark hair golden blonde, "but the bad area I live in has corrupted my thinking."

Beneath her arm she carried a photo album. We sat in a pew, elbows touching, as she flipped through the pages. They held crushed flowers and typical teenage snapshots, except in some the kids cradled Mossberg 12-gauge shotguns; in others they clustered around open coffins. TJ pointed out an old boyfriend in one casket. Then she drew my attention to a single Polaroid of a Chicano boy crouched menacingly on all fours, staring defiantly at the camera. The clothes were just as she'd described: baggy black pants, flannel shirt, black baseball cap cockily pulled low. She'd disguised herself as a man more than once to commit crimes, usually for a car-jacking or a house burglary, but on that night three years ago she did her makeup so perfectly that she couldn't resist a commemorative picture. The transformation was flawless.

Yet as a female, TJ was invisible. Deputies at the sheriff's station did not consider her a threat. One dismissed her as a neighborhood whore. But then a lot of cops don't see gang girls as much of anything. In a world of second-class citizens, they remain third-class. At best they serve as mules to carry the weapons and drugs boys pass them during police searches; at worst they are sexual punching bags. Even the word "gang banging," ghetto slang for fights between rivals, evolved from an ugly street term for gang rape. When it came to women, most guys from TJ's gang were in rare agreement with the cops: a girl was important only as long as an important boy wanted her—a philosophy I once saw summed up in three words tattooed across the forehead of a male gangster: TRUST NO BITCH.

For TJ, disguising her sex was a cheap price to pay for power, even if it was power she could not advertise and rarely exercised. "I only told a few of my homegirls what I did—and the guys who were there, of course," she said conspiratorially. "You see, the thing about me is that I'm always very sneaky and I get away with a lot more crap. Men just run out and do things. They don't think before their actions. Women sit down and calculate and strategically plan everything before they do it. But"—she gave a casual toss of her hair—"it turned out I didn't kill that guy. Afterward he took off for Mexico. Occasionally, some of his gang would come round the hood, looking to blast the guy who shot him."

She flashed a smile. "Guess they'll never find him, huh?"

Where the Girls Are

The first girl gang I encountered was in my adopted hometown of New York, a city that, in 1992, most cops would tell you didn't have female gang members. Loosely structured, short-lived corner crews and "posses," yes, but they'd point out these don't adhere to initiation rites, behavior codes, or symbolic colors. Ignoring the cops' dismissal, I acted on a tip and arranged to meet NFL, or Nasty Fly Ladies, a posse of high school girls whose turf was around Delancey and Essex Street, a part of Manhattan's Lower East Side known to police for chain snatching and strong-arm robbery. When I caught up with them, hanging out near a subway exit, the four girls looked too childish to be in a gang. Slouched against a wall, hands plunged deep into pockets of trousers so baggy that the crotches reached almost to their knees, they affected an exaggerated cool that only seemed to underscore their innocence. I had a lot to learn about appearances.

A hefty Latina girl with her hair in a high topknot introduced herself as Carmen in a voice so soft it was almost a murmur. She nodded toward the others: Tiny, Isabel, and Happy. Tiny took in my brown wool coat and hat and a smirk crept across her face. We locked eyes for a second before she quickly looked away. I didn't fit in here and we both knew it.

Inside a local Burger King, Tiny sat across from me. The littlest of the lot at five feet tall, she wore droopy pants and an oversized windbreaker, making her appear even smaller. On our way over, she'd bobbed and weaved behind me, aping my walk. "Tiny—she's the comedian," Carmen explained. "Her mouth's always getting us into trouble."

At sixteen, Tiny was sweet-faced with baby-fat cheeks, pouty lips, and smooth olive skin, except for the angry purple crescent on her right cheek. Another scar sliced her laugh line. She turned to reveal yet another that snaked below her ear. "They say they'll go away in about a year," she said, but this seemed unlikely. During a fight she was winning, her opponent surprised Tiny by flicking a concealed razor blade from her mouth. Her face burning, Tiny at first thought the girl had slapped her, only harder than she'd ever been struck before. She didn't realize she'd been cut from the side of her nose to just below her right eye until the girl jabbed at her again. This time Tiny knew. She frantically felt for the wound, blood seeping between her fingers. Suddenly, in self-preservation, she grabbed the girl's neck and, blinded by her own blood, began smashing her rival's head into the concrete until Isabel, hearing a siren, dragged her away. The girl had slashed Tiny's face eleven times.

Carmen rolled her eyes. "Tiny provokes fights." She sounded like a disapproving mother, complaining about a toddler misbehaving at daycare.

Tiny fixed me with a cold stare that wiped away any earlier impression of childish cuteness. "See, we smaller girls, we go for your weak spot." Her gaze moved across my features. "Your face. Your throat. Your eyes, so we can blind you. I don't care if you have more weight on me. I'll still try to kill you because, you know, I have a bad temper—"

Her words broke off. Outside a gangly redheaded girl sauntered by, then stopped. She peered inside the window, grinning oddly, then grabbed her crotch and thrust out her tongue. Tiny smacked the glass with her palm. "I'm going outside!" She started to slide out of the booth, but Carmen blocked her. "Not now." Her tone was firm. "We're talking."

I asked whether Tiny recognized the girl, but she shook her head. "Let me break it down for you: round here it's all about respect. Because people will disrespect you. Call you a sucker. And if you don't punch them in the mouth and say, 'No, I'm not a sucker!' they gonna keep picking on you. Nowadays the fists don't work no more. You gotta have a knife or a hammer. Or a gun. 'Cause my homegirl got shot in the stomach. Lost her kidney."

Isabel listened, gently rocking her head. "See, we formed NFL to protect ourselves." She tucked her chin in slightly, as if she would rather swallow her words than say them, and watched the redhead's back retreat down the sidewalk. "Nobody's out there we can trust but ourselves. And we defend each other. Ain't nobody else gonna do it for us."

At times, though, the Nasty Fly Ladies ran with the Regs, a male gang from a nearby housing project. The girls were constantly on the lookout for "hos" and "hoochies" who wanted to sleep with their men—especially the Hill girls, named after a Lower East Side neighborhood.

It was a Hill girl who autographed Tiny's face. Tiny wouldn't submit to her boyfriend's demands to have sex in the park, so he found a four-teen-year-old Hill girl who would, inviting his friends to observe them surreptitiously. After Tiny learned about the outings, she attacked the Hill girl. "She was crying and begging, but she'd disrespected me in front of *everybody*. We started fighting and she pulled that blade out—" Tiny shrugged. "I just wasn't prepared. You can't tell when someone's got a razor in their mouth. Anyway, I didn't have no Vaseline."

Sensing my confusion, Carmen spelled things out. "First thing you do if you know you're going to fight is pull your hair back and smear your face with Vaseline. That way your enemy can't scratch you."

How does one learn to carry a razor blade in one's mouth?

Happy, a stunning full-lipped Puerto Rican girl who had busied her-self biting the skin around her cuticles, suddenly came to life. "First time I saw a girl put a razor in her mouth, she was flipping it around with her tongue, not getting cut. I thought"—she placed one hand on her hip, languidly waving the other in a caricatured feminine gesture—" 'Oooh, that's for me!' So I got me a brand-new razor, put it in the side of my mouth and cut myself." She giggled. "A lot of blood! I waited for it to stop, cleaned the razor, and stuck it back in. 'Damn! Cut myself again!' I kept putting it in until, after a while, I got used to it." She returned to her cuticles.

I couldn't help wondering why Tiny directed her anger toward the Hill girl and not her ex-boyfriend. After all, no one forced him to go with this girl. My ignorance dumbfounded Carmen. "Round here, if you flaunt yourself in front of a guy, a guy's gonna take you!" she snapped. "His girl's gonna have to kick your ass to keep you away from her man."

"Round here," said Tiny, "pussy's pussy, no matter what. Pussy don't have a face."

Still NFL prided themselves on fighting guys as well as girls. Carmen fired up to provide an example. "One time the guys we were chillin' with tried to catch a herb." A "herb" means a victim, slang from an old

Burger King commercial featuring a frail milquetoast character named Herb, who became a symbol for an easy white mark. "And Isabel was looking for a herbette, but couldn't find nobody. So when her boyfriend and all his homeboys jump this herb, she's trying to jump him, too. She goes up with a forty-ounce bottle and smashes him on the head. It goes *ba-ding!*"

"I guess I didn't hit him hard enough"—Isabel leaped in—"because it didn't break. He started screaming and then . . . he started blowing a *whistle!*" Isabel cracked up at the ridiculousness of this attempt to get help, her eyes welling with tears. "I was like, 'Man, make him eat it. Make him eat that whistle.'" I thought about friends on the Upper West Side who wear whistles on key chains or around their necks.

Though minutes earlier the girls insisted they formed NFL only to protect themselves, they now gave in to adolescent swaggering, seeing themselves as urban bandits.

"If I see you coming down the street and I think you have money, I'll rob you," Tiny told me in lurching rapid-fire speech. "Out here we only go for Chinese or white people. They got money. I won't rob her"—she pointed to an elderly woman outside—"because she's old." The others nodded, silently agreeing with this moral code. "But I'll rob her"—Tiny poked Happy—"as fast as I'll rob you. It don't matter. We do it for fun. Sometimes to get high or to buy something to drink. If we go out dancing, we catch a herb first. We can have money in our pockets and we'll still do it."

"Do you ever feel sorry for any of the people you rob?" I asked.

Tiny looked puzzled. "No. Because . . . no."

This cavalier disdain for physical injury—their own as well as others'—was one of the hardest things for me to understand about gang girls. But acceptance of pain is a key to the terror they hold over their enemies. Tiny, a child with the energy of a small hydroelectric plant, had a huge advantage over the average middle-class citizen, who hasn't been in a fistfight since adolescence. Beaten by her mother, boyfriends, and other girls, Tiny would risk injury for a wallet or for fun with barely a thought.

Their explanation of the brutality in their lives possessed an eerie quality of inevitability. "Two years ago they shot my brother," Carmen revealed. "He was a big-time drug dealer. He was in his car on 16th

Street and they rolled up behind him. They just went *bang, bang*—six times in the head. That's when I got really violent."

As Carmen spoke, Tiny and Happy, who'd already heard this story, talked about Tiny's new boyfriend. But Isabel listened avidly to everything Carmen said, as if the two of them were in on the same secret. "They killed my boyfriend last December," Isabel now said solemnly. "We know it had to be more than one person, 'cause Steve would shoot you as much as look at you." For a brief moment, Isabel seemed to turn inward, staring at something only she could see. "But he never hurt me. His mother used to beat him, but he felt women shouldn't get hit. I guess because she used to get hit by his father."

Carmen leaned forward. "That's what I'm saying. My brother was very violent. You didn't have the money you owed, he'd put a knife in you and turn it both ways. He had no heart for anyone but his family. It was his business not to care."

I asked whether Carmen used drugs since her brother died. "You'd think I wouldn't, but I have. My family was all into drugs. When my mother used to get high on cocaine, little things would set her off. If I left dishes in the sink, she'd grab me and pound my brains out against it. She'd get so wild I thought she'd go overboard and kill me. You learn not to walk into your parents' scene when they're in there over the mirror. Or when your stepfather's shooting up in the bedroom."

Isabel shook her head. "They think because you're small you don't see. But you do."

Tiny jerked back into the conversation. "It's like the anger will kill you! Today I had a fight with my boyfriend and I pulled a knife on him. He tried to grab it and I sliced his hand. It doesn't matter when you have anger."

"We have gone crazy." Carmen looked down at her cigarette. There was a long, uncomfortable quiet. She crushed out the butt—she had smoked it all the way down to the filter—and toyed with the ashtray. When she glanced up, I gently asked her about their futures. To my surprise, they all eagerly contemplated the possibilities. When Carmen graduated—she was six months behind at a high school for business training—she hoped to study marketing at the Fashion Institute of Technology. Isabel, the girl who hit strangers with beer bottles, planned to be a nurse; she'd already enrolled at a junior college. Happy, only fifteen, intended to finish high school. Tiny thought she'd eventually study sociology or psychology. She went on to explain, "The violence, the robbing, all of this will stop when I find out I'm pregnant. Then I'll have something to live for. Right now it's just me and I'm taking care of myself. If I have a baby—" Tiny halted. Two men sneered through the window of the Burger King. "See what I mean? It never stops."

Their faces concealed behind dark glasses and hooded sweatshirts, the men swaggered toward the restaurant's entrance. The skinny redheaded girl who had taunted us earlier reappeared to join the men, along with another girl. Tiny spotted the redhead, yelling at Carmen, "Look! Man, you never listen to me!" The four entered together. The two girls hopped into a booth, but the men hovered around our table. Carmen and the others steadied themselves.

Finally Tiny addressed the intruders. "With all due respect, can you guys go?"

One of the men turned to his friend. "That scar-faced girl is cross-eyed."

Tiny heard him and hollered, "Crackhead-looking bum! Fucking faggot!"

The man leaned so close over the table that I caught the glimmer of a gold tooth in the back of his mouth. "I'll go home," he whispered, "get my gun, and when I come back, I'll blow you away."

The men returned to the redhead and her friend, who stared hard at our table. No one in Burger King noticed the exchange or at least no one was foolhardy enough to let on.

Happy and Isabel shifted nervously. Carmen slid over and put her arm around Tiny, but the girl drew away, gazing across the room in challenge. Through clenched teeth Isabel said, "Let's do something before it's done to us." She slumped lower in her seat. Not much, but noticeably. She asked Happy for a razor. I knew then they were not kidding.

Panic swelled in my own gut. I was worried about my bag, containing all my tapes and notes. I glanced out the window for a cab, but the streets were empty.

"Go on with your questions," Tiny ordered, not taking her eyes off the corner. I asked how having kids would change her life, startled by the strain I heard in my own voice. Would she move out of the neighborhood?

"No, I'd just ignore everybody. You roll your eyes at me, I'll keep walking. I won't fight over that because I have my child . . ." She noticed the girls at the other booth standing up. "Fuck you, too!"

Carmen started removing her rings, anticipating a brawl. "These are coming off. My mother's gold, know what I'm saying?"

I kept talking, believing if I acted as though nothing were happening, perhaps nothing would. I asked Tiny if she thought she would one day learn to ignore provocation, why not begin now?

" 'Cause we have nothing to live for, nothing to lose. When I'm with them"—she gestured to her friends—"I'm rowdy. But when I'm with my boyfriend, 'cause he has two sons, I'm calm." This was the same boyfriend she'd pulled a knife on earlier that day. "His sons come first. But right now I am going to ignore that table for your sake, 'cause if we fight, you will get hurt."

I suggested we leave. The girls said nothing, but Carmen seemed dour at this loss of face. Outside they kept checking to see whether the men were following. I wondered if I could drop them off anywhere. "Where we supposed to go?" Isabel asked before answering her own question. "Nowhere." Then I was in a cab, headed uptown, saved by a pack of teenagers. I turned to look back at them, but already they had vanished into the anonymous landscape of Delancey Street.

My interest in female violence had been triggered by the public's obsession with it. Throughout history the female criminal has been viewed as such an anomaly that many scientists and lawmakers of times past believed she suffered a severe biological defect. The cause of her sickness wasn't between her ears, however, but between her legs: "uterine irritability"—a quasimedical term for insanity—served as a viable legal defence up until the twentieth century. We continue to be fascinated by female crime, partly because people are curious about encountering the violent side of human behavior where we least expect it.

I met the Nasty Fly Ladies in June 1992 while researching a phenomenon *Time* dubbed "the summer of the formidable female" in a cover article about a trend in movies, such as *Thelma & Louise* and *Fatal Attraction*, that depicted beautiful female killers. A magazine commissioned me to find out whether there actually was an onslaught of female crime or if Hollywood had simply reversed a tried-and-true formula in search of new entertainment dollars.

Inside prisons on both coasts, I spoke with women convicted of homicide. The inmates were African American, white, and Latina; the oldest was a seventy-six-year-old grandmother with pop bottle glasses that obscured her eyes, the youngest twenty-four and as beautiful as a magazine cover girl. Yet their stories resonated remarkably the same. Unlike their glamorous fictional counterparts, these were terrified battered wives or girlfriends who, in one irreparable moment, could find no better solution than to shoot, stab, or otherwise maim their way out of their circumstances.

From the FBI and criminologists I learned that women accounted for only 12 to 15 percent of all homicides in the United States—a figure that has stayed the same for three decades. The bottom line: among all races, all classes, and in every corner of the globe, men are more violent than women. But a correctional officer at Sibyl Brand, the women's county jail in Los Angeles, told me if I wanted to find a segment of the female population where violence was increasing, I should look at teenage girls who belonged to gangs.

Uncovering reliable information on girl gang members, however, wasn't easy. In 1993 criminologist David Curry of the University of Missouri at St. Louis, attempting to verify an estimate that 10 percent of the approximately 650,000 gang members nationwide were female, polled seventy-nine law enforcement agencies around the country. Each jurisdiction varied greatly in how it defined a "gang member." Twenty-three of the largest police departments with reported gang problems didn't classify girls as gang members as a matter of policy. (Even as they failed to report statistics on female gang membership, police in Aurora, Colorado, attributed two drive-by shootings to girls.) Four other departments noted the existence of independent female gangs in their communities but kept no records of their activities. Some agencies relegated all females to "associate member" status of a male gang. On the surface, Curry's survey seemed to indicate a bias against acknowledging girls' activity in gangs.

Wanting to know more about those girls who bucked the stereotype, I interviewed social workers, cops, church leaders, and kids. The stories of gangs I heard overwhelmingly supported the notion that boys died more often than girls and took more thoughtless risks.

Girls had other problems. Many endured not just physical brutality in gangs, but also tended to be the primary victims of domestic violence, potentially even more devastating than the dangers of the street. Girls, who might become pregnant at thirteen and thrown out of their homes, encountered realities their male counterparts never had to face.

Angela, a teenage mother who desperately needed a home, accepted placement in a housing project teeming with rival gang members. One night a group of thirteen- and fourteen-year-old girls surrounded her while she carried her infant. After ordering her to put her baby on the ground, the teenagers set upon her, stabbing her with sharpened screwdrivers twenty times.

At fourteen Michelle ran away to join a gang after she became pregnant by her first boyfriend, a rookie cop, who raped her. At eighteen she was arrested for carrying a loaded gun and sent to jail, where she witnessed a group of women rape an inmate with a curling iron for crossing them in a drug deal.

I spoke to Daffney as she and her boyfriend lay in bed among a pile of shotguns, Mac 10s, and .25 automatics—a bed her boyfriend sometimes shared with Daffney's mother.

A girl named Ruby bore scars on her hands from the glass and cigarettes she used to slice and burn off gang tattoos so that she could apply for jobs. By the time she turned eighteen, Ruby had survived a bludgeoning with golf irons and had been riddled eighteen times by semiautomatic gunfire. She recalled lying abandoned in the street—her homeboys had run away—and the shock of hearing the air whistling jaggedly through the wounds in her chest with each breath. Despite this, when I asked what was the most pain she had endured in her short life, she answered without a moment's hesitation, "Giving birth to my daughter."

One day in L.A. a young woman came to the door of the Westwood apartment where I was staying. She was selling magazines as part of an exchange program between kids in South Central and Memphis, Tennessee, where she lived. South Central, of course, had long become notorious for its Crips and Bloods gangs. I asked her what the differences were between the two cities.

"Nothing," she told me. She said she belonged to a Memphis gang called the Lady Stones. Without prompting, the horrors poured out of her. "One of my friends has eight children and she's only twenty-four. She started having kids in elementary school. This other girl I know, she's sixteen. Her grandmother wouldn't let her have ten dollars, so she stabbed her to death. A Lady Stone, one of my friends, had a baby by her boyfriend who's in the military. He joined to get out of the gangs. She got hooked on crack after he left for the Gulf War. The day her boyfriend was coming back from Desert Storm, his little girl found a rock of cocaine on the coffee table—and babies are gonna pick up anything they can—and that baby swallowed it. Little girl's heart just burst. She died instantly. The boyfriend came home to that dead baby and beat the woman so bad she nearly died. That was his homecoming in my neighborhood." She grew silent. When she spoke again, she was talking to herself as though I were not there. "Just is no difference. It's the same everywhere."

BY now, I realized that female gang life possessed a scope and breadth that could not be squeezed neatly into a single magazine article. Each girl I met introduced me to others. Seeking a range of family backgrounds and personalities who could offer windows into a collective experience, I quickly learned that generalizations and stereotypes didn't work. Although most girls in gangs are poor and members of minorities—being cut off from mainstream society is among the reasons kids join gangs—I met white girls from middle-class homes who packed 9-millimeter semiautomatics. It's precisely the gang girls' similarity to other teenagers that makes their cruel behavior so haunting. They've contracted no disease or condition that sets them apart from the rest of the population. Not in a nation where some 2.3 million kids under eighteen are arrested each year.

There is no such thing as a typical gang. Each gang possesses a history that reflects the community where its members grow up, a city's most marginalized and despised teenagers struggling to adapt to a specific social environment. I wanted to focus on neighborhoods where gangs were entrenched and recognized publicly, at least in some small part, by local authorities. I chose L.A. to start with because it is the capital of gang warfare, where girls have achieved a notoriety greater than what I witnessed anywhere else. San Antonio came to my attention when a cop faxed me a shocking news story about girls playing Russian roulette with AIDS, submitting to a sexual gang initiation that allegedly involved sleeping with a teenager infected with HIV. I picked Milwaukee in my home state of Wisconsin because it seemed so far removed from the obvious locales known to have gang problems; if girl gangs also existed in a city of primarily Polish and German descent, they were clearly a phenomenon of national scope. In the end, all three cities, like many cities in America, had sizable immigrant and minority communities with persistent problems of segregation and racism.

Before I had actually met the girls, the prospect of entering their world frightened me. But once in their living rooms, hanging out on street corners, in the parks of housing projects, or cruising in a car, I never regretted my decision. It was true that some of the acts they had committed were undeniably vicious. But in time I would come to believe that most people can not be judged soley by their worst deed. They were not always easy to love. Hooking up with them could be frustrating, as many adhered to a loose Third World concept of time. Because they had no money, if an opportunity arose to make some, whether by a drug deal or hanging out with a friend who had just scored, I was forgotten. Yet with rare exceptions, these girls were playful, giving, and curious. They invited me into their kitchens for home-cooked meals, introduced me to their mothers, their children, and their boyfriends, and offered me makeup tips.

Like all teenagers, they ranged from the socially clueless to the articulate. Most, however, were startlingly insightful, speaking with a rhythm and dialect uniquely their own that poets would envy. They constantly surprised me. Urban troubadours, they knew they had a story to tell and wanted to get it out.

This is my attempt to tell their story.

PART I
Los Angeles

"Trust No Bitch"

My plane descended into Los Angeles one January morning in 1994, four days after a major earthquake. On the drive in from the airport, I passed highways cracked in two, churches ruptured off their foundations, car dealerships collapsed on top of Mercedes and BMWs, and crumbling houses with hand-scrawled signs hanging from shattered windows: APART- MENT DESPERATELY NEEDED.

Although the earthquake hit Northridge in the Valley, the epicenter of Los Angeles' social tremors was—and is—South Central. Here unrest has rumbled beneath the surface for years, finally erupting in April 1992, when the Rodney King verdict triggered the greatest civil disturbance in modern American history, ending with 59 deaths and nearly a billion dollars in property damage in one of L.A.'s poorest neighborhoods. In a city famous for having no seasons, residents now say there are four: floods, fires, earthquakes, and riots.

By 1994 there were other fault lines in the social landscape. A running turf battle between rival black and Latino gangs in the largely middle-class districts of Venice and Culver City left 17 people dead. In a big northern L.A. County jail racial riots broke out fifty-five times. Rumor had it one of the most powerful prison gangs, the Mexican Mafia, had spread the word to Latino street gangs to shoot African American drug dealers on sight.

Some 1,200 gangs roam the four thousand square miles of urban sprawl that make up Los Angeles; of the 100,000 members listed in police files, roughly 7,000 are females. Although there has always been adolescent violence, the current generation of L.A. gang bangers is distinct for its firepower. For the fifth straight year, nearly 800 people died in gang killings, the highest gang homicide rate in the nation. In one year alone, some 8,050 victims were treated at L.A. county hospitals for gunshot wounds—thirteen times the number of U.S. military personnel killed and wounded during the Gulf War. With more gun dealers than any other county in the United States, Los Angeles is armed to the teeth. In some schools, where spending for education has fallen from first to forty-second in the nation, children practice duck-and-cover drills to protect against gunfire from other children.

Known for setting many of the country's trends, perhaps no Californian cultural export has found greater success than gangster-inspired clothes, music, slang, and graffiti, moving beyond the ghetto into the suburbs. The spray-painted citations of the California penal code for murder—the numerals 187—painted next to a rival's name have become the lingua franca of street gangs across the nation, a symbol indicating the next enemy to die.

As the twentieth century edges toward its finale, L.A. suffers the worst street gang problem in the United States. It is a crisis that has been building for years. Gangs became the desperate effort of tragically unequipped children to create a family in a social vacuum. Without an effective national policy for youth, kids fell through the cracks in droves. Each new youth atrocity added up to a larger picture of societal neglect. America's answer was to be "Get tough on crime," the political rallying cry of 1994.

In his State of the Union address that January, President Bill Clinton declared we must tame our violent children and reclaim our streets from gangs, drugs, and guns by means of a new federal law with a catchy slogan: "Three strikes, you're out." Under three strikes, a third-time perpetrator of a serious crime would be locked away for life. But a state version of the law went into effect in California, where anyone with two violent felonies could be sent to jail for twenty-five years to life for *any* third conviction, no matter how minor (one man was imprisoned for life after stealing a pair of jeans). Even before the law, the state led most of the country, and at times the world, with the number of people incarcerated per capita, outdistancing prison populations in South Africa and the Russian Federation. Only the Israeli-occupied West Bank and Gaza Strip, with their fluctuating figures for jailed Palestinians, came close.

Like a thick layer of smog, Californians were blinded by an obsession with crime and punishment. In Sacramento lawmakers approved the circulation of petitions for a November ballot initiative that would require violent felons, once freed from prison, to wear identification numbers tattooed on their faces. Officers from the LAPD appeared on the evening news, urging tourists to stay away from Los Angeles because they could not assure their safety. The stunt later turned out to be part of a $19,000 public relations campaign to raise the salaries of union officers. Along with warning brochures for travel agents and airlines, the blitz included a billboard of a California blonde climbing into her car, unaware of the masked gunman behind her. The billboard popped up along twenty-two of L.A.'s most frequented roadways, among them on Crenshaw and 48th Street, the vortex of the 1992 uprising. It read: WARNING: THIS CAN BE YOU WITHOUT THE POLICE DEPARTMENT. Shortly after the billboards went up—with the police department still intact— gang members killed two Japanese students during a car-jacking. Within forty-eight hours the signs were painted over.

The shooting of the Japanese students had occurred not far from the home of the young mother and member of the notorious Crips gang I was headed to visit. Coco's South Central neighborhood was part of the LAPD's 77th Street division, considered the twelve most dangerous square miles in Los Angeles. At night, when the police gang unit returns from its patrol, each squad car cuts its headlights a block before reaching the station—to guard against neighborhood snipers.

Although I had lived in L.A. for almost three years in the early eighties, I'd never set foot in South Central. Now, as I passed neat but barricaded bungalows, seeing parents play with their kids under eucalyptus trees or wash their automobiles, this neighborhood so demonized in the media appeared fairly ordinary. But then what had I expected? Beirut? Soweto?

Coco and her family lived in a small back-lot house of white clapboard with faded blue trim that resembled a Norman Rockwell home under siege. Heavy security grates covered the windows, shutting out any possibility of sunlight, and a cast-iron gate concealed the door. The only view the house afforded was of the neighbor's trash; the "lawn" was no more than a patch of bare earth lining an oil-stained driveway.

A young boy with long curls framing a sweet dark face crouched next to a dilapidated Buick and poked a stick at a cat. When he spotted me, he scooted up the porch steps to the protection of a large teenage girl. The girl told me to come in, explaining curtly that she was looking after the kids while Coco and her boyfriend were out waiting in line for earthquake relief food stamps.

Inside Snoop Doggy Dogg blasted over mammoth loudspeakers. Everything in the room was hugely oversized, from a massive TV set to a monstrous ceramic panther holding up a glass coffee table. Later Coco told me the house had been robbed four times before she finally replaced her stolen possessions with furniture too heavy to steal. Decorated in black carpeting, white walls with black trim, and black drapes covering the windows, the place had the feel of a seventies drug den, albeit a spotless one. In the middle of the room, a tiny pigtailed girl sang along with Snoop, lyrics tumbling out of her ice-cream-rimmed mouth about "doing it doggy style."

When she saw me, she stopped, introducing herself as Tasha, four years old, though soon to be five.

There were four kids in all: Tasha, the curly-haired boy I had seen outside, a cherub-faced toddler named Sheba, and a diapered baby boy who Tasha now tortured by dragging him by his armpits, forcing him to dance. Coco's brood. I spotted a picture of Coco and Bird, her boyfriend, on the wall, and told the curly-haired youngster he looked just like his father.

Tasha rolled her eyes. "Bird's *not* his daddy. Philip has a different daddy."

Despite this faux pas, Philip decided I was okay, if a little dim, and asked for a piece of paper from my notebook to draw me a picture. Tasha and the toddler settled next to me on the couch. The girl I'd met at the door stuck the baby in my arms; his skin was burning. "He's got a cold," she said and disappeared into the kitchen.

Philip handed me two drawings. The first showed a man wearing a baseball cap with menacing eyes peering above a mask. "A mugger," Philip informed me. The second drawing was more abstract, a figure doubled over beneath the cartoon bubble: "*Oooh nooo!*" It was a picture, he said, of "a lady crying because her husband left her."

I stuck the sad pictures in my purse and thanked him, remarking that he no longer seemed so shy. Philip shook his curls vigorously. "I'm not shy. I just don't talk when I first meet people. It's not good to let them know your business."

His seriousness made me laugh, but Philip remained firm. "People know your business, they mess with you."

"That's right, you get messed with," Tasha confirmed.

"Who," I wanted to know, "messes with a six-year-old boy?"

"Two Mexican boys at school. They call me 'nigger.' "

He read the look of concern on my face. "It's okay. I don't care. I beat them up. And they're big, too! In second grade. But I whipped them. My dad told me to whip them." He got on his knees, preparing to stand on his head. "And I don't cry."

I started to tell him it was okay to cry but stopped. Who was I to give advice to a kid growing up in South Central?

A half hour or so later Coco and Bird, the children's parents, returned home. Coco disappeared into the kitchen to put away some groceries while Bird stood before the mirror, removing his blue bandanna to reveal a head as bald and as smooth as a cue ball. His shaved crown rendered him both threatening and striking, showing off his chiseled features. In the corner of one eye was tattooed a tiny teardrop in memory of a fellow gangster who died in the pen. He turned up the stereo so loud that Li'l Chick, the six-month-old baby, cried on the floor from the vibrations. But to Bird the sound was just there, like air, and he talked right through it. Snoop Doggy Dogg, he yelled, was his old high school classmate from Long Beach. The gangster rapper—who now faced trial for a 1993 murder—had been the class clown.

Coco emerged from the kitchen. When I had first met the couple during a previous trip a month earlier, they were actually part of a trio. Coco shared her boyfriend with another woman named Roylene. I'd worked up the nerve to ask whether both women slept with Bird and Coco smiled sheepishly. Bird also grinned.

"And you two," I addressed the women. "Can you sleep with other guys?"

Bird's grin vanished. "Hell no!"

Behind his back Coco winked at me.

Bird's two women were a study in contrasts. Coco was small, compact, and spoke in a sexy, throaty growl. She had a hair-trigger temper, frequently launching into a flurry of curses. For days she would stay away from home, preferring the company of her homegirls in Grape Street Watts, one of the city's largest Crip gangs. Roylene, on the other hand, possessed a soft voice at odds with her big-boned frame, painted red lips, and gold hoop earrings the size of donuts. While Coco gang-banged, Roylene watched over Coco and Bird's children. (Coco and Bird had the youngest children together; Tasha was Bird's from a previous marriage and Philip was Coco's son.)

Today, though, Roylene was conspicuously absent. Bird explained that she was grieving. A few weeks earlier her aunt had been split in two by a hit-and-run driver.

The aunt's death had forced Coco back into her role as a mother. She was at a crossroads: With four children at only twenty-four, she felt too young to be a mother but too old to be gang banging on the street. She referred to herself as O.G., or "Original Gangster," a term of respect in the ghetto for those who have paid their dues, either by fighting, hustling, or killing, and could now rely on younger ones to do their bidding—in Coco's case, girls like her teenage nieces, still earning their stripes, who I was about to meet.

Besides Coco's two nieces, Coco and Bird had also invited over Bird's cousin Alex, a Blood, to meet me. The Crips make up one half of L.A.'s two major African American gangs; the Bloods are their enemies. Both supergangs consist of hundreds of smaller gangs, or "sets," that take their names from streets or geographical landmarks, such as Hoover Street Crips and Piru Street Bloods. The Crip sets actually fight more among each other than with Bloods. Coco and Bird welcomed a Blood in their home because family blood was thicker than gang affiliation. Still, on the outside this tie meant little; whenever Bird drove with Alex, he feared sniper fire.

While Coco focused on cleaning the living room, Bird explained Blood language. Slobs, he said, using a derogatory term for Bloods, won't use the letter *c* because it stands for Crips. Instead of cigarette, for instance, they say "bigarette."

When a car pulled up, Bird went outside, gently lifting a man out of the passenger seat who hung limply in his arms like a small crumpled child. The man's pants slid down, revealing the bandage around his waist. Inside Coco placed a towel over the sofa seat. "Bird doesn't like me to do this," she said, her voice low, "but I just don't want no leaks." Some Crips had shot Alex at the corner of San Pedro and Manchester, not far from here. The bullet severed his spine.

Bird introduced me as his "homegirl" who was writing a book on girl gang members. Alex's face had deep-set quiet eyes and he nodded thoughtfully. Coco brought out a scrapbook and we huddled around it. She showed me a picture of herself as a small girl in Mississippi. She remembered her childhood as happy in the South, where survival depended upon helping each other out, sharing meals, taking in an orphaned child. Coco's mother often took in homeless kids, whom Coco called "cousins." Yet when she was a young girl, her mother packed up the six children in the night to flee from her husband, a Vietnam vet who took out his rage at being used in a white man's war on his wife. Coco was bitter about abandoning her father; her mother only told her about his brutality after his death and Coco alternately struggled to remember and to forget him.

The family moved to South Central on the tail end of a westward migration of hundreds of thousands of African Americans seeking the new black version of the California dream. While her mother studied to become a paralegal, Coco soon discovered that school was not a place for learning, but for fighting to survive. With 640,000 students, classrooms in the L.A. unified school district were more crowded than any in America and, in the inner-city school Coco attended, had a soaring dropout rate of 30 to 50 percent. In this war zone, Coco became a bully. She joined Grape Street Watts Crips, named after its original neighborhood turf of 103rd and Grape Street, although its influence spread well beyond its borders. By the time the principal convinced Coco's mother to send her daughter to a better school in the Valley, Coco was firmly entrenched in gang life.

There were other pictures. One was a studio portrait of a radiant young woman, Coco's good friend until she lost her to crack. She had died when her boyfriend beat her to death, then burned down the house, himself perishing in the blaze. Another snapshot showed one of Coco's homegirls in Grape Street Watts, a diminutive teenager known as Li'l K. She was now in prison for stabbing a girl. "The girl underestimated Li'l K, 'cause she's small," Coco said, "until Li'l K stabbed her sixteen times."

A picture fell to the floor. "Oh my God," Bird said softly, picking up a color photo, turned yellow with time, of a tiny smiling boy. He glanced over at Alex. "I'm gonna show you something, but you can't keep it."

Alex squinted at the picture, as though not recognizing the image. Slowly his face betrayed an expression of terrible bewilderment and he threw back his head, covering his eyes with his hands.

Coco whispered, "He can't stand seeing pictures of when he could walk."

HER nieces Jade and Wanda were due any minute. Coco complained it took them hours to get "G'd-up," or gangster dressed in Crip blue. Gang members once universally distinguished themselves by their color coding of shoes, T-shirts, and bandannas—blue for Crips, red for Bloods. Meaningless to outsiders, the color war was taken dead seriously—the L.A. media reported the shooting death of a baby because the infant wore red shoelaces—but over the last few years, the ritual of dress has faded considerably. The older gangsters grew wise to the fact that colors made them a walking bull's-eye for their enemies, or worse, the cops. An O.G. who'd already proven herself, Coco was wearing crisp new jeans and a white fake cashmere sweater with VOGUE emblazoned across her chest in gold-lamé letters. "But the young ones, they want to make sure you know they Crips."

Jade and Wanda made their entrance a vision in blue: blue jeans, blue flannel shirts, blue sneakers, and blue bandannas tying up their hair. Wanda strode past me, head held high, wearing the classic teenage sneer, and changed the channel on the TV to a music video. Her sister Jade, a long-legged colt of a girl nearly six feet tall, swaggered in behind her, thin hips swaying to the music's rhythm. With her hair pulled back, she appeared almost Asian, almond eyes gazing out from a long, sculptured face.

Coco, with three generations of gang bangers and potential ones assembled, could not resist claiming her place as O.G. She admonished Jade and Wanda for getting G'd-up on the 53 Bus, which ran down Central Avenue, the main drag through Blood territory. "Someone's gonna fuck your ass up on that bus! I got cut on the 53." Standing in the middle of the room, she flew into a tirade, like some wild-eyed perspiring preacher, about the female enemy who stabbed her. "I started yelling,

'I'm stuck! I'm stuck!' My shirt was full of blood. My shoes were caked with it."

Her chubby toddler Sheba waddled up next to her and began parroting her movements.

"My friend stabbed that *bitch!*" Coco yelled, stomping her foot.

"*Bitch!*" Sheba echoed and stomped her own tiny foot.

"I mean, she got that ho *bad*—"

"*Ho!*" screamed Sheba. Jade and Wanda exploded with laughter and Sheba clapped her hands. Coco looked down, noticing her child for the first time, and scooped her up. "Tell Mama you ain't gonna cuss."

"*Ho!*" Sheba cried out happily.

Coco kissed her and returned to the story. "My homegirl wound up putting that girl in a coma and she died. I don't even know if she was the one who stabbed me. I think it was her friend." She set Sheba down to display her wound, but it was hidden beneath the girdle she wore since Li'l Chick's birth. As consolation, she showed us some buckshot scars in the back of her neck.

When she was finished, she turned to Jade and Wanda. "When I was your age, I was banging hard. When you get old, you realize that bus ain't cool."

But the girls barely listened, the way kids tune out when their mother tells them to come home early. Jade absently examined her wristwatch. "I took this off a girl at that bus stop."

Coco waved her hand, "I don't bother robbing people for things like that. I robbed to pay my bills. Never for fun."

"What about when you were my age? Did you beat people up?" Jade asked, knowing the answer.

"Yeah. It was more fun to beat them up than to rob them. But if somebody owed me money? Once this bitch owed me a hundred dollars and I went to her house. She came to the door, talking shit. I said, 'You-all don't pay me my money, I'm gonna come in your house and shoot your kids.' See"—she looked at me—"she didn't say she didn't *have* the money, she said she wasn't going to *pay* me. So I shot into the house three times. Shot *up* that motherfucker!" Coco's pitch reached a crescendo, then fell back to normal. "I wouldn't really have hit her kids, but I got my money. Don't fuck with me because I will smoke your ass." She pointed to Sheba, crawling into Jade's lap. "I was pregnant with Sheba at the time."

Jade laughed. "Someone don't give me my money . . ." She mimed aiming a machine gun and began to buck in her seat: "*Pah-pah-pah-pah!*" Sheba began firing her own imaginary weapon.

Coco looked ready to tell another story, but Jade abruptly left the room. I followed her into the bedroom, where Tasha attacked me with a dollop of hair grease. I tried to explain that my Caucasian hair was different from a black person's, but it was too late. While the little girl braided my hair into a sticky mess, Jade launched into a litany of who she had robbed: other girls, liquor stores, the chains off elementary school kids. I stopped her when she mentioned "old people" to ask about her technique. "You just say"—Jade's voice turned steely—" 'Give me your money.' And if they don't . . ." She shrugged. "You just gotta click your gat. Soon as they hear that click, they hand it right over."

Jade anticipated my next question, insisting she came from a good home. Her mother gave her money, she just wanted more. Like so many kids in the ghetto, she sometimes felt crazed with wanting. "I want money, so I can buy whatever I want. Jewelry! Gold! Shoes, so I look fresh. I just want to never want for anything."

Jade grew up amid the greed and glory of the go-go eighties, and the materialism she and her homegirls displayed was unsurprising. Like so much of America, they were hypnotized by the equating of money with power and fashioned gang hierarchies on things like clothing, gold-plated AK-47 pendants, and expensive Nike air shoes.

We returned to the living room, where the TV was tuned to the trial of the Menendez brothers, the young men who murdered their wealthy Beverly Hills parents. Bird watched the tube with Philip at his feet. "See that?" he told his son, as though telling a fable. "If they were black, you wouldn't be seeing this on TV. If they were black, they'd be fried by now."

SOMETIME during the afternoon, Jade and I left to pick up food at McDonald's. No ghetto is without the superfranchise, although there are mile-long stretches without law offices, supermarkets, or safe schools, you can always find a liquor store and a fast-food joint. As we turned onto Manchester's bustling thoroughfare, a woman of indeterminable age, barefoot and wearing nothing but a cotton robe, scrambled across the intersection. Jade pointed a slim finger at the woman, one of the hood's numerous crackheads with the characteristic jitters and haunted eyes that stare without seeing. "I sell rock to people like that," Jade announced flatly, meaning rock cocaine or crack. "They pay me with food stamps, shoes, clothes—if I think the outfit's decent and ain't nobody been in it, I'll take it."

The woman ducked into a darkened doorway. "Women like that," Jade went on, "sell themselves for crack. There used to be this cop who'd make the crackheads give him blow jobs for free. He'd be over here with his partner, see them hanging round, then come back alone. One time this woman didn't want to do it. She was like, 'Fuck you' and started crossing the street. He just ran her over with his car and kept going."

In the ghetto, I would learn, there are hundreds of independent "rock house" franchises. Jade sold crack only occasionally, using an abandoned house, earning ten to twenty dollars a pop. Even so, it made more sense to her than a menial job, which was a stepping-stone to nowhere. Dealing provided more prestige and instant reward. Most gang members who sold drugs were not growing rich. Some dealt to help pay the rent while their mothers looked the other way. Few were high rollers.

Crack became the drug of choice for the poor because it's cheap. Before 1981 a kilo of cocaine in L.A. County cost $55,000 to $65,000. When production rose and imports grew, the drug began to flood the market. Cocaine switched from a drug for high-powered Hollywood partygoers to a turn-on for the middle class and prices plummeted. By 1984 you could cop a kilo for as little as $12,000 to $16,000.

Tons of the stuff crossed the border. To unload the excess, the drug trade created a new product: rock cocaine, or crack. If freebasing pure cocaine was the equivalent of an expensive champagne, crack was a cheap rotgut wine. More addicting than any other street drug, including heroin, crack provided a fifteen-minute high that left users craving more. The new drug devastated the ghetto through addiction and the violence associated with dealing. It also exposed an awful class and race bias. Under federal statutes, defendants convicted of selling 5 grams or more of crack, worth about $125, received a mandatory minimum of five years in prison. It took, however, 500 grams of coke—nearly $50,000 worth—to land an equivalent sentence. Someone caught with a relatively small amount of crack, most likely a poor defendant, could receive a sentence two to three years longer than a person convicted of possessing nearly 100 times that amount of the more expensive powdered cocaine.

AT McDonald's we watched another cartoon crackhead frantically scuttle from one car to the next, begging money. He spotted us and, twitching and rocking, put out his hand. Close up, I could see his singed eyelashes and the burn on his mouth, most likely from a bad pipe. "*Shiiit*," Jade hissed. "He's just gonna use the money for more dope. Don't give him nothing. Men like that make their women turn tricks."

Her voice turned quiet. "My cousin was a nice girl. Then she went with this guy who got her hooked on dope, had her turning tricks. And then . . ." Jade glared at the man and he backed away. When she spoke again, her voice was a fusion of pain and anger. "She sold her three-year-old daughter to men for dope. We found out 'cause the little girl's vagina was bloody. She was a good mother until that guy. We don't know where she is now. My other cousin wanted to adopt the baby, but I think she's in a foster home."

No place existed in Jade's emotional geography to make the connection between her own crack dealing and the addict who had forced her cousin to whore. Neither of us said anything for a moment, then I asked if all women were at risk in the hood. "Yeah, but not as much as the guys. Even so, guys still shoot a female in a flash—it's called a 'bitch slap.' Like once some Blood niggers gave a party, and some sly females ended up there to spy, you know how bitches do that shit. A Crip bitch went in there and didn't never come out. Her own homeboys didn't give a fuck about her, 'cause they never went to look for her or nothing. Whosever's house it was, when the woman opened up the closet, the girl fell out dead—and it was her friend's daughter. They'd put an AK-47 to her head and just blew her whole face off."

"How do you know this?"

"She was a bitch we used to cheer with."

"You were a cheerleader?"

"Yeah, Wanda and I cheered from '85 to '89. Then it got too competitive."

• • •

IT was dark back at the house, the only light from the TV bathing the room in a shifting silvery glow. Bird told tales of guard beatings, rape, and gang fights in the L.A. County Jail. The children, except for Li'l Chick, who was asleep in the bedroom, sat with their feet tucked under them, listening raptly. Coco suddenly spotted Tasha with Wanda's blue bandanna, trying to tie it around her head, gangster style, like the older girl. "Give me that!" Coco snatched the rag away and threw a look at Bird. "Letting your daughter play with a dirty Crip hanky."

Wanda and Jade laughed as Tasha danced out of Coco's reach. Leaning back in a chair so far her long legs dangled off the ground, Jade announced to the room, "I'm gonna be gang banging for life. My husband's gonna be gang banging and the baby's gonna be gang banging!"

Although she had just finished admonishing her daughter, this idea invigorated Coco. "When I be seventy-five years old," she hollered, "I'll still be a Crip!"

"What about them?" I pointed to Tasha, Philip, and Sheba, who gleefully watched their mother.

"They ain't gonna be like us," Coco insisted.

"Though there's kids joining at eight or nine," Bird cut in. "I was walking to get me some chicken and this little nigger—nothing but nine years old—pointed to my Rollin' Twenties cap and said, 'Fuck that nigger.' I said, 'C'mon, little cuz. I know all your big homeys.' He just says, 'Fuck you.' So I'm like, 'Fuck you then.'" Bird's eyes grew wide. "Right there, that little nigger pulls out a gun. I couldn't run at first. I just stood there for a minute"—he mimed standing still, frozen in disbelief—"and he was shooting!"

I looked again at six-year-old Philip, now drawing pictures in my notebook. "How could anyone trust a kid with a gun?" I asked.

"You can trust him," Bird assured me. "If he's from your hood, he's from your hood. He was trying to put in work, shoot me because I'm O.G."

"And always will be!" Coco said, on a roll. "If I come across some motherfuckin' old Blood and she's still in it, I'll . . . I'll . . ."

Bird filled in for her: "Hit her with your cane!"

The two smiled at each other.

It was late and Bird offered to walk me to my car. I asked if he was strapped—carrying a gun—mostly out of curiosity. He smiled, left the room, then returned with a small silver gun. I recognized the caliber as a

.25. The first time a gang girl showed me a .25 automatic, it looked so small that I mistook it for a novelty cigarette lighter and she snatched it away before I pulled the trigger. A cop told me that despite its miniature size, a .25 could potentially do the damage of a high-powered machine gun—the bullet madly ricochets inside your body, lacerating your lungs, heart, spleen, any organ it hits.

Just then four-year-old Tasha caught sight of the weapon and leaped up from the floor, her eyes dancing. She dashed across the living room and jumped for Bird's hand. He raised the gun in the air and absently shooed her away with his free hand. But the child kept jumping, reaching, reaching for the glittering toy.

THE MAKING OF A MENACE

TJ sat in a booth in the Denny's on Hawthorne Boulevard in Lennox, drawing a diagram on a napkin to show the structure of her gang, Lennox-13. Large Latino gangs, she explained, consisted of smaller "cliques," groups of thirty to fifty kids around the same age. "See"—she leaned toward me, straining to be heard over a howling infant in the next booth—"Lennox is kind of an umbrella term for the whole gang." She scribbled LENNOX-13 at the top of the napkin, then drew lines branching off it like a family tree. "You've got a bunch of cliques like the Tinies or the Pee Wees—they're youngsters. The Winos, they've been around for a long time and have the most pull." Beneath each branch she marked in bold block letters the name of a clique: THE JOKERS, THE TOKERS, THE NIGHT OWLS, THE MIDGETS, THE DUKES, and her own, THE PLAYGIRL GANG-STAS. Nine in all.

TJ wore glasses and an old-fashioned rose-print dress and her once waist-length hair now fell only to her shoulders, a haircut that at the time caused her to burst into tears. Two years had passed since she revealed to me how she camouflaged herself as a man to shoot a rival. We'd kept in touch through letters and phone calls, but once back in L.A. it took me weeks to find her. I tried her mother's house on several occasions, though I didn't know that the dark-haired woman who appeared at the door surrounded by three mongrel dogs was her mom, because each time she told me that no one named TJ lived there. TJ laughed huskily when she heard about her mother's attempts to dodge me. Bill collectors constantly called her after TJ had ended up in the hospital, nearly dying from complications surrounding appendicitis.

Now twenty, TJ seemed as chatty and likable as the day I met her. With many gang kids, the sense of hazard always lingered; it was part of the air they breathed and they were deliberately hard on strangers. Not TJ. She was a full-lipped, fair-skinned girl with a cocky tomboy air, not the acrid malice of a hard-core killer. She held strong opinions about everything, blessed with an intelligence for expressing them. In her letters, she sometimes enclosed samples of her art, pencil drawings of wild mustangs or a portrait of Malcom X. I enjoyed her company and also believed that she could open my eyes to why someone who possessed talents and options was attracted to gang violence. More and more she seemed to grow introspective. Her lingering illness made her question her gang involvement, and frequently she found herself seeking solace in church. Still, she became my Virgil, guiding me through the hell of life in Lennox.

By traditional standards, TJ's gang, which formed in the early 1970s, is relatively young. Most Lennox-13 members are first-generation teenagers born of Spanish-speaking parents who crossed the border from Mexico, El Salvador, or other Central American countries. The gang takes its name from its neighborhood of Lennox, an unincorporated area of 1.5 square miles located in Los Angeles' far West Side, just minutes away from LAX, with a population of some 24,000 mostly Latino residents.

Each Lennox clique cultivates its own identity, and its members usually hang out among themselves. For funerals, weddings, or crucial meetings, however, someone passes out Xeroxed announcements and all the cliques may assemble, some 300 gangsters—tattoos on their foreheads, behind their ears, snaking up their arms, or crawling down the length of their spines—crammed into Lennox Park or the parking lot of a local burger and burrito stand. In their oversized Ben Davis shirts, the boys' baggy pants slung low to expose their boxer shorts, they mill about and throw up their gang sign, thumb and forefinger extended to form an *L* for Lennox, shamelessly courting enemy bullets.

Sometimes these invitations are answered. Death decimates the cliques as their members grow older, but gangs can also dissolve in other, slower ways. Prison may finish off many members, along with heroin, as finding a fix overrides all other concerns. For women, premature mother-hood exacts its toll.

The organization TJ described is no different from that of 18th Street, White Fence, El Hoyo Maravilla, or hundreds of Latino gangs that have sprung up since the 1930s. Even the clique names have stayed the same; most gangs include a Dukes, a Tinies, a Jokers. Nicknames, too, have lingered on. I met several Goofys, a pair of Flacos (Spanish for "skinny"), and three Sleepys.

The history of gangs is a history of fear—the fear of outsiders. Al-though their skin was darker, their faith Catholic, Latino gangs grew in Los Angeles for reasons that most street gangs do everywhere, including the white Italian and Irish gangs of Chicago and New York in the mid-1800s and later the German and Jewish gangs—as a result of swift demo-graphic change. In the 1920s, thousands of Mexicans streamed into Cali-fornia to answer the need for cheap labor on farms and desert mines and to find *una vida major,* "a better life." Their port of entry was the *barrio,* Mexican settlements in unincorporated terrains of hills, ravines, and hol-lows. In the shadows of foundries and railroad yards, families swelled in shacks of scrap lumber and tin, their children left to play on dirt roads.

When the Depression hit, Mexicans were no longer needed. Unlike the white immigrant gangs, which eventually disappeared as Italians and Irish youth were absorbed into the larger economy and society, Mexicans remained outcasts, facing more intense discrimination than the most despised white immigrants. California began repatriation, forcing immi-grants back across the border.

Throughout the 1930s and 1940s, neighborhood street gangs formed for protection and identity. Their members were called *cholos,* "people trapped between worlds," originally referring to those on the fringes of indigenous Indian and Spanish colonial cultures in Mexico. In America it meant poor second-generation kids whose parents remained Mexican at heart while their children desired, yet were denied, full American citizenship.

Misunderstood in their own homes and unwelcome outside, they fell into the companionship of misery. The gangs' first uniforms consisted of zoot suits, ballooning trousers, and exaggeratedly long coats. In the early 1950s, they created the look still seen today in parts of L.A.: chinos or cotton work pants called "dickies" (requiring a ritual of ironing the trousers inside out with starch so that the crease was so perfect the pants could stand up on their own), topped with a white T-shirt and plaid Pendleton shirt. They cultivated their own walk, a controlled saunter of graceful machismo, and talk, a blend of Spanish and English street slang. Black kids later adopted the cholo look and remolded it into their own style, which the Latinos eventually borrowed back. Although black gangs also existed by the late 1940s, mainly in response to attacks by racist white kids, the Crips and Bloods didn't arrive on the scene until three decades later. While some of the black girls I met had fathers in a gang, Latina girls could brag their *great*-grandfather had been a cholo.

Wherever teenage boys get together, girls soon follow. The early *cholas* wore short skirts, mesh stockings, and pompadours. In the 1960s, they grew their hair long and teased it, lined their eyes in black-and-white raccoonlike circles, and slithered into hip-hugging black skirts. They participated in gang life as the sisters and girlfriends of male gang members, although soon female cliques, or auxiliaries, emerged. Though they took their name from the feminine version of a male gang's name— the Diablas, for instance, spun off from the Diablos—they acted, for the most part, entirely on their own. In some cases, girls formed completely autonomous all-female gangs, like Las Monas or the Black Legion, who bonded for partying and dancing, a girls' club without a clubhouse.

Although both early male and female gangs were primarily social, occasionally breaking out into chains and knife fights, the Los Angeles police treated them like a corrupting force. One sheriff's report in 1942 characterized Mexicans as "biologically" predisposed toward criminal behavior. When street kids adopted the short-lived fashion fad of wearing expensive zoot suits, the police and press reacted as though they'd donned war armor. The term "zoot suit" became synonymous with Mexican lawbreaker.

On the evening of June 4, 1943, a group of soldiers and sailors, angry over a dance-hall brawl three weeks earlier, invaded L.A.'s barrios and beat anyone they found in a zoot suit. One of their first targets was a group of Mexican-American kids on their way home from a meeting at a police station to discuss ways to preserve peace in their neighborhood. The attacks exploded into a four-night campaign of sartorial feuding as servicemen in uniform pummeled Mexicans, although blacks, dark-complected Caucasians, or anyone who had the misfortune to wear a zoot suit were also targets. The newspaper coverage blamed the Mexican kids, including cholas, quoting one "slick chick" as swearing to fight until the death.

By June 7 the tabloid media had whipped the servicemen into a frenzy. They descended upon downtown Los Angeles armed with sticks and weighted ropes, a civilian mob and police in tow. *Time* magazine reported:

> Scores of Mexican youths had been stripped of their pants (some of them on the stages of movie houses), beaten and then arrested by the Los Angeles police for "vagrancy" and "rioting." The police practice was to accompany the caravans in police cars, watch the beating and then jail the victims.

The federal government responded by vowing to crack down on illicit trading in zoot coats and pants, saying they contributed to "hooliganism." The Los Angeles City Council passed an ordinance making the wearing of a zoot suit a misdemeanor. Patrol cars cruised the barrio for offenders.

A half century later L.A.'s racial politics had changed little. The LAPD still shook down and harassed kids who looked like they might be gang members, making little effort to differentiate between an awestruck wanna-be and a hardened killer. Many of the gang programs that cropped up periodically had disappeared in the 1990s, when education, early childhood prevention, job training, and drug treatment were often dismissed as liberal cant. By the end of 1994, Californians would vote yes on Proposition 187—ironically the same numerals as the California penal code for murder—a bill aimed to kill medical and educational services for illegal immigrants (i.e., Latinos). The Lennox Zip Code had the worst unemployment rate in the country. Kids found few jobs or opportunities to climb out of their decayed neighborhoods. Street gangs remained as entrenched as ever.

Since childhood, TJ wanted to be something more than a wife or mother, the traditional aim of many Latina girls in her neighborhood. After all, her mother had worked and raised TJ without a man. Her father split before TJ's second birthday, leaving her only a dim memory of looking up at him, the sun in her eyes rendering him a faceless silhouette.

She was bright and did well in school, attending a campus in El Segundo near the beach until the ninth grade, when her mother moved to Lennox for cheaper housing. TJ transferred out of the beach school to what she considered a ghetto school, where tattooed rivals roamed the halls, "mad-dogging" one another. She detested the new environment. Her grades plummeted until she ended up "in the stupid classes."

Special education served as the school's dumping ground for troubled children and in its classrooms TJ came face-to-face with gangsters. They didn't frighten her. She felt attracted to the muscular cocksure boys who liked her body and used her brains, cheating off her papers. Soon she found herself partying with them at night. She'd always been what mothers call a wild girl, stealing candy from the corner store, sneaking out at night; the young gangsters liberated her from the false femininity the world forced upon teenage girls. "See, the gang accepts anybody: handicapped, ugly, fat, homosexuals . . . Well"—TJ reconsidered—"gay *girls*, not guys, but almost anyone. A nerd would have to shave his head and put on khakis. We got people in wheelchairs—Sidekick was even kind of retarded. He got killed on the Ave. But safety comes in numbers. So if you're a wimpy type, 'cause there's a lot of wimpy quiet girls who get more rowdy once they get alcohol and drugs, you'll join for the drugs and to get closer to the guys. Mostly, you get into gangs to fit in. 'Cause some of these girls, they come from really abusive homes and they're just looking for some comfort"—she paused for effect and rolled her eyes—"in the sweet words of a gang banger."

In TJ's new neighborhood, girls faced the same risks as guys—poverty, drugs, unemployment, violence. Most of their mothers had been teenagers themselves when they gave birth, and without strong female role models to emulate, their daughters looked to the boys. In this world, the strongest cholo, the one "crazy" enough to take the dare—snipe at the cop, deal the big bucks, wipe out the enemy—survived. So you found a guy who was crazy or became crazy yourself.

A girlfriend offered to hook TJ up with a twenty-one-year-old homeboy in prison named Shotgun, who had no one to write to. TJ felt sorry for him and was intrigued. Each time a letter arrived, she raced to school to show it off to her friends. Yet when Shotgun was released and the two finally met, she was unimpressed. He looked like all the other boys, if more pumped and tattooed from time in the pen. Her feelings changed when she saw how other homeboys feared him. Back on the street Shotgun, cursed with an unpredictable temper that ignited at unsettling speed, soon rose to the rank of shot caller.

In turn, TJ experienced the vicarious power that comes with a connection to a "successful" man, receiving respect and protection. She saw Shotgun the way no one else could, as vulnerable, emotional. When he was scared after a drive-by or a death, the only one he could tell was TJ. And TJ was smart. She kept his fears to herself.

But she'd attracted a girl gangster's attention. Fresh out of prison and unofficially the leader of Lennox's PlayGirl Gangstas, Angel set out to recruit Shotgun's new girlfriend into her gang. Angel had formed the PlayGirls, whose members' nicknames reflected muggish teenage braggadocio—Miss Crazy, Bambi, Dreamer—to follow her rules. At nineteen she already had two children, who'd been bundled off to relatives "in white man's land." Her body bore tattoos of her kids' names alongside the names of both male and female lovers and street battle scars. Her mouth, however, bore the most vivid testimony to the violence of the life she led. Her two front teeth had been knocked out; of those remaining, many were chipped and most were crooked—they had either grown in at strange angles or been redirected by powerful blows. "There ain't no difference between guys and girls in gangs," Angel once told me. "We kill people, too. You know—six feet under, no more Mommy for you." Though some of this was typical gang bravado, Angel had done hard jail time for knifing two girls.

At their height in the late 1980s, the PlayGirl Gangstas counted about ten hard-core members, but during Angel's stint in jail they'd fallen apart and needed new blood. Angel wanted TJ in the gang, and TJ had little choice. If she refused to be "jumped in," allowing the PlayGirls to punch and kick her in a ritual pummeling, she would lose respect and face beatings every time she ran into Angel.

As a PlayGirl, TJ excelled. She learned how to break into houses by watching crime shows on TV. She especially liked stealing cars and could jimmy an ignition and start one without a key in under a minute. At her peak, she broke into four cars a day. One night she hit upon the idea of dressing herself like one of the homeboys; as a girl, she'd always be more easily remembered by witnesses. An exceptional art student, she applied her talents to transforming her face, drawing on a mustache with eye pencil, slicking back her hair, wearing gloves to conceal her dagger nails. Her newfound power—power based on her own exploits, rather than Shotgun's—bolstered her confidence. Her grades shot back up and she relished her double life of schoolgirl by day, gang girl by night.

Her gang didn't seek out violence; it was just a normal part of life in their always contested landscape. What they did most was simply hang out, drink beer, gaze dead-eyed at rock videos, waiting for something, anything to relieve the boredom. But eventually the realization hit TJ, as it did all gang bangers: the life extracted a terrible price. A half dozen Saturdays each year were spent raising money for funerals. TJ would turn brown from the sun in the bikini top and shorts she wore for the benefit of passing motorists as she held a large CAR WASH sign. She would hand drivers a flier explaining they were raising money for the funeral costs of Little Solo—or Flyer or G-Dog. "His family doesn't have the cash to buy a coffin," she would explain, neglecting to tell the driver that Little Solo was a member of Lennox-13, killed by a rival gang in retaliation for a drive-by. She'd collect the money in an engraved silver cup from her high school prom.

With each death she changed incrementally, desiring to do more than raise money. She wanted to retaliate, get payback. When her homegirl Rosa's little brother Danny was killed, it gave TJ a chance to act.

Her boyfriend Shotgun scoffed at her attempts to impersonate a male gang banger. He was furious that TJ had joined Lennox-13, though there was nothing he could do—initiation was akin to baptism, it could not be reversed. Instead he monitored her comings and goings, beating her afterward if he came home and found her absent. That New Year's Eve, as the couple headed out to a party, TJ invited along a homegirl. Not in the mood for company, Shotgun dragged TJ into a park, knocked her to the pavement, straddled her, and beat her head against the ground.

The next morning TJ could not see out of her left eye. The doctor diagnosed a concussion. It left a protruding blue vein on her forehead, which years later still pulsed visibly when she became angry. A day later she became ill in the bathroom. Gazing at the mass of flesh and blood she'd expelled in the toilet, a form "the size of a puppy," she collapsed on the tile floor. She had not known she was pregnant.

TJ refused to tell the police about the beating. In her neighborhood, no one ratted. Because Shotgun forbade her to leave, she stayed with him until the cops hauled him away one day on a robbery charge.

Her new boyfriend was simply a grunt in the gang, a small quiet boy who turned shy and goofy whenever TJ came around. She picked him because she knew he wouldn't beat her. But that ended, too, a year and a half later, when a crackhead's bullet hit the boy in the face and blew out the back of his head. TJ remained at his bedside for three days until the life passed from his sunken face. Afterward she designed his tombstone, drawing his portrait; once more she collected the death fund in the silver cup from her prom.

When Shotgun had killed her unborn child the year before, she sliced out the tattoo of his name on her leg with a scalpel she stole from the hospital. After her second boyfriend's funeral, she heated up a spoon and burned his memory off her arm. She grew so accustomed to the numbness in her life that she almost welcomed the pain that jerked her awake one night, screaming in agony. The appendectomy for which she was rushed to the hospital did not go well, and complications developed that kept her bedridden for weeks.

Her illness allowed her time to think. Outside on the streets, Angel was on the lam for stabbing another girl. The remaining PlayGirls were now mothers or wasted from rock cocaine. For the first time, TJ thought seriously about moving out of Lennox. Sometime earlier, she had traveled up north to visit some homeboys in the state prison and had been awestruck. "I saw scenes I never could imagine! The ocean crashing on the rocks. Seagulls. Beautiful houses. I mean, there's always Rodeo Drive around here," she said, referring to the shopping lifeline of Beverly Hills, only minutes away, "but you know you're not going to get there."

ALTHOUGH TJ was capable of great violence, she and her gang adhered to a strict moral code, however misguided. Like other gang members, she was quick to describe acts of revenge but usually reticent to talk about the reasons for them. Yet whenever she recalled the night she disguised herself as a man to avenge the murder of twelve-year-old Danny, her voice filled with the black-and-white moral certainty of adolescence and the ancient logic of revenge. "The guy was at that party, probably bragging about it to some girl, when I found him. But he survived." She broke off and seemed, for a moment, to lose her composure. When she spoke again, though, her voice was soft, controlled. "If I had it to do over again, I'd shoot him in the head."

I was still not certain I believed her story of payback. Despite the boasting of gang members on talk shows, I had learned by this time that truly hard-core kids do not admit to murder—or in TJ's case, attempted murder—as there is no statute of limitations for homicide.

I suspected that the story might be one of the lies TJ told about herself in order to hide uglier truths. I once asked her if Danny's payback was the worst act she ever committed for her gang. To my surprise, she paused. "The worst?" She looked at the ceiling. "No, I've done worse. One night Angel and ten of us in the back of a pickup truck we stole drove into Inglewood, looking for the enemy. Somebody spotted a carload at the 7-Eleven. We took off after them, chasing them to La Cienega, where they crashed into a pole. We all jumped out of the truck and charged their car.

"There was four of them, two guys and two girls. I get out. I had this long steel pole sharpened to a point. I used it to smash the windshield. Some of the guys jumped on the hood, kicking the glass. I opened the door where this fat chick sat and whacked her on the shins—" TJ was animated now, reliving the event. "You could hear her bones cracking. *Pop! Pop!* She was screaming. Then I took the pole and rammed it between her legs."

TJ let out a laugh. I listened, slack-mouthed, trying to reconcile the innocence of her face with the ugliness she described. I steadied my voice, careful not to convey the horror that was welling up inside me. "What do you mean, 'between her legs'? Inside her vagina?"

"I don't know. I pulled it out and there was blood, about a foot of blood up the pole. I remember laughing, 'Ha! Bitch!' "

She pushed aside the sandwich in front of her, warming to her subject. "Meanwhile everyone was kicking the shit out of the other guys and girl and we all ran for the truck. I remember looking down and there was this big crack of blood going down this chick's face. And the guys with her looked the same way. Their noses were broken, their lips busted. It looked like a river of blood.

"We took one of the girls with us. I don't even know which one. I was sitting on the edge of the pickup, trampling her face with my boots as hard as I could"—she stopped to demonstrate, stomping her feet underneath the booth—"just busting up her whole face. Then"—she stifled a giggle—"this is the *really* funny part. We're driving along and this car sees what we're doing and follows us, honking its horn, flashing its lights to get someone's attention. We drive past a cop giving a ticket—and he totally ignores us. This happens with two different cops! Sees what we're doing and does nothing!

"I was like, 'Throw her out! Throw her out!' First I told them to get her rings, I noticed she had jewelry. So everyone is taking off her rings. I didn't want one. I just wanted to throw her in front of the car following us, 'cause then it would have to stop. I guess we were going about forty-five, we tossed her out, and she kind of bounced over to the side. The car, though, kept after us all the way to the hood. So we jumped out of the truck and took off."

She took a sip of water. "I spent the night at my homegirl's. In the morning, my shoes were covered with blood, my hands caked with it. I called up my friends and they picked me up with a change of clothes, 'cause I had to clean up the blood, hide it. The sheriffs were everywhere, looking for us. A rumor went around that a bunch of Lennox dykes had kidnapped an Inglewood girl, raped her, and threw her in a Dumpster, something ridiculous like that. I mean, *that* fat ass? Then I changed and went to school."

I felt sickened, soiled by what I heard. I needed an excuse for this excess of human conduct.

"I wasn't wasted. I was like buzzed, blowing in the wind in the back of the truck, like 'Hey, I'm cool.' I knew exactly what I was doing."

"Did you feel bad about this?"

"No. I laugh about it. I never worried about it. I guess I just didn't care. Whatever happens, happens."

Her voice never faltered; her face revealed no emotion. I asked if she could turn on someone she cared about.

"Not any of my family members. To tell you the truth, when I caught my boyfriend in bed with someone else, I just walked away. But see, I started training myself when I was about twelve to control my temper with people I know, 'cause I have a really bad temper. I get quiet on the outside, but on the inside I just get kind of hateful. Being in a gang, it's like when you're in the military and you just have to do it. Like sometimes I'll think I've got to do this for my country. I'll think about my old pets that have died. I'll just think of things that get me, like something I would fight for. You know?" She took the first bite out of her sandwich. "And that fat girl? That's what she got for being from the wrong hood."

THE next time I mentioned the truck incident when I phoned TJ, she sounded distant, withdrawn. I reminded her that she had laughed while telling the story only a few days earlier. "Nervous laughter," she corrected me as though ashamed. "Sometimes I want to forget, you know?" She repeated several times, "That was my old self."

Her voice reflected a numbness common in occupations familiar with death: cops, firemen, doctors, morticians, the droning monotone of the confessed killer. The more you could feel, the more you cared, the greater chance of self-destruction. It was not coincidental that many of the kids in gangs took drugs or drank. Drugs helped protect them from things that would, if fully perceived, drive them crazy. Although rarely a user, TJ found ways to shield herself just the same.

She existed as two people. In a mob or with the support of a few homeboys, she cultivated a ruthlessness that allowed her to act with almost limitless violence—a brutality she was incapable of on her own. It was an attitude she probably needed in order to survive, at least as a player, in the hood. Alone, she was likable and funny.

On the phone she reiterated that she had been going to church. If a gang member is serious and not hiding behind the altar, religion, like motherhood, is one of the few ways a gang will allow you to leave. I asked how her absence would affect the girls in Lennox-13 if she managed to break free.

"I'm about the only older girl who's not a mother." By "older," she meant over nineteen. "Right now there's only one young girl who is a true gang banger, the real thing, as high up or higher than the most important homeboys. Everyone calls her Shygirl. She's the only female allowed in an all-guy clique. Well, she's not a female, really—when you run around and look just like a dude, there's less friction, you know? She carries a loaded gat; she's down. I hear she's trying to organize some younger girls into forming their own clique."

TJ was quiet again for a beat or two. "There'll always be someone ready to take your place. 'Cause nothing changes. Dying never stops."

CALIFORNIA GIRL

Sometime after I'd come to know her, Shygirl told me the story. She woke up in her makeshift bed from an explosion of gunfire one night and realized she was dreaming again. The shots that she often heard on the street sounded no more frightening than a car backfiring or a kid lighting a firecracker, but in the dream they shook her like an earthquake. This night her eyes snapped open and she jerked upright in bed. The silence felt shocking. In the darkness, she looked toward the other side of the living room where her father slept, her ears primed for trouble.

A moment later there was another noise. Someone knocked at the door. Shygirl glanced at the clock: 2 A.M. Knocks at this hour brought bad news.

At the door a teenager, one of her older brother's friends, looked down at her. "Wake up your father," he told her.

"Why?" she asked, rubbing her eyes.

"Just wake him up."

She let the boy in, and he walked to the couch and gently shook her father, speaking to him in Spanish.

"They shot Jose in the neck over on the Ave."

Shygirl did not react when she heard the news about her brother. She stood still as a shadow, face drained of emotion, steeling herself for the familiar pounding in her temples, until a voice reached her from far away. "Let's go," her father was saying, standing in the middle of the room, holding his coat.

Not again, she thought.

At the hospital her mother bent over Jose's pillow, crying and pleading with God. Shygirl wondered why her mother was so hysterical—the pulsing respirators, the beeping heart-rate monitors, the intravenous lines were proof Jose was, at least, alive. But after staring at her brother's prone, motionless body for a few minutes, she understood. Nothing stirred. Not a hand, not a finger. A tear made its way down his cheek and stayed there. Her father desperately tried to talk with his son, demanding over and over, "Who did this to you?" as if the question were the key that would magically spring open Jose's frozen mouth. He instructed Jose to blink his lashes, twice for yes, once for no, but the boy's tears made even this communication impossible. Shygirl saw her father's inflamed expression as he gazed at his son's ruined face and left the room.

Outside her father grabbed her arm. Where, he wanted to know, could he get a .38?

"What do you want a gun for?" she asked.

"Find out how much." Her father broke into sobs. "I want to know who did this."

Shygirl begged her father not to get involved. But a night or so later she sat next to him in the car as they slowly cruised the street, searching for the enemy. Each time they passed a circle of boys, her father whispered, "Who's that?" hoping it would be someone, anyone from the gang who shot his youngest son. At last Shygirl recognized her rivals, three or four teenagers huddled in front of a bodega. The absurdity of the situation hurt her head—her father soliciting his daughter's help in a drive-by. As they approached the boys, again he asked who they were. Shygirl sunk slightly into her seat and peered at the group outside. One could be the triggerman.

Her father interpreted her silence as a possible yes. His voice quivered. "Is it them?"

Finally Shygirl answered. "No. Those are some of us," she lied. "They're from Lennox."

But when they got home, Shygirl went to her bed and removed a .45 automatic from a hole under the mattress. Her father didn't hear her slip outside. She stole down the street to her homeboy's house. Together they left in a car to return to the bodega where she'd spotted the enemy, the gun resting in her lap.

"I didn't want my dad to do anything." Shygirl related to me as we drove in my car along the same streets she had hunted that night. "I don't know why, I felt like it was my responsibility. My dad, he's not the type, he doesn't understand why these things happen. I don't want him to get caught up in this gang. I mean, if that had happened to my kid, I would have done the same thing. But I told him we would take care of business."

■ had heard all about Shygirl before I ever laid eyes on her. Wherever I went in Lennox, her reputation preceded her. One gang banger boasted Shygirl jumped him in. For a sole female to participate in a boy's initiation beating was unusual; I wanted to know whether Shygirl had hit as hard as the others. "Hell, she threw the first punch! She had her arm around my shoulders, then all of a sudden—*boom!* She hit me in my face with her right, knocking me to the ground. She's crazy."

Another one warned, "She is the real thing, the most real you will ever get. She can act low-key, but when she gets angry she just snaps. It's like she gets tunnel vision, her eyes narrow, her whole face changes. She will take down anyone in a minute; she does not care. She eats, sleeps, and lives Lennox."

The gang unit at the Lennox sheriff's station also knew her. One officer kept a Polaroid of Shygirl in her patrol car, but in four years they had failed to pin anything on her. "We know for a fact she's been involved in some shootings, but without evidence, there's nothing we can do," said Detective Ralph Garay. "A guy from Inglewood had gone on a rampage in Lennox, and one day some of the Lennox guys recognized him on the street. They opened fire in broad daylight, like the O.K. Corral, Shygirl being one of them. We tried questioning her, but Shygirl's a poker face. I mean, you get no emotion. You sit there and talk to her—she just gives you a blank stare. Like stone. As far as her gang's concerned, it's probably one of her best attributes."

The detective also said she was a "dyke." "She looks just like a dude. You can not tell her apart from the homeboys."

One night the sheriffs deputies took me on a run of the neighborhood, offering to find her, but turned up empty-handed. They suggested I try the Lennox Middle School. Although seventeen years old, Shygirl still visited her old junior high, as did other high-school-aged gang members. The middle school failed to keep them out of gangs once they left its walls, but it provided a safe haven and counselors who offered a rare, sympathetic adult ear.

As I entered the school parking lot one afternoon, a yellow motorized security cart pulled alongside my car. A woman behind the wheel wearing blue sunglasses and a nose ring asked if she could help. I hopped in, and she introduced herself as Brenda Muse. I noticed a tattoo on her wrist—three dots, the symbol of the gang motto: *"Mi Vida Loca"* ("My Crazy Life"). She caught me staring at it. "You can take the girl out of the hood, but you can't take the hood out of the girl," she said. Now thirty, Muse hailed from Lennox-13, a former leader during the late

1970s of a female clique. "I'm not proud, but I'm not ashamed. I have regrets, but not many."

She wore a faint reminder of regret on her left cheek from the night an enemy caught her in a parked car and slashed her across the cheekbone with a box cutter. The gash never healed properly, and Muse constantly covered her disfigured face with her hand. Then a plastic surgeon who felt sorry for her offered to fix her face for free. Thankful for a second chance, Muse spent lunch hours during her senior year tutoring younger kids at her old junior high. Fifteen years later, she still worked with kids as campus supervisor at the Lennox Middle School.

"I never accepted the new girls around here," Muse said as we cruised the playground and manicured lawns, "the TJs, the Angels. They were into the heavy metal rock crowd, then switched to gangs."

The level of girls' involvement in the Lennox cliques went in cycles over the years. At times the boys' gangs welcomed girls, at others they pushed them aside, denigrating them as whores, bitches, snitches, and spies. Girls frequently found themselves in a catch-22: male leaders would order the prettiest to infiltrate an enemy party to set up or lure a rival—at high risk to herself—only to resent her and all females for making men vulnerable. "Right now girls are at the bottom of the totem pole. They've been reduced to nothing," Muse said. "Except Shygirl. I could see her shoot somebody in a heartbeat."

At the school she introduced me to Rachel Romero, a counselor who had known Shygirl since the sixth grade. Until a few months ago, Shygirl had shown little use for Romero. Then her best homeboy was killed in front of her and she almost fell apart. It was the first situation Romero had witnessed that Shygirl could not handle herself.

When I finally saw her, Shygirl's appearance fit the descriptions I'd heard. She looked like a Latino boy, slouched unsmiling in a corner, her husky frame draped in a striped shirt that hid her breasts. Downy hair covered her upper lip like the debut mustache of a teenage boy. Shockingly, the word LENNOX was tattooed on her forehead in indigo blue.

I was unprepared, however, for her pale perfect skin and her thick black lashes, all the more noticeable because her eyes seemed perpetually downcast. Shygirl had agreed to talk with me in Romero's presence. I began with simple questions about the neighborhood; she turned expectantly to Romero, awaiting a translation. At first, I thought she did not speak English. But Romero was translating my inquiries into barrio slang. When I asked where Shygirl hung out, Romero said, "Where do you kick it?" A question about how many girls were armed became "Who's strapped?" I hadn't experienced any problem communicating before. Shygirl intended this not-so-subtle putdown to keep me at a distance.

Romero, however, was used to making misfit kids feel at ease. She grew up not far from Lennox in Gardena. Her father rumbled with gangs as a teenager; her uncle was a victim of the zoot suit riots, publicly stripped and beaten. Beyond her duties as a counselor, she served as mother, advice-giver, and chauffeur to gang bangers, maintaining daily contact with at least ten. As a result, she averaged around four or five hours of sleep a night. Today she was angry with Shygirl because the high school had suspended her for a week for beating another girl on school property. Shygirl insisted to Romero that the girl had disrespected Lennox-13 by dating rival guys. "She says things she shouldn't have; she sleeps around. The girls don't respect themselves. There's a time to party and a time to take care of business."

Without thinking, Shygirl swirled toward me with indignation. "This girl was behaving scandalously!" Gang lexicon reserves the word "scandalous" for the most amoral act. "We don't want the message out that we don't have control over our women, that they go back and forth between gangs like toss-ups. I have a lot of love for my hood. I don't want the girl to fuck it. So I made her bleed."

Romero cut in. "From what I heard, five security guards couldn't stop you."

The disappointment in Romero's voice turned Shygirl's face vivid crimson, and now her nickname fit. From beneath the raw exterior I glimpsed the child who deferred to adults. "Shygirl waited two hours to tell me what happened," Romero explained. "I told her not to allow people to manipulate her. Other guys in the hood could have taken care of this girl, but Shygirl feels tremendous pressure to prove her allegiance constantly, as the only true homegirl. She has it harder than most boys. The girls from other neighborhoods constantly try to fight her. To pull Shygirl down would build their reps exponentially. The rival guys hit her because she's the only girl."

Recent events further complicated Shygirl's life. During a gang summit in September 1993 that both press and some 1,000 teenage gang members attended, the Mexican Mafia, or *La Eme* (after the Spanish letter for *m*), a brutal organization within the California prison system with a strong influence on Latino street gangs, ordered a truce among youth gangs and an end to drive-by shootings. Anyone jailed for a drive-by—although this part of the edict was not expressed to reporters—faced death or maiming once in prison.

Many felt the truce would end one of the bloodiest cycles in Mexican-American street gang history. Bangers were now to fight face-to-face, careful to protect innocent bystanders. In the immediate months after the summit, homicides did fall in some of the worst neighborhoods. The more cynical law enforcement officials believed that the truce was designed merely to improve drug trafficking—*La Eme* was long tied to heroin distribution—and end brown-on-brown gang banging to take over lucrative turf now controlled by black gangs. (The word was that *La Eme* gave the green light on shooting black drug dealers.) Whatever the Mexican Mafia's intentions, street gangs took its edict against drive-bys dead seriously. Whenever I mentioned *La Eme* to gang counselors or to kids, I was met with stony silence. One counselor warned me not to write anything in my notebook about the Mexican Mafia.

For Shygirl, the truce brought calmer nights to Lennox—she could now eat in a fast-food joint in enemy territory with her back to the door—but it also attracted more kids to the gang because you could win prestige without having to put yourself in the line of fire. The newcomers did not do drive-bys; did not steal cars; did not write graffiti in enemy hood; in short, did little to prove themselves. Shygirl was furious with these wanna-bes who saw themselves, on an investment of nothing, as urban guerrillas. "There's just girls everywhere who say, 'I'm from Lennox.' You ask who jumped them in and they're like, 'I don't have to get jumped in, 'cause my brother's from Lennox.' That don't matter. If you say you're from the neighborhood, you got to show me you're down for it. I didn't get my fame because of my brothers. I got fame because I did it on my own."

Her fame came with a cost: she surrendered her sexuality. She made it clear that she did not date the homeboys, nor did she have sex with them. Reluctantly, shyly, she admitted she once had a crush on a boy in her gang: Smokey. It was his death that compelled her to come to counselor Romero; the two of them visited his grave each month. In school Shygirl still daydreamed about him. "He was the sweetest person. He was a gentleman. We could talk about anything."

Yet when Smokey was alive, she was terrified that if he realized she liked him as more than a homeboy, their talks, their friendship would end. She was determined to excel in the neighborhood as one of the boys. She long ago gave up wearing dresses and in sixth grade horrified her teachers when she showed up one morning with her head completely shaved. She volunteered for the gang's riskiest jobs, breaking into cars, pulling robberies, or invading enemy territory. She earned a reputation for backing up her homeboys.

Smokey, who started the clique, was the one who allowed her in the Tinies, the only girl ever permitted to join. To Smokey, Shygirl was a friend, a backup, a homeboy who just happened to be female. "I wasn't really into that girl stuff," Shygirl said. "I got into the violence, the fun stuff. Nobody came near me. I was the only one putting in work. The girls would just kick it, come to the parties. The guys never asked them to do nothing. I'd be like, 'Let me go. Let me do it.' 'Cause all I cared about was gang banging. Sometimes I did it to get my mind off problems at home. I'd get mad—whatever—and go and take it out on anything."

A question had been bothering me and now that Shygirl seemed more relaxed, I finally, gingerly, asked it. Given her mannerisms, had people thought she were gay? She grimaced. "Hell no. I don't think so. I may be dressing like this"—she squirmed, an arm disappearing inside her shirt to rub her neck—"but I ain't doing that shit. I get mad when people say that. That's why I made some changes. Like my hair. I started to think that people were getting the wrong idea, so I was like, 'Fuck it. I won't shave my hair.'

"There was a time I thought I should change more," she said suddenly. "My sister-in-law cut feathers in my hair and put makeup on me and I put on a dress. I was all embarrassed. It felt weird!" Her face betrayed an uncertain smile. "In a way, it felt good, but . . . I went outside and they all made fun of me." She grinned broadly, her features red, and for an instant seemed vulnerable, even girlish. The moment passed quickly. "But those guys who made fun of me?" She smacked her fist into her palm. "They got the picture." She laughed and she and Romero high-fived each other.

Many male gang members welcomed lesbians in their ranks with an acceptance that extended beyond anything I'd witnessed in mainstream society. Though at first this surprised me, in time it made sense. Both boys and girls in gangs prize aggressive masculinity above nearly any other trait. Extremely butch homosexual women win respect precisely because they appear almost indistinguishable from men, favoring the same clothes, right down to their boxer shorts. They stay active far later in life than straight women because usually they do not have kids.

Conversely feminine attributes are disparaged. "Bitch," "girl," or "faggot" are the worst insults one can sling at a man. The notion of femininity is complicated, even for gang girls. Although some feminine girls secure a role beyond that of seductive informer or spy—I have encountered petite, frail girls who could reduce many men to a pulp, their seemingly innocent faces an effective surprise weapon—inevitably their biology holds them back. Sooner or later, most become pregnant and in Latino gangs a woman on the street who has children at home is an object of scorn.

I don't think Shygirl knew herself whether she were gay or not. Romero told me later she believed Shygirl was asexual out of survival. "It would be real interesting if she ever came across a guy who would accept her for her. I can see her completely falling apart, because no one has ever tapped into those emotions. A floodgate would open."

So far no one had been worth the risk to Shygirl. Respect was something hard-won, easily lost, and thus something that constantly needed to be guarded. You had to fight for your place in the world. "She's done good for so long, she survived the whole gang, and now she can be an original ganster," Romero told me when I asked what she thought would become of Shygirl. "But I don't think that she'll ever get out of the neighborhood. That's all she's got. It really, really is."

SEVERAL nights later I drove down Inglewood Avenue, passing young men in baggy pants and flannel shirts posed like border guards on every corner. I became lost and stopped midstreet, squinting in the blackness at the house numbers. A figure in an L.A. Raiders jacket limped toward my car. It was Shygirl. Relieved, I jumped out to apologize for my lateness, but she only laughed, her cheeks reddening, the corners of her eyes crinkling. "I was worried about you. I thought something happened."

Shygirl settled into the front seat like an old woman. Her leg was asleep, she explained, the one that was hit during a drive-by. The bullet remained lodged in her thigh, a souvenir. "I can't run that fast. It's worse when it gets cold, 'cause the bullet gets cold."

At the local Denny's Shygirl shifted awkwardly in her seat. I asked if her leg still bothered her. "Naah," she said, reaching down to adjust the fabric in her crotch. "I'm strapped. It's tucked between my legs in my underwear." She blushed again, as though she were talking about menstruation. "It's a .380. Like a .25 in shape, but bigger with bigger bullets. It's ready to shoot. I just reach down and pull it out."

Shygirl had roamed the streets since the age of twelve, although, unlike some of the kids in the neighborhood, she had a home. She preferred the "Ave.," as she called Inglewood Avenue, because she was known there and the chaos on the street was more predictable and less personal than the pain at home. Her family had moved to Los Angeles when she was an infant, fleeing the civil war in El Salvador, but misfortune had followed them north. When Shygirl was four years old, her older sister took ill and died. Afterward Shygirl talked out loud to her dead sister, frightening her baby-sitters. Her mother gave birth to another girl, but the addition did little to improve the mood of the household. "Before my mom left, my parents would fight in front of everybody. I was ashamed. My dad would start drinking, then beat up on my mom. Once, I think I was like eight or nine, we were at my aunt's house right here in Lennox, and my dad was too drunk to drive. My mom wanted to go home, they started arguing, and I don't know what happened, but my dad started punching and kicking her. He cracked her head open and knocked her teeth out. I remember my aunt grabbed me and just covered my face. I was screaming."

Her father's behavior made Shygirl increasingly cynical. Everything and everyone was failing her. "There was a time when everything would be going good, the family would be getting along. During those times, when I went to school, I would just concentrate on my work and stuff. I don't know, I liked school, it was all right. It still is. I liked to stay after and help the teachers. But I was always scared, saying to myself, 'Oh, I hope nothing bad happens,' and then always something came up."

While Shygirl was still in elementary school, her brothers Tito and Jose arrived from El Salvador with stories about bodies piled up like junked cars. Their native country's civil war prepared them well for the streets of L.A. and almost immediately they joined Lennox-13. Tito, the older brother, cultivated a reputation as a street fighter who wore flamboyant trademark red Vans sneakers.

Smokey and other boys her own age wanted to emulate Shygirl's teenage brothers. In the beginning their antics were little more than childish pranks: returning bottles for deposit that they had stolen from the store owner. But they could be vicious, hunting stray cats, swinging them by the tail over their heads or running over them with their bikes. Once, while digging through her brother's dresser to borrow his clothes to dress "crazy," Shygirl found Tito's .357 Magnum. She sneaked out of the house armed with the six-shot revolver to show her new friends. "At home they were all going crazy. I'd go outside and see my homeboys. It made me forget about my problems."

Gang life became Shygirl's religion. Lennox gave her courage, faith, told her how to live. It gave her the sense of something greater than herself, of some higher purpose. At thirteen, despite her brother's warning, she got jumped in to Lennox's Tinies clique.

The night of her initiation, word spread that a rival gang had launched a drive-by on the neighborhood. The shooting was Shygirl's first encounter with gunfire and she felt both exhilarated and frightened. By the time she got there, the police had already sealed off the area with the strangely festive yellow crime scene tape. Kids spilled onto the street. She tried to peer through the cops, the paramedics, the gawkers to glimpse the body, but she was too small—she could see only a pair of blood-soaked Vans sneakers abandoned on the pavement.

"Damn, Shygirl," said Smokey next to her. "Those look like your brother's shoes."

Another one agreed. "Yeah, isn't that Tito?"

Shygirl laughed awkwardly. Her brother was too tough. After the ambulance crew loaded the body onto a stretcher, the crowd broke up. When the other homeboys saw her, their faces grew dark.

"They shot Boots," one said.

Shygirl did not recognize the nickname. "Who's Boots?"

"Man, Shygirl, they shot your brother."

She walked home in a daze. Her mother and father were watching TV in the living room. For a minute or two, Shygirl didn't say anything. She felt stupid. She didn't know what to say.

Finally she said, "They shot Tito."

Her father looked at her. "Shut up," he said and turned back to the television.

"They did," Shygirl insisted. "I saw his shoes on the street."

Her mother told her to quit saying such things.

They sat in silence until moments later Shygirl's cousin knocked on the door with the news their oldest son Tito was in critical condition with nine bullet holes. Shygirl's mother turned and screamed at her for not telling them.

After that, the nightmares started. They were always the same dream: she was being shot.

ONE evening, while parked in my car eating burritos, Shygirl told me she wanted to start an all-girl clique called the Tiny Locas. "But it's hard to find a girl who's really down. Not some hoochie. A girl who knows when a problem comes up not to talk about it." She considered recruiting her cousin Annie, but Shygirl worried about her, like a mother worrying about her child. "I don't like talking about what I've been through, all the shooting, 'cause I don't want to make Annie feel bad." She admonished Annie for hanging out with the wrong people. Shygirl could be bossy, ordering Annie around when Annie briefly dated a young black man, a pairing she and her homeboys refused to tolerate.

But the Tiny Locas never got off the ground, in part because Annie showed more interest in "taggers"—bands of teenage graffiti artists with no loyalty to turf—than in Lennox-13. Shygirl felt that Annie constantly tested her, forcing her to choose between her cousin and her gang.

The fact was, Shygirl seemed to care too much about everything and everybody. During the day she was fine, but at night her dreams were mean-spirited. After rough nights, when she walked around with dark bags beneath her seventeen-year-old eyes, she would allow Romero to talk about taking her away from the neighborhood for a while. A friend had moved out of L.A. to Riverside; Shygirl envisioned it as a real-life version of *Little House on the Prairie.*

Memories proved dangerous for Shygirl. Her description of Smokey's murder made her sound eerily like a traumatized war veteran. "Smokey and I were together." She crossed two fingers to indicate their closeness. "When he got in trouble, I'd back him up. When I got in trouble, he'd back me up. I don't know how to say this, but I got so close to him that I loved him, you know? That was the hardest thing. We were going home from a party, we got drunk. We were in my homeboy's car, and some-body outside was shooting. Everyone started running out of the car, we were all so drunk—he and I just stayed inside. He got hit. Shot in the head. If I hadn't been drunk . . ." Her voice quivered. "He told me he was going to die. I looked at his hands and they were clenched white. We called the ambulance, but these cops, they come for every little thing, but if somebody gets shot, they take their time. By the time they got there . . ."

She made a small choking sound. Her body was wracked with deso-late, uncontrollable sobs. Tears streaked her cheeks. She looked very young and alone.

I drove her home soon afterward. She limped around the backyard of her uncle's house to the converted garage where she and her father lived. Although her father had beaten her mother for years, the anguish he showed over it afterward would win his daughter's pity, and she pledged never to abandon him. He, in turn, had not taken a drink for two years and now attended night school.

"I can't promise my father or Miss Romero that I'm gonna stay away from the gang. I can't promise them that I'm going to be good, that I'm going to get out. The only thing I did promise was that I'm not going to drop out of school. Which I'm not. I want to be something. I want to have a job. A good-paying job. Not on welfare or food stamps. Be proud, you know, of the money that I earn.

"When this all started"—she waved her hands to encompass the neighborhood and its chaos—"I didn't know the truth. When they shot my older brother Tito, the night I got jumped in, I was like, 'Why did they shoot him?' I didn't know that we shot at them *first*. I didn't know how serious it was."

Out of habit, she glanced over her shoulder at the street. "That's why I'm tripping out. If we can have this truce now, why did we ever start shooting at each other?

"I have a guilty conscience. I dream"—she sighed heavily and looked up at the stars—"I dream I'm kickin' back and the cops raid us. Or I see myself not making it to my house. I see myself get shot. When I try to scream for help, nothing comes out of my mouth." She shivered, as though trying to shake off the thought. "But what really trips me out is I never see the sunlight in my dreams. I can't see people, only their shadows. I trip out, damn, I want to see the sunlight, but I'm trapped in the dark. I get scared, you know?"

Then she walked into the shadows where I could not see her.

COLOR WARS

"You're too nice, Gini." Coco sat in the backseat of my car as we sped down Broadway through February's twilight, beneath a sky the color of pink grapefruit. L.A. in winter is discernible only by the absence of human life—in summer, packs of kids rule the street corners of South Central. Now many of them cruised Broadway inside big cars: Cadillacs, Buicks, Monte Carlos. Cops call them "gangster cars," stopping them for a broken taillight or a missing windshield wiper before searching the trunk for stolen guns.

I had let Bird drive. He maneuvered the wheel with one hand, the other arm draped gracefully out the window, his sculpted profile a picture of elegant machismo. Both he and Coco showed little patience for my driving skills. They offered tips for navigating through South Central, advising me to try to never stop at a red light—someone could leap inside your car, put a gun to your head. Time it so you roll through.

"You're just too friendly around here," Coco went on. "You got to be careful."

Bird glanced sideways at me. "You can't trust no one," he said protectively. "Like, we go to clubs and say we meet some guy who's got money? We'll be real friendly to him. Call him up, start hanging out with him. This might last two nights, might last a month. Then one night we'll call him, say, 'Come on over. Let's party.' When he shows up, me and my homeboys jack him. Take all his money."

"Isn't that hard to do to someone you've gotten to know?"

"Don't matter," Coco piped up again from the back. "Got to put food on your table."

"How do you know he doesn't have to put food on his table, too?"

Bird snickered. "I jack people who got money."

"How come you never jacked me?"

Coco, taking in the baggy jeans and T-shirt I'd worn every day, didn't miss a beat. " 'Cause you don't have shit, Gini."

We all exploded into laughter.

I was clearly an outsider in South Central, as much as I occasionally imagined otherwise. Coco and Bird often made comments revealing how little they believed whites knew about black culture. Bird almost fell on the floor, punching my shoulder playfully, when I'd recognized Snoop Doggy Dogg and Dr. Dre on the radio, even though their popularity was hardly restricted to the ghetto. Another time I used the expression "pissed off" and Coco accused me of picking up ghetto slang. They viewed my refusal to drink or smoke weed as another example of my whiteness, not as a matter of personal choice.

Race was one obstacle for me in South Central; another, almost greater hurdle was class. I grew up in an all-white community in Wisconsin, the child of well-traveled professionals, the product of college and graduate school. Coco knew her way through the bewildering labyrinth of welfare offices, mean streets, and criminal courts. She was intrigued to learn that I had black friends in New York—journalists, television producers, lawyers. On my street in Brooklyn, my middle-class black neighbors roughly shared my income level.

White faces were so rare in their South Central neighborhood that if not for the access Coco offered, I would have encountered almost insurmountable obstacles in my attempts to have strangers to open up. Q-Mac, a girlfriend of Coco's, spelled it out for me: "We be aware of white people in our area 'cause not many come down. Most people would think you an undercover cop or something and they'd rob you. Or figure you here to buy drugs—the druggies get money from people like you."

For the most part, however, people eyed me curiously when my rental car passed by. Occasionally, teenagers stared with open hostility. As a kid, I would have been terrified of these youngsters and their icy glares. But as an adult, I was not frightened, not because I am particularly brave, but because I was an outsider and at relatively low risk. I was taking a certain chance: if a gang member decided I was an informer for the police or an enemy gang, he or she wouldn't have hesitated to rough me up. And you could always get caught in a cross fire. But most often the victims of these teenage gunmen are children just like themselves: their former playmates, their neighbors, sometimes their relatives, but rarely, if ever, white reporters.

Trapped in a society that fears and quarantines them, ghetto teen-agers survive as best they can. This acute sense of isolation perhaps explained why a few girls shunned me, among them Coco's nieces Wanda and Jade, who grew aloof after our first encounter at Coco's house.

I finally asked Coco about their attitude. She sighed. "The girls, when they're into this, are meaner than the guys. Distant. They're even distant from me sometimes. But I know where they're comin' from. They don't want nobody to tell them what to do 'cause they don't give a fuck. See, when you go to school here, you have teachers who are racist and shit. They say they want to help you, but they come down on you." Coco's anger ordinarily rumbled near the surface, and she communicated it at ear-splitting decibel levels, but she spoke these last words in a tone that betrayed only weariness. "The girls don't give a fuck about life itself 'cause the simple fact is, they've been hurt too much."

ONE afternoon my frustration led me to show up unannounced at Wanda and Jade's house, hoping to talk with them. At first I feared the girls had given me the wrong address. The place looked abandoned, the curtains drawn, the shades pulled. A green sign on the window read something about earthquake inspection in English and Spanish. Chicken wire, along with a general air of dilapidation, surrounded the dirt lawn, where a brown mutt with a gaping open wound on its leg dozed near the gate. I placed my hand near its nose and the dog raised its head just high enough to take a disinterested sniff before returning to its nap. I opened the gate and let myself in.

Through the screen I made out a darkened empty room. Suddenly a little girl appeared. I asked if her mother or Jade were home. Twice she shook her head. "Wanda?"

This time she nodded yes and opened the door.

Out of the dimness a shadowy figure moved toward me.

"Did she let you in?" the voice asked.

"Yes, I'm looking for Wanda."

She stepped into the sunlight, her shoulder glued to the phone. "I'll call you back." Wanda slammed down the receiver.

"You are going to get whipped!" she hollered down at the little girl. "I'm telling Mama when she gets home and you are going to get whipped hard!" The child looked up at Wanda and trembled. "Mama just whipped you this morning for following that meter man outside the gate. That's how little kids get snatched and raped!"

The child was too scared to make a sound; her eyes glistened with tears. She had no idea what getting snatched and raped meant, but she knew Wanda was terribly angry. Wanda marched her to the porch. "Sit on that front step and don't move."

Inside Wanda grabbed a broom and attacked the carpet as though cleaning house could clear her mind, all the while mumbling about snatching and raping. A day earlier the remains of a five-year-old boy were found encased in concrete in a Dumpster a block away from Coco and Bird's. Almost a year ago to the day, the boy's sister was found in an identical gruesome cast. Their mother was the only suspect.

Though I could barely see inside the house, Wanda made no move to turn on a light. She swept up toys—a Barbie with knotted blonde hair, a hot-pink miniature backpack, a jump rope—throwing them in a heap in the corner. From the waning caramel light seeping between the cracked curtains, I could make out that the room was beige, the paint blistering with age or perhaps from earthquake damage. Still, the house looked neat, considering the fact that a toddler lived there. The sofa was shrouded in heavy yellowed plastic, almost as if the occupants moved out long ago.

Sweeping furiously, Wanda informed me that she had talked to the homeboys in her hood and could not bring me there. In Wanda's case, "hood" did not refer to the neighborhood where she lived, but rather a street corner some twenty blocks away, where she hung out with the Crips. "They're like, 'Oh, Wanda, so now you're spreading our business?' She stopped and leaned on her broom, wiping dust from the corner of her eye. "See, some might boot you out of the hood, kick your ass, or kill you. First thing they said was 'Don't bring that writer to the hood 'cause she won't look the same when she leaves.' Some other homeboys, they were like, 'She's writing a book about us?' " She mimicked one of them nodding his head and rubbing his chin thoughtfully. " 'That's cool.' Those homeys aren't worrying about shooting Bloods. All they worry about is gettin' money."

I asked whether the boys told her what to do. "The older homeboys, they watch over all of us," she conceded. "But you got to make them respect you. See, some homeboys, they can fuck you up. Tell you to put in work: give you a gun and tell you to shoot so-and-so. But I tell them, 'You don't own me. I'm not going to jail for you.' If a girl does that, puts in work just 'cause some guy tells her, they've lost respect for her. They know she's weak. And those people get caught and go to jail. They might just kill one person, but they'll take the rap for like nine people and be gone for life."

She cracked the screen door to check on the little girl, who remained frozen on the steps.

Wanda and her sister Jade, although Crips, grew up in Blood territory on the East Side—the designation for anywhere east of Main Street, the dividing line in South Central. The East Side was poorer and more dangerous than the West Side, where Bird and Coco lived, although this distinction was not readily apparent to outsiders. Crips outnumbered Bloods by almost seven to one. The Bloods, however, were considered "crazier," more committed fighters.

"When me and Jade was little, we used to have to fight everybody. It all started on 27th. Over there Bloods are on one corner, Crips on the other. Bloods used to whip me every day, just because me and my sister used to walk by. We'd get beat back to 28th Street. I started to avoid the area. I was scared to go, afraid somebody was gonna fuck with me. It took me a long time to go down there, probably five or six years. I haven't been gang banging a hell of a long time. Like '89, the middle part of '90. That ain't a long time. But in that time I've learned a lot of things. Before I couldn't take death; I was scared I was gonna get killed. When you in a gang, you can't allow that fear to fuck you up. You end up not being scared of shit by being in a gang.

"Soon as I started hanging with my homeboys, they started teaching me you can't be weak in this society. They showed me how to hit people to kill them or knock them out."

Wanda walked over to the TV set and brought me a photo of Jade in a bright yellow cheerleading uniform from a collection of family pictures. "Now my sister Jade ain't never been no punk, she always wanted to have her name known. See, everybody cries when they fight, when they get mad, but not Jade." Wanda assumed a fighting position in the middle of the room, one foot in front of the other, fists high. "You're nervous the first round like, 'Damn, is this bitch gonna hit me or am I supposed to hit this bitch?' With Jade something clicks and she's like *kill, kill, kill*"—

Wanda pummeled the air—"and when that happens, she just wants to sock harder and faster. She ain't gonna let nobody talk shit to her.

"My sister, she was never the type to show me right from wrong; it was always my mother. My homeboys showed me how to be rough, but all in all, my mama put the heart in me; she's the one who took all the fear out of me. She said, 'Don't be no punk.' If we did the wrong move, she'd say, 'Don't do it like that. They'll fuck you up. Do it again.'"

Having refused to talk to me at first, Wanda now unleashed a verbal torrent. "People say kids join gangs 'cause they came from a bad home; that's a fucking lie. People join gangs to get what they never had. Some guy in a gang hangs with a homegirl, he ain't probably never had no sister. My two half brothers were murdered. My oldest, who lived with my daddy, was killed when he was seventeen. He got shot seven times in the head by the police. I didn't even know he got murdered. I didn't find out until two or three damn years later. All that time I'd been writing him letters and shit. But now in my gang I have lots of brothers to love."

She rarely mentioned the girls in her gang. When I asked about them, she said that there were ten altogether, then added that girls couldn't be trusted. She and Jade were different, she claimed. They were like the homeboys, not like those other bitches, who talked too much and scared quickly. It was a sentiment I'd heard a number of times. Worst of all, Wanda said, girls set up her homeboys.

"Like when my homeboy Baby G got killed?" Her voice unexpectedly rose in the darkness. "A female set him up." Wanda paused a moment, then I heard the broom swish against the carpet. "I was on the phone with him when he got killed. He was high, calling me from the street. He wanted to come over here on his bike. Like I said, this is all Blood territory here, we surrounded by Bloods. I told him not to, he'd be risking his life."

While Wanda and Baby G argued, she heard a noise that caused her to jerk the phone away from her ear. "I thought he was hitting the receiver against the phone booth 'cause it was like—*bam, bam, bam*. I was like, 'Baby G, stop that banging!' Then I stopped and listened."

Wanda stood still in the darkness. "I had my fingers crossed, thinking, 'Please don't let this happen.' I thought maybe someone shot at him and he ran away. I yelled, 'Baby G!' I heard this deep breathing." She released a slow raspy gasp. "I went, 'Oh shit.' I cried, 'Don't die, cuz! Don't die!' I hung up the phone and started putting on my clothes. I was gonna ride my bike to where he was, but then my phone rang. A voice said, 'Wanda, Baby G is dead.'

When she arrived at the phone booth, she saw that the neighbors had covered Baby G with a bedsheet. "The police?" she asked rhetorically and laughed bitterly. "They were somewhere eating donuts and coffee. I got there thirty minutes later and the paramedics hadn't even got there yet. The motherfucking police rolled by the scene two times and didn't even stop. Baby G collapsed under that telephone stand, police cars passing him by, and died."

She sighed deeply. "That experience on the phone, I *never* went through anything like that. That was like a baby dying in my arms. November 2, 1993, at seven o'clock."

She went back to the door to peek out at the little girl. In the light I scrutinized Wanda's profile for tears, but her cheek was dry. She settled in the sofa opposite me. "All the homeys were at Baby G's wake, right? To see the dead body? We were just sitting down, and Big G, that was Baby G's big homey, said, 'This shit ain't happening. My little nigger ain't leaving.' He got up to the casket and opened up the fucking lid! They had Baby G tied down. Big G cut the motherfucking rope and took him *out* of the casket, threw the body over his shoulder, it was heavy as a goddamn board! Hard like this." She knocked on an end table. "Baby G was wearing a suit, but no pants, just white shorts, and his suit was split up the back. When Big G took him out, his shorts fell down, his booty was wrinkled and shit. Big G carried him out of the damn mortuary, going, 'My homey ain't gonna die. I'm taking my li'l homey home with me.' He wouldn't put him back after the man said to, so the man called the police and they came like a SWAT team, running in with Mace and shit, yelling for everyone to come out. After we went outside, Big G still wouldn't let go of the body for nothing. They finally got Baby G's body away from him, and he got so mad he went and shot up the funeral home. But the police knew that he was grieving, so they cut him some slack."

Wanda made a clucking sound with her tongue and nodded. "Big G's still around. He's doing good now. He still believes his homeboy's here.

"And all this—because of a *female*," she spat, the last word oozing disdain. Baby G, she said, was on the phone for only ten minutes. "That was a fucking setup." Wanda smacked her thigh. "This bitch saw him on the phone and called her homeboys. Her and Baby G had got into it 'cause she was hanging around the Bloods. I was the one that first said, 'Let's kill this ho.' I wanted to kill her, but I really couldn't, 'cause one of the girls from our hood, that was her relation.

"But even so, her own cousin helped me set her up, 'cause she don't like her. She called her, and I got on the phone, pretending I was a Blood, and she started running off at the mouth about Baby G. I caught her that night. Until they pointed her out on 42nd Street, I'd never seen her, but I watched her ass all day. Finally I caught her strolling down an alley by herself. I walked in after her. With the way I was dressed, and I was talking to myself, she thought I was some crazy pipehead. As soon as she turned her back . . . *Whoomp!* I smacked her right across the head. Then my homegirls came running down the alley and we fucked her up! I was beating on her rib cage, hitting her in the ankles—*bam, bam, bam*—hitting her in the knees, make sure she don't walk again. I didn't want to kill her; I wanted to let her know that you don't set up one of mine and get away with it. We beat her for twenty minutes—"

I interrupted her. "And no one stopped you?"

She exhaled loudly. "This is the East Side. Nobody gives a fuck what happens here. Afterward, we wrote the name of some other Crips—our enemy—on her face with a marker so the police wouldn't look for us. Her mouth and ears was bleeding, scared the shit out of me. I thought I'd killed the damn girl. We rode by a little while later and seen them putting her into an ambulance. She was in the hospital for two weeks. When she got out, she had casts on her legs and a neck brace." Wanda's voice filled with self-satisfaction. "I don't know what my homeboys did to the guy that shot Baby G, all I know is what I did—'cause niggers ain't the only ones doing work out here."

Later I would hear a different version of Baby G's death that made Wanda's story even more disturbing, if that were possible. Q-Mac, a member of Wanda's gang, told me that some of the gang members believed that Baby G himself pulled the trigger while he was on the phone, pleading with his girlfriend not to leave him.

But I did not know this other version of the story that afternoon. When I pointed out that using the girl's cousin to set up an ambush for a nearly lethal beating was precisely the behavior Wanda hated in females, she quoted from the Bible: "An eye for an eye." She assured me that God was on her side: "You in a gang, you lie, you sin, you can get forgiven for all that. I say, 'As long as you have faith in God, you win.' I can go out here and sit on my front stoop, and if someone rides by and shoots me, I'm going to heaven. That's how I feel. That's how much faith in God I got."

Interpreting my silence as skepticism, Wanda grew animated. "Gang banging ain't no sin," she insisted. "Where's that in the Bible? Now, killing is a sin. But you'll be forgiven for killing. You'll be forgiven for everything you do. Except for killing yourself. That's despair, taking God's business into your own hands, and you can't be forgiven. I think all those motherfuckers that are in hell are the ones that committed suicide."

She stepped out on the porch. The little girl now sat on the bottom porch step, tears rolling down her cheeks. "What you crying for!"

The child recoiled.

"What you do? Did you pee on yourself?" Wanda pulled her up by her arm and felt her bottom. In a flash she hauled the toddler inside. "Girl pees on herself and she's three years old! Now you are going to get a whipping!"

Wanda stomped into the back room, dragging the little girl. I could hear Wanda spanking her, accompanied by her faint cries. Wanda reappeared, shaking her head. "That child is in big trouble when my mother gets home."

Minutes later Wanda's mother, Mrs. Franklin, arrived home from her new temporary job at the phone company. A few months earlier she'd been one of the thousands of employees laid off from Sears, where she had worked at a warehouse for twenty-one years, beginning her day at 3 A.M. and returning home at 10:30, long after her daughters had left for school. She looked tired and wary of strangers.

The little girl, having survived Wanda's wrath, reappeared in fresh clothes and crawled next to her grandmother on the couch. At thirty-nine Mrs. Franklin was only three years older than I, yet she carried herself as though she'd lived much longer. She possessed a warm smile and the skin of a young girl's, yet her eyes, like the eyes of so many mothers here, looked like they had seen too many things that one should never have to see.

Mrs. Franklin had grown up in South Central, her own mother out-lasting three husbands to raise thirteen children. Her memories of the old neighborhood were vibrant and lively. Central Avenue, the main strip where Mrs. Franklin and her daughters now lived, had been known in the 1930s as the dazzling "Jazz Street," but in the 1970s, it was still a hot spot, lined with raucous nightclubs where Tina Turner and James Brown turned crowds wild. Even the prostitutes on Central in their high heels and furs seemed glamorous. Now Central Avenue was merely one long stretch of graffiti-covered gas stations, liquor stores, and storefront churches with long-winded names.

"When I was young, my best friend was white," Mrs. Franklin said, recalling the differences between the South Central of her youth and that of Jade and Wanda's. "She grew up with me, lived above the cleaner's on the corner. When children are born, they know nothing about race; they go out and play together and have a good time. It's the parents that feed them this garbage about race; this is how all the shit comes about. Back then, it was a community thing. We had problems"—she nodded her head vigorously—"my husband got addicted to heroin and my brother joined a gang. But he never fired a gun, it was fistfighting. And we had Officer Kelly. He was a police officer, he was black, and he lived in the neighborhood, right on 55th and Compton. A nice man, always involved."

Mrs. Franklin had watched and held on as her neighborhood slowly decayed. First the area's whites fled to the suburbs, then the middle-class blacks. Businesses moved as well. In two decades Los Angeles lost more than 25,000 jobs in the rubber, steel, and auto industries.

Without jobs or opportunity, gangs became the last resort for thousands of forsaken youth. The Crips' forerunners were the Slausons, the Outlaws, and the Gladiators of the 1950s, who formed for protection, often against white teenagers who didn't want blacks moving beyond the boundaries of the ghetto. From the ashes of the Watts riots (when the Slausons and Gladiators joined forces against the police as the Crips and Bloods would do almost thirty years later after the Rodney King verdicts) arose the Black Panthers. The teenage Crips that came to power in the 1970s would share none of the Panthers' ideals or political goals.

The Bloods banded together primarily to defend themselves against the Crips. Because Crips wore blue bandannas to disguise their faces during missions, the Bloods adopted red ones. As more neighborhoods gave birth to gangs, Crips fought other Crip sets as well. Legend has it that one of the first Crip-on-Crip struggles was over a girl.

Although much smaller than the Latino gangs, the Crips and Bloods made up what they lacked in numbers and organization in the ferocity of their color wars. By the late 1980s the major imports into South Central were guns and crack cocaine, pouring in by the trunkload. Meanwhile local politicians pumped huge sums of money into corporate downtown Los Angeles, its glistening skyline visible from the Franklins' door. Despite its proximity, or perhaps because of it, Mrs. Franklin and her neighbors felt abandoned.

WHEN I asked Mrs. Franklin about the gangs her daughters had joined, she smiled patiently. What I viewed as gang members, she saw as neighborhood boys she'd known all their lives. "The first one I ever knew was a gang member," she recalled, "was Scrappy. They grew up with him, they beat him up, he beat them up. He used to play football and they were cheerleaders. They started hanging around Scrappy and it just kept going as the years went on." Mrs. Franklin toyed with the pink airplane barrettes in her granddaughter's hair. "I do not want Jade and Wanda to go up and hit somebody or take something from someone that don't belong to them. My children are not hungry, they're not homeless, they're not looking for no money, they're not looking for no love. Unlike a lot of children who are in families where there is no love or no one there for them, their family is behind them."

Her daughters talked big, Mrs. Franklin admitted, but they weren't bangers, not really. "You can be minding your own business and be caught in a drive-by shooting. My oldest daughter's husband, that's how he got killed. Drive-by shooting.

"Where's your daddy?" she suddenly asked the child seated next to her.

The little girl pointed skyward.

"She thinks he got wings. He's dead," Mrs. Franklin said, "shot by a friend high on PCP." She cuddled the girl. "When I was a kid, people died, but it was always the older people, never our friends. I never seen other kids get shot."

Was she worried how this would affect her daughters? Mrs. Franklin remained philosophical.

"Jade and Wanda got so many obituaries on their wall. I think death bothers Wanda more than it bothers Jade. Jade, she don't care. When

Wanda goes to a funeral, she'll cry. Jade won't. You're dead, you're dead. It's your time. Jade wants to be a mortician." She let out a dry laugh. "She'll pick up a chicken heart or a gut and throw it at you. She'll pick up a dead rat and throw it on a plate.

"Let me tell you something. Jade had a boyfriend named Fear. One night they were playing cards and he said, 'You know, Jade, I have to tell you something.' He sounded real serious. She said, 'You gonna go kill yourself or something?' And he said, 'No, Jade, this is serious. When I was about ten or eleven, my father attacked my mother and slit her throat. And then he slit the throats of the twins and the baby. I wasn't home at the time, so he didn't kill me.' Well, he said, his father went on the run. Then when Fear was about twelve years old and his cousin was eleven, they tracked down his father and those two boys shot him to death. Fear felt bad about killing his own father, but he felt he had to be a man. He started crying when he told Jade that story. So Jade has heard a lot."

LATER that afternoon, when her mother had retreated to her bedroom, Jade came home in high form. She danced into the living room, arms and legs waving like pinwheels. "Hi, Gini! What's up?" she greeted me. Then she shouted to no one, "If I don't get a job soon, some white people are gonna die!" She fired her invisible weapon into the air, before bursting into laughter and collapsing into an armchair.

The little girl ran to Jade, pointing under her chair.

"There's a gun in there!" she yelled.

Jade's mouth twisted into a half grin. "There ain't no gun here."

"Yes, there is. There's a gun in there!"

"Shhh." Jade lifted up a corner of the cushion. "Look! See? Nothing."

The little girl wasn't having it. She crossed her arms. "I know there's a gun in there."

Jade pulled the child to her and lowered her voice. "If you tell Grandma, I'll tell her you picked that gum off the Laundromat floor and ate it."

The girl weighed this. "You'll tell her that I *ate* it?"

Jade nodded.

The child quietly crept away.

Jade looked relieved for a moment, then her expression switched to annoyance. She sat up and peered out the window. "Oh, my trick is here." She clarified for me. "My boyfriend. Ice Capone."

A tall lean black man, Jade's male counterpart, with legs like bean poles, a blue T-shirt, and Puma sneakers identical to hers, strode in without knocking. "What's up, cuz?" he said to Wanda, then studied me, sitting on the couch. "I heard about you. You like hanging out with black people?"

I must have looked flustered because he gently tapped my knee and grinned broadly. "I'm just playin' with ya." Ice plopped down on the arm of Jade's chair, his long legs splayed in front of him.

The little girl again shouted, this time for the young man's benefit, "There's a gun in there!"

"Mom!" Jade started to yell. "She ate—"

Her pint-sized opponent immediately surrendered. "No! No! I'll be quiet."

Just to make sure, Jade toughened her threat. "You say anything to Grandma and you're gonna sleep outside with Jimmy." Jimmy, I learned, was a rat that resided in the walls. The girl blanched.

Satisfied the child wouldn't squeal, Jade looked at Wanda accusingly. "You showed it to her. Now she can't shut up."

The gun belonged to Jade's boyfriend and was loaded. I asked Jade if she were afraid her little niece would injure herself.

Jade remained unfazed. "She won't play with it with us here and she's never alone. It's too heavy for her to lift—a 9-millimeter—and the safety's on."

"Does your mom have any idea of the gang stuff you've done?"

"No, 'cause I keep it shady. She be telling me, 'You don't got to rob and steal. You come home. I'll give you money. I'll give you clothes. You don't got to sell drugs.' But I do it 'cause it's my choice. It's what I want to do."

Wanda cut in. "My mother says we're gonna grow out of it. Ain't nothing but a phase. All gang bangers, once they reach that age where they see it ain't getting them nowhere, gonna go on with their life. Just some people, who want to get out, get killed before they can."

I heard this same logic from Coco, who, at twenty-four with four kids, still seemed to be hanging on to this "phase." But Wanda saw a difference between herself and Coco. "I'm gonna tell you something about

Coco. She is crazy. Coco will fight anybody. Her first husband?" Wanda referred to the father of Coco's son Philip, now in prison for attempted murder. "Coco beat the shit out of him. Stabbed him and did more than that to his ass. Coco don't take no shit off nobody. She don't care who it is, female, male, mama, daddy, granny, sister. She don't give a shit. And her little girl Tasha gonna be exactly like her.

"We," she said firmly, "ain't got anything to worry about."

FAMILY MATTERS

Spotting my car as I pulled up in front of Coco's, Tasha came running. She looked strangely unbalanced, with one side of her hair neatly pig-tailed, the other tousled and wild—evidently she'd made a successful dash for freedom from her mother's comb. Another girl raced behind her, halting abruptly at the sight of me, as if a big stray dog had just appeared in the yard. The woman in the front house shuffled onto her porch, magenta housecoat wrapped around her heavy frame, to call me over. "My unemployment check didn't come. I need money"—flashing a queasy smile, she pointed to Tasha's playmate—"for my niece."

The woman looked in my direction with bulging eyes that refused to focus. Bird had warned me his neighbor was a "shermhead," addicted to marijuana cigarettes dipped in PCP. One night after smoking, the woman and her boyfriend had exploded into hallucinatory rage, smashing every window in their house. Coco and Bird jumped out of bed, terrified of another earthquake. "That little girl don't mean nothing to her," Bird said when I relayed our encounter in his living room. "She's the daughter of her current boyfriend. They just want the money for drugs."

In a neighborhood where many boys father children, then disappear into street gangs and death, Bird remained devoted to his kids. He went into the kitchen to dole out ice cream for them. A tattoo peeked out above his collar on the back of his neck: TASHA. He had it done, he told me, in the pen, where he nearly went crazy from missing her.

He was dressed in Crip blue, with a plaid shirt and jeans fashionably baggy but spotless, pressed to perfection. Like his stepdad, Philip, too, was decked out hip-hop style, sporting a tiny pair of Timberland boots and gigantic trousers that his belt, tightened to the last notch, couldn't keep from slipping over his knobby hipbones. The pants, Philip confessed, were really his mom's shorts.

Eating his ice cream, Philip declared that he wanted to be a paramedic when he grew up. I asked if he knew what that was.

"They carry out dead men."

"How do you know that? From TV or seeing it on the street?"

"On the street!" Tasha shouted brightly.

Bird shooed the kids outdoors. "You all beat it out of here while we smoke cigarettes."

He lit a joint, sticking it under my nose to make sure I knew it was weed—"herbal" as he called it, not a "primo" laced with cocaine. "Anything that comes from the ground can't hurt you." Going over to the huge stereo, he put on Snoop Doggy Dogg, the bass rattling the door frame. The baby Li'l Chick had finally learned how to sleep through anything.

Coco was out picking up Bird's mother to baby-sit. While Bird waited for them, the landlord, an elderly white man in a suit and aviator glasses, dropped by, leaving a minute or so later with his $575 rent. For a little more money, Bird and Coco could find a safer, better-kept place, but unspoken rental discriminations against families with many children kept them here. Besides their rent, they paid about $80 a month in gas and averaged $100 for their phone. Each month Coco received $200 in food stamps and $663 from AFDC toward the care of Philip, Sheba, and the baby; Bird received $490 for Tasha—he had won custody of his daughter after the court deemed his first wife unfit because of drug use. Together Bird and Coco totaled $16,236 a year from Aid to Families with Dependent Children for their family of six. AFDC excluded women from welfare if an employable man lived in the house. Bird and Coco were not married and, though they did not always live together, would be penalized, or cut off for trying to keep their family intact, if discovered under the same roof.

At the moment neither was working. The year before, after serving as a cook for the school board for six and a half years, Coco quit when her employer slashed the staff's pay 10 percent and reduced her schedule to two and a half hours a day. At that rate, the job did not even cover the cost of gas or baby-sitters. Bird had worked as a certified nurse's aide in a convalescent home, gang banging after midnight when he got off, until a few months earlier when he broke his hand while lifting a patient into a wheelchair. He received workmen's compensation, but his boss threatened to fire him if his hand did not heal soon.

While looking at the photo album on that first day I visited them in L.A., Bird had shown me a picture from his childhood: a joyous boy, captured midflight in a back flip, his feet a blur as he hurls himself skyward. As a kid, Bird could barely stay on the ground. His family lived in the Valley, near the Famous Amos Cookie Company, one of the few black entrepreneurial success stories of the 1970s. One day a man from the company brought Bird's mother some cookies and announced that they wanted to sponsor her son in gymnastic competitions. The next day he took Bird to a gym where he introduced him to a white boy who Bird recognized from a TV commercial. But soon afterward, Bird's mother and father moved to Long Beach and he had no way to return to the Valley to train.

"I could just flip like a motherfucker!" he had recalled excitedly. "I could have been in the Olympics!" He turned to a photo of himself flexing a well-toned bicep next to a prison wall. I would come to see many such pictures—absurdly pumped-up, bored incarcerated men who built their pride with barbells. Bird traced the picture with his finger. "Now I'm O.G. Bird, so it's all good, but . . ." His words trailed off.

In Long Beach he had met boys who introduced him to the Rollin' Twenties, a Crip set. By junior high he was "robbin' and shit, but I kept thinking, 'I'm not ready for this.' Then one day one of my homeboys got shot. From then on, I was in it to the fullest." He was twelve.

At sixteen he was sentenced in juvenile court to the California Youth Authority for assault with a deadly weapon for striking four people in the knee caps with a baseball bat during a gang mugging. A year later he and his friends robbed a credit union with a toy gun, too nervous to use the real thing. Under the Step Act, which demands the harshest sentence possible for a known gang member, Bird was tried as an adult and sent to state prison at a time when California officially shifted the emphasis of imprisonment from rehabilitation to punishment.

Two years later he was back in his old neighborhood and a cold job market, now with a criminal record. He wanted a job, but question six on the application always tripped him up: "Have you ever been convicted of a felony?" In the living room, Bird excused himself, a moment later returning with what looked like a bundle of play money. Food stamps. He asked if I'd drop him off at work after Coco returned. Bird's "office" was the corner of Manchester and Broadway, open Mondays and Tuesdays, where he earned his living selling food stamps. He bought them from neighbors at a discount, then hawked them to someone else. The stamps were traded again and again, with each person taking a cut. The offense was a federal one, as illegal as drug dealing, but Bird considered it less "nasty."

As a "little homey," he had sold drugs for a living ("You keep the weed in a plastic bag up your ass. It might stink a little bit, but you make your money."), but now was too scared. He had struck out twice under California's three strikes law. One more strike, depending upon the mood of the prosecuting attorney, could separate him from Tasha and his other children for life.

ONE night Bird took me to meet his homeboys in Long Beach. We pulled down a residential side street, stopping in front of a small apartment building where a pack of young men milled about, decked out in the Rollin' Twenties colors of black-and-gold, adapted from the uniform of the Pittsburgh Steelers. He introduced me as a friend who was writing a book and the two young girls in the crowd immediately vanished. At first his homeboys avoided my questions with harmless teasing—Maybe I wanted to go out with one of them? Did I like their clothes?—then they simply forgot about me. They affected relaxed attitudes, perched in a row along a cinder-block wall surrounding the apartment building where one of them lived. A pint-sized teenager with a motormouth named Baby Crazy stood up and began writing ROLLIN' TWENTIES with a Magic Marker on the wall of the building. Jay, the boy who lived there, did a double take.

"You're not writing on my house?" He peered through the darkness to make sure he was seeing right. "Nigger, you ain't writing on my house, are you?"

Bird grabbed his gut. "Baby Crazy is crazy!" he roared. "Nigger, you just went up a stripe!"

"Man"—Jay stuck a hand on his hip—"just *let* the police know where I'm at."

Baby Crazy ignored him, jumping down to the sidewalk, his baseball cap sliding over his eyes. "Hear about Cass?" he asked. "The girl is smokin' crack." The news turned the boys solemn. Bird recalled the time when Cass and he were selling weed on the corner together, and she saw the police headed their way and without a thought shoved the dope between her huge breasts, locking Bird in a spine-crushing embrace until the cops passed. Jay remembered how, after her man got arrested, Cass hustled, sold dope, anything to get the best lawyer for him. Though this same boyfriend had once car-jacked Bird, putting a .38 to his temple, Bird still held the girl in respect for her loyalty to her man. He cringed at the thought of such a woman chained to the pipe.

Suddenly a kid called Li'l Dog bolted from the wall. Jay looked down the street. Sure enough, a black-and-white cruiser was approaching.

"Don't run!" he hissed. "They gonna stop for sure!"

Li'l Dog jerked to a halt. He turned back slowly, casually resuming his place on the wall. But it was too late. The black and white screeched to the curb, followed by an unmarked police car—unmarked in name only, since every man, woman, and child in the neighborhood could spot one. Twin sets of headlights blinded us. Someone on the wall groaned, then every boy went still. A blond-haired cop stepped out from the unmarked car. In the middle of his forehead was a round Band-Aid like a third eye.

I knew exactly what was about to happen. These cops were members of CRASH (Community Resources Against Street Hoodlums). I had ridden with several of these cowboylike gang units, all of which operate under the theory that constant surveillance, harassment, and suppression in target areas will break up gangs. They may rely, on occasion, on helicopters, thermal-imaging devices, and made-over armored vehicles to destroy gangs, but the daily routine goes like this: officers pull over groups of kids, often on petty pretenses. (During one patrol I was on, two teenagers were stopped for a broken taillight and a group of men for drinking beer in their yard.) The detainees knew exactly what to do, passively lifting their arms in the air, clasping hands with fingers intertwined in the approved manner behind their necks, adopting a blank expression. Even the tiniest frail nine- and ten-year-old brothers caught outside at midnight with two men knew the routine and stuck up their hands and assumed that vacant look.

Most of these kids weren't left with new respect for the law or a desire to leave their gangs, but with even more hatred of the LAPD. During one stop, a crowd had gathered on the street, among the onlookers a young woman with angry eyes that bored into me. "Who's *she?*" she had asked the cops, not breaking her sulfurous stare. "A new undercover?"

I answered for myself. "I'm a reporter."

"Don't matter." Her face contorted in an ugly sneer. "You with them. I seen you. I know who you are. Don't come around here."

I had made a mental note of what block I was on, deciding to stay away for a few days. She was enraged because I'd witnessed her neighbors being treated with so little regard for their dignity. I was about to get an inkling of what she felt.

"EVERYBODY ON YOUR KNEES!" the blond cop now barked at Bird and his friends.

Simultaneously a large dark-skinned Latino cop exited the black and white cruiser.

"Niggaz, on your knees!"

Immediately each boy hit the ground, arms in the air.

Behind the officers a bespectacled man with a receding hairline and a paunch, an undercover cop or maybe a reporter, eased his way out of the patrol car's backseat.

The dark cop began at the far end of the line, searching each guy, sticking his hand between the boy's legs and pulling down on his balls.

"Don't break my cigarettes," one kid told him.

"Oh, excuse me. I thought I was squeezing your dick."

"You keep going, and you will." The kid laughed. The dark cop laughed right back.

He reached Baby Crazy, G'd-up in black-and-gold with his Steelers cap and jacket. The cop leaned over the kid from behind, so that his big broad face must have appeared upside down from Baby Crazy's vantage point.

"You wouldn't be a Rollin' Twenty, would you?"

"Steelers just my favorite team." Baby Crazy smiled.

"Yeah, I thought so."

Meanwhile the blond cop turned to Bird. It flashed in my mind that Bird had smoked a joint in the car. Was he carrying drugs on him?

"You, I remember your face." The blond cop was taunting him. "Your name?"

"You know him?" the dark cop asked Bird, tilting his chin toward his partner. "He ever jump down from a tree on you? He used to wait in a tree for guys like you."

The blond flashed his teeth. "I'm a psycho!"

If Bird did have any marijuana, the cop missed it. Then the blond turned his attention to me sitting on the wall, where I had remained since they pulled up. Somehow this didn't seem real. And I couldn't see this as having anything to do with me.

"Who are you?"

I indicated Bird. "A friend of his."

"Then get on your knees."

I fell to my knees and raised my hands. The action felt strange, humiliating. I noticed how much it hurt on concrete. The other thing was how absurd it seemed—but then I had nothing to hide. I had done nothing and I was white. During the time I'd lived in L.A. I'd never had an encounter with the LAPD, other than seeing them in the street as they passed in RoboCop stride, eyes hidden behind mirrored sunglasses. These men gave me the creeps. Unlike cops in New York, where I usually felt reassured to find one patrolling my block or riding on my subway car, L.A. cops always made me feel as though I'd done something wrong. How much more intense that feeling had to be for a black or Mexican kid.

"What were you doing here?" the dark cop growled at the kneeling line.

"Just having a party," someone answered.

"Well, the party's over. I can haul you in for trespassing." Although one of the boys lived on the property, no one dared contradict the officer. "I can take you all into jail or you can leave."

The boys rose and headed into the backyard of the apartment complex, away from the sounds of muffled laughter and car doors slamming. In the dark they talked quietly.

"Man, I hate getting on my knees," said one.

Bird shifted from foot to foot. "Don't you hate to get fucked with?"

"What we have to do," said Baby Crazy, "is get smarter than the police."

"Yeah," they all agreed.

Coco's relatives criticized her choice in men. Bird was "cool," Jade and Wanda thought, but needed more direction. And they rolled their eyes at how Coco shared him with another woman. "Fucking the same nigger your homegirl is fucking?" they'd say. "And Coco got two babies by the fool and doesn't know if Roylene will get pregnant by him? No, cuz, that shit ain't cool."

But Roylene, the other woman, had still not come around in weeks. Bird did not explain why, just said she acted distant. Then one afternoon Coco announced that Roylene was having a party and invited me along. When I arrived to pick up Coco, I was surprised not to hear the familiar bass pounding through the locked door. I recognized Tasha's timid voice and identified myself.

"Hi." She peered out from behind the screen. "Come in."

The room was dark, the shades pulled. Sheba reigned happily in the center of the room on her potty seat and Philip and Tasha colored on the floor. Once my eyes adjusted, I made out Coco's collapsed form facedown on the sofa. She stirred slightly, then opened her eyes, wearily pushing herself up by her arms as a torrent of bread crumbs and chicken bones rained on the floor.

She studied the mess for a moment. "The kids must have covered me with food while I was asleep." She looked around the room. "Which one of you did this?" she snapped, only half-angry. Tasha, the obvious suspect, backed into a corner.

Coco dragged herself into the bedroom to change for the party. As she went inside, another woman came out. For a moment, I mistook her for a man; she was flat-chested and wore men's clunky black boots. This was Bird's mother, Coco explained. Both mother and son shared the same high cheekbones, which were striking on Bird but made his mother appear skeletal, the skin stretched too tightly over her gaunt features. She said hello, revealing a sad collection of rotted teeth, then vanished into the bathroom.

In preparation for Roylene's party, Coco poured herself into a fawn-colored velour dress that barely covered the top of her muscular thighs, but she seemed ambivalent about going. When she'd called Roylene earlier to tell her we were coming, Roylene had only responded, "The drinks cost." The party's entertainment came with a fee to help Roylene make this month's bills.

Bird's mother resurfaced from the bathroom, a thin curl of acrid smoke trailing behind her. Coco led me into the bedroom and lowered her voice. Bird's mom, she lamented, refused to baby-sit unless Coco coughed up ten bucks, which she didn't have. I had no problem loaning

Coco the money, but I suspected that the funny smell coming from the bathroom might be crack. I glanced out the door. The woman sat quietly on the couch while Tasha and Philip danced in the living room, singing along with Snoop Doggy Dogg.

"Is that okay?" Coco was saying, pleading a little. "I'll pay you back."

I handed the money to Coco and she immediately gave it to Bird's mother. "Nothing's for free," the woman said as she counted the crumpled bills. She looked up, her eyes meeting mine for the first time. "Don't stay too long. She's got young kids, you know."

In the car I asked Coco about the woman's smoking in the bathroom. "Lord, I hope it isn't crack," she said, sighing. "I told her if she did that to take it outside. I don't want her to do that in my house." Her tone betrayed resignation. "She stares at you all crazy, like she's paranoid." Coco popped her eyes out in imitation, rocking her head in tiny frantic motions. "Scares me when she gets like that."

My ten dollars was probably helping to support her habit.

Before we reached Roylene's, I asked Coco what was going on between Roylene and Bird. She sounded vague. "I don't know. Maybe she and Bird had words. Or maybe she's upset because of her auntie's death." Bird, she volunteered, had cheated on her with Roylene almost from the beginning. She had not known. When they met, he was only seventeen, though he lied and told her he was older, showing a fake ID his mother made for him on her job at the DMV. They'd flirted at a McDonald's drive-in. Bird had tapped on her car window and asked, "Can I have two or three minutes of your time?"

Two or three minutes would turn into years. He paged her that night while her boyfriend was visiting at her house. When she hung up from Bird, she asked to borrow her boyfriend's car. "For business." She drove to Bird's house in Long Beach, not bothering to come home for four days. Coco burst out laughing at the memory. "I just didn't like that boyfriend."

Soon she was pregnant with Bird's child. She was already raising Philip, her son by her first husband, and Bird, by this time, had custody of Tasha. "I accepted Tasha, but I didn't want any more kids. But Bird said, 'Have them, have them. I'll take care of them.'"

She gave birth to their daughter Sheba. Not long afterward, she learned that Bird was sleeping with Roylene. At first Coco was furious, but the two women agreed to meet. Roylene, like Coco, had "lived the life." As a teenager she claimed Four Trey Crips, but quit banging after serving time in women's prison on drug charges. She respected Coco because they were both mothers and offered to help with Coco's children. Eventually, Coco said, they grew to love each other. "Lots of people wonder why we have this arrangement. But Bird takes care of his kids, sometimes with Roylene. And I don't know if I'd be with him if it wasn't for the kids. I love him, but not the way I used to. There's too much pain behind it."

Less than a month after Sheba was born, Coco found out she was pregnant again. This time she was determined to change the outcome. She started rearranging heavy furniture in her house, jumping to the floor from a table again and again, picking fights with rival gang girls. But the little intruder proved stronger than her will. Finally she went to a hospital run by the Seventh-Day Adventists to rid herself of it once and for all. There, she recalled, a nurse made her watch a film on abortion. Coco, idly looking out the window, suddenly turned to face me with an expression of awe. "It showed what happens when a baby is killed at three weeks. And they *cry*, Gini. Just like a puppy. They make this moanin', screaming noise."

I thought a crying three-week-old fetus seemed highly unlikely, but Coco wouldn't budge. "After that, I knew there was no way I could abort it."

And so she gave up. While she waited to give birth to Li'l Chick, she would sit by herself for hours in a locked parked car, just to be alone. Her mother had told her that's why the baby always looked forlorn; he'd felt her despair inside her womb. The loneliness wore her down and finally she and Bird broke up. Bird said she could leave if she wanted, but not with his kids—he'd kill her first. "That last pregnancy tore me up. I was rebelling from motherhood. He wanted all those kids, he could take care of them. The majority of time I lived in Watts with my homeys from Grape Street Watts Crips, gang banging."

Nine months pregnant, Coco got into a fight with Philip's father. In a rage, he punched her in the stomach, slamming her up against a light pole. Bird found out and went crazy. "I didn't think he cared about me anymore, but he went after Philip's daddy, saying he was going to kill him.

"Bird told me he would always care for me," Coco said softly. "I was the mother of his children." But now that she was back with him, he was telling her what time to be home or demanding to know where she'd been. Coco didn't like anyone telling her what to do.

ROYLENE lived in the middle of a battle zone between two warring Crip sets. Just days earlier, a twelve-year-old boy down the block took a bullet to the head. At night she'd barricade herself inside her large bungalow, once white but now covered with layers of yellow-brown dust, surrounded by dying eucalyptus trees.

The living room resembled an old-fashioned bordello, with black carpeting and red satin drapes festooned with plastic poinsettias. Several men lounged silently on twin red leather sectional couches; none looked up as we entered. I recognized the coffee table, a huge ceramic panther holding up a plate of glass, as identical to one in Coco's house. On the wall hung a portrait of Philip and Tasha seated next to a little boy with a shaved head—Roylene's son, Coco explained. The child's father was murdered by car jackers five years ago when Roylene was pregnant. Coco whispered to me that the little boy suffered from sickle-cell anemia.

In the dining room, which displayed original dark wood molding, exposed beams, and built-in shelves with leaded glass, Roylene had pushed a table to one side and lined it with liquor. Here the women mingled. A very pretty girl, who was wearing men's pin-striped trousers and a matching man's vest with no shirt but a push-up bra supporting impressive breasts, sat apart from the rest, eyeing me.

"You dance?" she asked finally.

"Not well," I responded.

Coco and the others giggled. Coco explained that the girl wanted to know if I was a stripper. A former exotic dancer herself, Roylene had invited some cronies to perform at her house for a percentage of their tips. As the only white woman in the room, I was assumed to be one of them. This led them into whispered obscene chatter—interrupted by howls of laughter—about how white girls called a man's penis his "cock." To them, Coco said, cock meant "pussy."

Roylene emerged from the kitchen, her large figure voluptuous in a cream-colored suit, and touched my elbow. When we were alone, I asked her about Bird. She said he couldn't understand why she had become fed up with him after all this time. "I'll still take care of Bird's kids 'cause I love them," she said, "but I want someone there for me."

From out of a back room came a tank of a man, head bald as a bullet, tattoos covering nearly every brawny inch of both biceps, twin billboards for Eleven Deuce Crips. Roylene saw my startled expression and laughed. "This is Ducky."

Ducky was Roylene's new boyfriend. Roylene explained that he held a steady job in construction after spending fifteen years in Folsom, Pelican Bay, San Quentin—nearly every prison in the state. He knew Monster Kody and Charles Manson personally. "A nice guy, Charlie," Ducky told me.

The pretty girl in the man's vest now slithered into a corner, where she began to strip, pelvis gently undulating for the benefit of a frail old man in a baseball cap and a younger man wearing a cowboy hat. The one in the cowboy hat stuck some bills in her waistband. We had no money to pay for our drinks, because I'd given my last ten bucks to Bird's mother. Embarrassed, Coco looked relieved when Bird's mom called with a message from a friend who owed Coco money. As we left, a woman in a red leather bra and a painted-on black leather skirt poured herself a drink at the table, singing to herself in a bluesy voice about how she was just a victim of the ghetto, headed nowhere.

"Sing it, Beverly!" Roylene cried.

"I *am* singing it." The woman lifted her glass. " 'Cause I sure as hell ain't goin' fuckin' nowhere."

Coco promised Roylene that she'd return after she picked up her cash, but now changed her mind. "I didn't want to stay at Roylene's." She gazed out the car window. "I can't stand women. They talk too much."

Her friend with the money had left by the time we reached her house, so Coco had me drive her home to dig through her car for a pair of new auto brakes she'd purchased the day before. We took them back to the store, where she returned them for cash to buy the baby Pampers. Then with her food stamps she purchased a giant carton of Kool-Aid, packs of frozen Ball Park franks, microwave chili, macaroni and cheese, and a heart-shaped box of Valentine chocolates for her mother.

Coco looked exhausted on the ride home. "I'm so tired. I can't take this pressure." She rubbed her temples. "I think my mind snapped when I had all these kids. The doctor told me I'm nervous and need to be on pills. That I need time alone."

Coco gripped the dashboard and stared down at her lap. "I never believed when women hurt their babies it was 'cause of too much pressure. I heard stories like that. I thought it was bullshit. But since I've had them all"—she raised her hand, fingers grasping at the air—"I'm afraid I might hurt them. No woman who hasn't had kids can know how much pain it causes you. First physically. Then it can make your mind unstable."

She took a deep breath and closed her eyes for a long moment. "That's why I can't stay with him. I don't know what will happen, now that Roylene's acting funny.

"And now he wants another son! I told him, 'There's no guarantee you won't get a daughter.' I just can't—"

Coco stopped, pointing out the window. "Look, Gini! They got her purse!" At the corner three teenage girls surrounded another, taking turns kicking and swinging at her. One grabbed hold of the girl's waist-length cornrow braids, yanking them so hard that her head snapped backward. A lone boy stood off to the side, then stepped up to throw a punch.

I was in the middle lane, stuck in traffic. Coco and I watched the fight as if we were at a drive-in movie. "Those girls trying to get them nappy braids 'cause they can pull your hair out from the roots," Coco noted absently. Neither of us made any move to interfere. I had already judged the fight not too serious; the numbness to brutality, I was learning, was infectious.

Coco turned away from the girls' circle, her expression solemn. "I worry about my kids. About Tasha. She worries me the most. I love my boys, but your girls—you want to raise your girls to be better than anyone. Tasha is fast. She's not afraid of anything and she uses bad language. We call her Nana, like a grandmother, you know, because she's so old for a child." She tapped on the window with her nail in a nervous, rhythmic beat. "I don't want what happened to me, all this gang stuff, to happen to her. I didn't get to be a child. That's what the ghetto does to you. You got to be fast in the ghetto, can't be slow. Can't be soft."

Traffic inched forward and Coco looked back to where the girls beat their teenage victim. The tormentors had broken up and fled, leaving her doubled over, struggling for breath. Coco twisted around and sat up stiffly. "You soft, you'll go under."

A few days later Coco called me.
"They arrested Bird. He's in jail."
Strike three.

LIVING WITH THE LAW

Bird was one of thousands of African American men listed as gang members in the Los Angeles police and sheriff's gang files. In 1992 the L.A. district attorney's office released a report giving the explosive statistic that police had identified nearly *half* of all young black men in L.A. County as gang members—that is, 47 percent of all of those between the ages of twenty-one and twenty-four. Gang workers, police critics, and civil liberties advocates doubted the accuracy, stating the tendency of cops to overstate gang affiliation by stereotyping and singling out for arrest black men simply by their clothing and where they live. (In 1988, during a high-profile attempt to suppress gangs called Operation Hammer, some 25,000 African Americans were stopped and searched in a matter of days. More than a thousand were arrested and later released without being charged.)

In contrast, investigating female participation in gangs takes low priority, if any at all, for law enforcement. One explanation is that many gang girls are minors. Police officers have less incentive to haul in youngsters based on the belief that the juvenile justice system treats those arrested for vandalism, theft, and misdemeanor assault with notorious leniency. Girls, they reason, are much less a threat than boys and will be handled even more indulgently in court (although, in reality, females may receive harsher sentences because "they should know better"). This attitude leads to both an overidentification of those boys only on the fringes of gang activity as bona fide gang members and an underrepresentation of girls.

The L.A. County Sheriff's Gang Manual lists criteria for identifying a suspect as a street gang member. On page 21, the manual describes the male who is flirting with the idea of joining a gang:

The third level of membership is that person who hangs out with members of the gang but is not directly involved with the gang's criminal activity. He may or may not be dressed in gang attire, but associates with members of the gang. Many people will say this person is not a member of the gang and that he is merely a wanna-be; but, in fact, he is a member of the gang. He is aware of the gang's criminal activity, associates with members of the gang by hanging out at the gang's gathering places, and is often a victim of rival gang violence. The reality is: *If you associate with gang members, dress, talk, and act like a gang member, you are, in fact, a gang member* [italics mine].

The same manual, seven pages later, describes females who claim gang membership this way:

If one was to talk with a so-called female Black gang member, it would be thought that the female plays a major role in Black gangs. The reality is that females play an extremely minor role. There are just a handful of females who actually participate in the activity of these gangs. It is rare to find a female that has actually been "jumped in" to the gang. They rarely hide suspects, narcotics, or firearms for gang members. There have been a few female Black gang members who have participated in gang violence against rival gangs, but the number is not remotely proportionate to Black male participation in the gang. In some of the most hard-core Crip gang neighborhoods, you can find females wearing red attire. These same females say they are members of the local Crip gang, however, evidence has shown this is not to be so.

Appended to the manual is a report on female gang members by a young female deputy of the gang unit at the Lennox sheriff's station. In it, she urges officers to take girls seriously. Anyone reading the manual is left, at best, with a mixed message.

The fact is, boys receive more attention from cops, counselors, the justice system, special programs. Much of it is negative attention—detention and arrest—but it signals who's more important in the system. Girls fall between the cracks in terms of how the police handle youth and in prevention programs—there is no equivalent of midnight basketball for girls. The few social programs for girls typically focus on hygiene and manners or become available only once they are pregnant.

While the crime rate for girls lags far behind that for boys, it has been rising much faster. The arrest rate for girls under the age of eighteen rocketed 82 percent during 1989 to 1994, according to the Justice Department, compared to 25 percent for males. During the 1980s, the number of adult women in state and federal prisons jumped from 12,331 to 43,845, an increase of 256 percent.

Women who are arrested in Los Angeles end up at Sybil Brand Institute, the women's county jail. At any time the population averages 1,800 inmates, which includes minors sentenced as adults. The day I visited the count hit 2,124, with the deputies identifying 702 women as gang-affiliated. Both prisoners and sheriffs do time at Sybil Brand, a beige concrete facility with the institutional aroma of disinfectant on good days and the nostril-assaulting stench of sweat on bad. Gang deputy Rachel Jimenez, however, asked to work here. In charge of the gang unit, Jimenez grew up among cholas in East L.A. She never gang-banged, "out of respect of my mother and fear of my father," but she understood her neighborhood. She witnessed police beating gang members and dreamed that one day she might become a cop who could make a difference. But at eighteen she married and two years later was raising two kids. Not until she turned thirty, after her marriage disintegrated and her children were grown, did she join the sheriff's department.

Jimenez operated out of a closet-sized office, crammed this morning with too many bodies. She listened while a mannish woman, geometrical designs shaved into the sides of her buzz haircut and a teardrop tattooed below her right eye, recalled how she became "president" of her clique. "The leader, she had cancer and was dying. She couldn't hold up during a fight. So me and another girl boxed to see who would take over."

The room was so narrow, stuffed with file cabinets and boxes labeled GANG MONIKERS, that Jimenez and the inmate almost touched knees. Behind the inmate, drawings of cholas with huge exposed breasts and cascading hair, like comic book superwomen—which didn't resemble any of the girls I'd met—papered the cinder-block wall. On the deputy's side were hundreds of Polaroids of real-life gang girls. In the far corner was the wall of death: pictures homicide detectives had taken of bloodied homeboys sprawled on the front seats of cars or in street gutters.

Throughout the morning Jimenez spoke with inmates who belonged to gangs: one's mother had committed suicide; another grew up in foster homes; yet another, who had five children by three different fathers, none of whom she married, just lost her infant niece to a drive-by. Her daughter was also in prison—for murder. The fourth woman was nine months pregnant. A friend promised to take the baby until she was released; when that would happen she did not know.

After the last woman left, Jimenez turned to me. "These girls are likable, when you take them away from their neighborhoods, their drugs. But put them in a pack and they're evil." Jimenez sat down on the edge of her desk, folded her arms. "It's true females will never achieve the strength of guys. Once in jail, they'll talk the talk and walk the walk, empowered by the fact there's no men here to call the shots. But you listen to the complaints of women in jail, their primary bitch is their love life. They have boyfriends on the outs." She nodded toward an area of the wall decorated with photos that the inmates' boyfriends sent of themselves, bare-chested, pumped, and tattooed. "In female prisons what matters most are matters of the heart. With the males, it's power and money. The gang world is just like the corporate world.

"We had to fight to get a gang unit here. A lot of people don't believe there is such a thing as a hard-core female." Jimenez leaned over and tapped one Polaroid on the wall of a boy, about fourteen, lying in the street, literally soaked in his own blood. "It's true boys have it worse. They're expected not to run if someone puts a gun to their head. But a girl will kill for her neighborhood, too. Meet you in the alley and take you out like nothing. How much more of a threat do we need?

It was a question I heard over and over from female officers. As I left the jail, one deputy took me aside to speak anonymously. "This attitude that girls aren't anything? You'll hear the same thing from male cops about female officers." She cracked a small smile. "Because there's a thin line between cops and gangs. Just like gang bangers don't trust anyone but their homeys, cops don't trust anyone except another gang officer." The woman gave a little shrug. "But while there are both males and females in law enforcement, when they need a SWAT team, who do they send? The elite of the elite—who are all men. Like women everywhere, women in gangs will always be second-class."

IN the parking lot of the Lennox sheriff's station, I ran into Deputy Karen Shonka, leaning out the window of her cruiser. Shonka was one of the few female members of the sheriff's department's Gang Enforcement Team. She held a special interest in girl gangsters, writing a report on them for the department's gang manual. She was mildly shocked to learn that I was reporting in Lennox, home of both TJ and Shygirl, on my own. The working-class neighborhood was deceptively calm by days, with row upon row of bungalows on palm-lined streets. At night, she warned, the children take over.

About to begin her shift, she invited me along. She introduced me to her occasional team member, Bobby Delgadillo, who, it turned out, had grown up in the middle of gang territory in the Aliso Village housing projects in East L.A.

I asked Delgadillo why he thought kids bang. "It isn't banging, it's your culture. It's a way of dressing, of talking, of living. I understand these kids. There's nothing for them. Unless somebody shows you the way"—Delgadillo stopped in midsentence to turn around and face me—"and you *want* to be shown the way. I dressed like the cholos." He chuckled softly. He was young and handsome; you could see how good he'd look in his khakis and white T-shirt. "But I didn't stay in it. The girls I knew didn't like that look and I liked girls too much."

"What happened to those girls who did like gang members, the cholas?" I asked him.

"I go back home and they're all divorced. Or dead. Heroin was easy to get and wrecked their lives."

As twilight approached, the patrol car slipped into Lennox. Residents stared at the car, their faces tight with distrust. We neared a group of youngsters, no older than ten, playing kickball in the street. Shonka turned the siren off and on to clear the road. As we slowly passed by, the kids gazed into the opened windows. "Sorry," said a boy with the ball tucked under his arm to Delgadillo. "We'll get out of the street."

The cop smiled. "Nah, that's okay. I used to play ball in the street myself."

The next group of younger children waved the instant they saw us, excited the way they undoubtedly were when they spotted the postman or the ice cream man. They'd not yet become infected with suspicion, which sooner or later boiled over into hatred. Shonka waved back.

When we cruised by some teenagers leaning against a parked car, the friendly demeanor of both deputies vanished. Delgadillo glared at the boys in their hoodies and baggy jeans, then flipped on the loudspeaker: "GET OFF THE STREET!"

Shonka stuck her flashlight in their faces, more, it seemed, to irritate them than anything else. "Seventh grade is when gangs start around here," she said. "The Lennox Middle School has them under control until then. Problem is, their mothers don't recognize it, especially Mexican parents. You have to go to their home, take them into their kid's bedroom, show them the gang graffiti on the wall, the pictures of their girls holding guns with the guys."

Seventh grade had marked the turning point for Shonka, too. It was then that her family—half-Mexican, half-white—finally moved out of the neighborhood where the gang girls taunted her daily. One day, surrounded by a group of them, Shonka had at last fought back and wound up at the police precinct. "I remember thinking, 'I'm gonna get back at all these idiots for beating me up.'" She laughed. "Now I'm taking gang members to jail."

She was one of five women out of the 115-member staff of Operation Safe Streets, the sheriff's department's gang bureau that began in 1979. Shonka belonged to the Gang Enforcement Team (GET), the uniformed patrol division that cruised the street, though she dreamed of rising in the hierarchy to the investigative unit. The odds were not great; so far, only one of the five women had made detective.

In the backseat of the car she kept a folder, one section containing Polaroids of gang kids, with captions giving their gang names, real names, and addresses; the other displayed close-ups of gang tattoos. Among the photos I found a Polaroid of Shygirl. "The most notorious female in Lennox," Shonka confirmed.

The sky darkened from hazy blue to indigo; now the deputies' real business began. Delgadillo turned down an alley between 110th Street and New Hampshire. Gang graffiti covered every inch of the alley walls, warning intruders whose turf they were entering. "This is Sox Los territory," Shonka explained, like a tour guide deciphering hieroglyphics. She nudged Delgadillo. "Flash your headlights on and off. That's their code. It drives them nuts when the police use it."

The dispassionate voice of the radio dispatcher broke the quiet in the alley: trouble at an apartment complex at Century Boulevard and Van Ness. Shonka recognized the location. A few nights earlier they had responded to a triple homicide there. Now, according to the frantic 911, someone roamed the complex, brandishing a Mac 10 machine gun.

We arrived ten minutes later, just as another squad car pulled up from the other direction. A third car nudged us from behind. Sheriffs crawled out of the vehicles. Two held rifles. Shonka and Delgadillo pulled out 9-millimeter semiautomatics. The officers turned to assess what faced them: a sprawling apartment complex with a labyrinth of paths leading into darkness, porch lights the only illumination. They walked in circles, unsure where to begin. The sergeant in charge suddenly spun on his foot, facing me.

"Does she have a vest on?"

Earlier, given the option of wearing a bulletproof vest, I had declined because of the heat. Delgadillo escorted me back to the car and outfitted me. "High Time Hustlers have been trespassing here for the last few weeks," he explained as he fixed the Velcro attachments at my waist. "Intimidating apartment dwellers."

Apparently the intimidation was working. A sheriff interviewed the manager, the man's eyes bulging in fear as he constantly checked behind him. He gripped his chest with his hand, letting the officer know that he was armed with his own handgun for protection. I followed Delgadillo back into the complex. In the blackness an orange glow appeared at the top of a stairwell. A woman leaned against the railing, taking a bored drag off her cigarette as the cops below provided the night's entertainment. A rerun.

Twenty minutes later the sheriffs piled back into their cars empty-handed. Shonka and Delgadillo drove off cautiously between the row of cars parked in front. Suddenly Delgadillo hit the brakes. Peering out at him from the open window of a dented green Oldsmobile was a little girl.

Delgadillo looked around, unwilling to believe his own eyes. "Is this kid *alone* out here?" He turned to the child. "Where's your mommy?"

The little girl stared, mute. A second head, belonging to a tinier boy, hardly more than three years old, popped up.

"Where is your mommy?" Delgadillo repeated to the girl.

But the child just gawked at the deputy, her fingers grasping the half-open window, her feet kicking the upholstery behind her.

"Well, Mommy doesn't care about you too much," Delgadillo said to himself. "What's wrong with this kid?" He faced Shonka. "Where's her mother?"

Shonka opened the car door and stood in the street, looking one way, then the other. I could see her mind at work—the nut with the machine gun could still be on the loose. She ducked beside the Olds so that her nose nearly touched the girl's.

"Did your mommy leave you here?"

"We're going to our grandma's for a party!" squealed her brother.

Shonka returned to the car. "I can't figure this out."

Delgadillo hit the steering wheel with his palm. "I'm ready to explode!"

Five minutes later a door opened somewhere and a woman appeared carrying several overstuffed bags and two balloons. She looked no older than twenty, a large heavyset girl with a quiet face. She lumbered under the weight of her packages.

"There she is," Delgadillo whispered to Shonka. Once again Shonka climbed out. "Yell at her, Karen!" Delgadillo added loudly as she shut the door.

"Ma'am, are these your kids?" Shonka called out. "There's some asshole out here with a Mac 10—a 10-millimeter machine gun. There was a triple homicide here a few nights ago."

"Oh, I didn't know that," the woman said softly.

"Well," Shonka said, unsure where to go, "these kids could have been kidnapped."

"Thank you," the woman responded, with the same blank expression as her daughter. "I didn't know."

Now Delgadillo got out of the car. "Ma'am, she spent nine months in your belly. Shouldn't you be more responsible?"

The woman's childlike face and tone did not change. "Thank you for the warning."

Shonka started to say something but did not. She and Delgadillo got back into the car.

BACK on the street, we passed hair salons, video parlors with their blinking yellow lights, the No Gang Banging Ice Cream Shop. Then the patrol car turned off Normandie and crawled down a side street. There were no streetlights here and the houses, dark and barred, looked deserted. Shonka absently flicked her flashlight on. A man sat on a porch alone, staring unblinking into the light, as though his night had not been interrupted.

She turned it off and the street went black.

We headed into the intersection of Normandie and 107th Street, passing the Malcom X Dry Cleaner's, when three pops broke the quiet in the car.

I heard myself yell, "That's a gun!"

From out of nowhere a small figure dressed entirely in black darted in front of us.

"That's him!" Shonka cried.

Delgadillo jerked the wheel to follow the kid into a parking lot, sending me flying across the backseat so fast that I grazed my face against the metal grate that separates the front and the back.

The cruiser rocked to a halt. Before I could lift myself up from the seat, Shonka and Delgadillo were gone. Led Zeppelin played softly on the radio. I was alone, in the backseat of a cop car with the keys in the ignition, the front doors open, in the middle of a Crip neighborhood where a gunman was on the loose.

"GET YOUR HANDS UP!" Delgadillo shouted from somewhere down the street.

Then nothing.

A few moments later Shonka returned. She slapped the hood of the car. "That fucker's gone!"

She circled the parking lot, squinting at the ground, hoping against hope that the guy tossed the gun when he saw their car. Failing to find anything, she slumped into the front seat and reached for the radio.

"We heard a lot of shots. Suspect is in black jacket and pants, black beanie, slim physique. We can go back over to the apartments where he ran, but that fucker's gone. Fucker did a walk-by." Shonka slammed down the radio. "Just a little kid, too, earning his stripes."

Delgadillo reappeared at the car. "You actually see his gun?"

"No, but it's just too coincidental—a barrage of shots, some kid comes running out of *nowhere*, then boogies when he sees us?" She exhaled loudly. "Man, that pisses me off. He shot someone. People are gonna second-guess us about not being able to catch him."

Already a helicopter roared overhead, its alien beam combing the urban landscape for the gunman.

Finding the shooter's victim required less-high-tech equipment. Delgadillo simply followed a woman's screams. Two or three black-and-white cruisers, both the sheriff's and LAPD's, were already slant-parked in front of the house, along with an ambulance, its red-and-blue beacon spinning in a dizzying whirl.

Shonka studied the figure lying belly-up in the driveway, then gazed back down the street where the gunman fled. "What an animal."

Paramedics were busily cutting the shirt off a large black man as scarlet blossomed beneath him. Another huge man, his T-shirt soaked from sweat despite the chilly night air, stood over his friend, looking down at him, then at his own hand, which one of the bullets had grazed.

"Victim's been shot three times, but he's pretty coherent," a sheriff said into his radio as we walked up. He turned to Shonka, then tilted his head toward the guy standing over the victim. "He was slingin' dope out of the backyard. They're all 107 Hoover Crips. The knucklehead who got shot is named Evil Dog. He's paralyzed. For life."

Shonka nodded. "So now Evil Dog is Crippled Dog."

"A guy from 105 Street Crips shot him. Apparently some kid, trying to earn a rep—he fired sixteen rounds—but these people aren't saying much. They want to get him themselves."

Shonka headed back toward the car. "I'd rather have shot that kid's ass than know he's in the wind, running with a gun in his hand."

A woman scuttled across the street with the characteristic jerkiness of a crackhead. "What's up?" she called to the crowd in the driveway.

The deputy elbowed Delgadillo. "She's from the gang that shot him. I saw her hanging out when you were running after the perp."

Shonka smirked. "Some lady. She's coming over here to make sure they hit their target."

• • •

WE stopped at the Firestone fire station for a break. A voice cut through the crackling static of the car radio: "Gunshot victim. Hispanic female on 88th Street and Budlong. Suicide attempt." Although this wasn't a call that the gang unit would normally investigate, we were close enough to respond. We climbed into the car and two other gang teams did the same. On the way over Shonka provided a monologue in ghetto slang. "What's up, cuz?" She mimicked the Crip greeting. "Shooting *yourself* now? Things can't be that bad."

The lights on 88th Street bathed the neighborhood in an eerie yellow cast. In the shadows two figures sat on a cinder-block wall. Without warning, one leaped off. I caught my breath—he was only three feet high and walked on all fours like an animal. As my eyes focused, I realized that it was a boy with twisted and malformed legs. Balancing on his arms, he lifted his truncated lower half onto a skateboard and pushed himself to the driveway.

Both boys were Mexican, probably seventeen or eighteen and nearly identical—except for the one's deformity—with shaved heads and faint mustaches.

"Those must be her sons. They called 911," Shonka said under her breath.

The taller boy, arms crisscrossed around his chest, as though holding himself together, evaded Shonka's stare.

"How she doing?" she asked.

He darted an angry look at the deputy with red, wet eyes. "She's dead."

He threw a nod behind his shoulder to indicate his house in back.

The sheriffs lumbered past the front house, slowed by the weight of their urban talismans: nightstick, radio, 9-millimeter Beretta. In the yard a man poked a flashlight under a car hood. He glanced up at them, his face revealing little. The tiny bungalow next door was close enough to touch, yet all the shades were pulled. While the shooting of the neighborhood drug dealer attracted a small crowd, this was a domestic incident, too common to cause a commotion. Another desperate person had blown her head off. The air seemed strangely silent, save for the hushed voices of the officers and a dog in back somewhere, barking without stop.

The front door was open, all the lights and the TV set on. Inside a burly man with a thick black beard rested on a sofa arm. He lifted his head slightly to tell the deputies that his wife was in the bathroom.

"What happened?" Shonka asked, almost whispering. "Was there a fight?"

A ripple ran up the man's arm and he absently rubbed it back into place. No, he and his wife were getting divorced—he'd given her the papers today. The family was watching TV when his wife said, to no one in particular, that there was a light on upstairs and left the room. A few moments later they heard the shot. The weapon she used had been his; he'd received it from a guy who owed him money. He, in turn, had given it to his wife. For her protection.

He cradled his face in his hands. I stood stupidly in the middle of the room, embarrassed to witness his grief. Shonka touched my shoulder.

"Do you want to see the body?" She looked at me expectantly.

I did. I wanted to understand how the girls I met could experience death up close. My gaze drifted beyond Shonka toward the man, worried he could hear us, but he sat motionless, head still in his hands. I followed her to the back, where the dead woman waited. Two sheriffs stood guard at the bathroom door. Shonka went into the room, then popped her head out, telling me to come in. Before I entered, I locked eyes with one of the sheriffs, waiting for my reaction.

I bent down to take stock of what only minutes earlier had been a middle-aged mother of two. My eyes traveled first to the red jellylike blotches bubbling on the tiled floor, then downward to the woman's white boots, then up her legs, running over her peasant dress, her body twisted on its side next to the tub, finally resting on her face.

She was turned toward the floor, as though embarrassed. Her matted hair and the blood seeping down her cheek hid her expression. A 9-millimeter gun, the kind the police carry, lay in her lap, her childlike fingers gently curled around the clip.

Shonka appeared at my side. "See that in the bathtub, that little piece of gray stuff? That's her brain." She was paid to try to view this body not as a woman who had left behind her sons, but as "Hispanic female, deceased." A piece of evidence. "Over there's part of the skull."

After listening to dozens of girls' accounts of bloodshed without witnessing them myself, experiencing the dismal scene in the bathroom seemed a rite of passage. Shonka, still young to the job, considered her work a grim but exciting privilege: being paid to encounter the most intimate details of human struggle and death. I sensed this feeling from the gang girls, too, the adrenaline rush, the jittery thrill of living on the edge. But both police and gang children eventually become immune to all the death and what once made them step back in awe begins to pass before their eyes unseen.

We went outside, where an officer instructed Shonka and Delgadillo to stay put until homicide detectives arrived, while he took the relatives in for questioning. No one suspected that this was anything other than suicide, but procedure required a cursory investigation.

In the yard the two boys stood mute against a police car, along with a young girl I hadn't noticed earlier who was crying, barefoot, and shivering. A cop went inside the house and returned with her shoes and a sweater for the trip downtown. Then I turned away from them, following Shonka and Delgadillo back to the house.

Family pictures covered the walls: the father cradling his wife in his arms; the father and his crew on an oil rig; the father receiving his black belt with a martial arts class; the sons standing proudly behind their seated mother.

One of the officers plopped down opposite an upright piano, which hid the boy's collapsed wheelchair, and started to play chopsticks. The clunky piano sounded startlingly loud, barging in on the dead woman's silence. A few minutes later someone yelled through the door that the homicide detectives had arrived and we could leave. Abruptly the music stopped.

Outside I caught the unexpected sight of the boys. I thought they'd been taken in for questioning, yet they were still leaning against the cop car. When I had looked at their mother, I was able to distance myself—after all, I didn't know the pathetic figure crumpled on the floor—but the heat of those accusing eyes burned through me. Surely they had heard that absurdly irreverent piano music. Shonka turned to say she was sorry, then we ducked under the fluttering yellow strip of tape that caged them in their death scene.

Shonka fell quiet a moment, then spoke again to Delgadillo. "Some bodies you get used to. Gang members, they're a menace to society. But women and children . . . ?"

The next day's newspaper would not print a line about the gang shooting or the suicide. Life and death would continue unmarked, as usual, in Lennox.

WOMEN WITHOUT MEN

Coco stubbornly refused to acknowledge her good fortune. The D.A., instead of charging Bird with a federal offense for hawking food stamps—his third strike that carried the possibility of a life sentence—had offered a plea bargain. If Bird pleaded guilty to a misdemeanor, they'd drop the federal charge. He'd probably receive ninety days. But Coco, convinced that the D.A. didn't have enough proof Bird was selling the stamps—even though he'd been caught with $1,350 in his pocket when the cops picked him up at his corner—believed he could get off. She had seen prosecutors routinely overcharge suspects, threatening them with long sentences in order to force them to cop to lesser charges. "If he says he's guilty, they're gonna take my money." She seethed visibly at the thought of losing the $1,350.

She had begged me to go with her to court. "He didn't do anything!" she'd told me, lumping me in with cops, lawyers, judges, authority figures to whom, on automatic pilot, she protested his innocence. I waited inside the courtroom with Tasha, Sheba, and Li'l Chick while she argued with Bird's attorney in the hall. "Bird's gonna plead no contest 'cause he wants to see his kids," she whispered angrily afterward. "I wish I could talk to him. I don't want this on his record. But his lawyer says he has to plead something." She stopped, listening to the friendly conversations between Bird's lawyer and the prosecutors up front. "They all in this together! They play games with your life!"

In the end Bird pleaded no contest in exchange for forty-five days in jail and twenty-four months probation. "Fuck this!" Coco had cried as they led him away. She hoisted Sheba on her hip, grabbed Tasha's hand, and scurried toward the door while I trailed behind with the baby. Outside the hall echoed with her curses.

VISITING hours at the L.A. County Jail ended at seven o'clock Saturday nights. Coco arrived with just twenty minutes to spare. Beneath the grim four-story windowless monolith that devoured blocks of downtown L.A., the basement parking lot was jammed. She took the stairs to the street level at breakneck speed, two at a time, only to hit the end of a long line that snaked down the sidewalk from the jail's double doors. A crowd of wives and girlfriends clutched photos and toddlers' hands while they waited to see their men. Teenagers were decked out in their hip-hop best, with Pelle Pelle jackets and Puma sneakers, as though on line for a rock concert. One kid wore a tuxedo.

Coco had sleeked her hair back, showing off her high mahogany cheekbones. Her skin smelled like roses, having baptized herself in the car with the perfume she always carried. She wore the same open-toed white platform shoes and red-flowered dress she'd carefully picked out the previous day for Bird's appearance at the Criminal Courts Building, conveniently located next to the jail.

A few minutes before seven she entered the double doors beneath a sign that read: NO GANG SIGNS, COLORS, OR VERBIAGE.

A sea of church matrons and miniskirted girlfriends flooded the large linoleum waiting area. Coco knew the routine from past experience. First, the stop at the info desk for a visitor's request. Second, the items she'd be allowed to bring in: up to five photographs, three-by-five in size, but no Polaroids or photos of men (they might be gang members); one pair of prescription glasses; and a maximum of forty dollars, which could include five dollars in dimes. The jail provided a change machine for this purpose, on which was posted another list of warnings: USE MACHINE AT OWN RISK. DON'T BANG ON MACHINE. DON'T ASK DEPUTIES FOR CHANGE. Handwritten replies decorated every available inch: FUCK YOU. BLOW ME. Coco had brought Bird his entire amount in one-dollar bills, the only denomination the candy and soda machines accepted—snack food being a necessity for inmates faced with prison fare. She counted her dollars over and over, each time coming up two short. "The guy at the store cheated me. And he looked so innocent."

Bored, she joined a group of women who were looking through the inmate roster to see who they knew. "There he is!" she cried out, pointing to Bird's seven-digit booking number, as though she'd come across his picture in his high school yearbook. Then she looked for celebrity criminals, finding Erik Menendez (booking number 1878449).

At last the deputy called out inmates' names, Bird's among them. Coco and the others filed into a long, narrow room lit a sickly fluorescent green. A countertop lined with stools on both sides ran the entire length, separated by army-green metal partitions with windows of inch-thick bulletproof glass that extended up to the ceiling, cutting the room in two. Behind the windows men were already seated.

Coco and Bird didn't bother to pick up the telephone in Booth 13. Palm to palm, they touched through the glass. His hair had started to grow in, along with a spotty beard and mustache. "I haven't brushed my teeth since I've been in!" he hollered. Without cash, he couldn't buy toothpaste or a brush.

Next to Coco in Booth 12 a young woman in a short denim skirt and red high heels perched on a stool, holding a magazine to the glass. The pages displayed giant photographs of engagement rings beneath the word SALE!!! "Guess how much this one costs?" she cooed into the phone.

Kids chased each other up and down the narrow space. In a vacant booth a little boy pretending to be a prisoner slouched on his stool, thumbs cockily hooked in his belt loops. His sister played the role of dutiful girlfriend—"Are you eating? Do you need money?"—but she quickly grew bored. "I want to be in jail!" she demanded.

Coco and Bird spoke in hushed tones, the first time I'd heard Coco so subdued. Her voice sounded low and sandpapery, pleasant to hear. In a few minutes it was over. "Let's go!" a guard yelled.

As Coco lined up to leave, Bird rapped on the window. "Bring me photos!" he mouthed.

On the way home she sobbed softly in the car. "Bird has got a good heart. He wants me to bring photos of his kids next time. He's talking about going back to school." Gang members, she went on, go to college. Gang members hold jobs. Yeah, some are ruthless. Like the guy who'd shoot you for stepping on his foot or for talking too long on the pay phone. But others, like Bird, wanted to better themselves. It was just so hard.

She slumped against the car door, resting her head on the window as though it were too heavy for her body alone. Her prettiness slowly faded, leaving in its place a sad, drawn stare. When she spoke again, her voice was steely. "Next time I go to the jail, I'm bringing him a picture of the kids, then that's it. I'm not going back there. I hate going to the jail. And when Bird gets out this time, I'm gonna give him his kids and I'm going away. Back to my gang in Watts. I won't let my kids down until he's home, but when he is, I'm out of here."

We stopped for a light and a little white boy stared at her from the backseat window of a car. "Get out of my motherfucking face!" she snapped.

At her house, toys littered the floor. Alongside a spilled bowl of cereal, the potty seat held stagnant urine. Coco's thirteen-year-old cousin sat in the dark, watching TV. Tasha and Philip looked up and, reading their mother's face, tried to stay out of her path. Philip took Sheba's potty seat, solemnly emptying its contents down the kitchen sink, while Sheba stood behind him, whimpering.

Tasha tugged at my hand, whispering. "My daddy's in jail 'cause he drove his car real fast," she said, her breath warm in my ear. "I want my daddy out of jail. My mama's gonna get him out," she assured me, nodding her head. But she gripped her fist so hard her fingers turned white.

Coco paced, mumbling to herself. "What am I going to do with Bird in jail?" She wilted in front of us, like an undernourished flower. She needed a night out with the homegirls, she said.

Coco and her homegirl Q-Mac parked behind Sizzler and smoked a joint, lazily eyeing a pair of cops climbing out of their patrol car, amid the fleet of black and whites in the lot. The restaurant is a favorite haunt of South Central police, located on Florence just a few miles from the Normandie intersection, where an LAPD cruiser was caught on the TV news abandoning Reginald Denny to his fate at the hands of rioting gang members.

"Never was a day of peace between the Crips and the Bloods in L.A. until the riots," Coco said, leaning back against the headrest, smoke crowning her hair. "Until they joined forces against the police." She pronounced it *PO-lice*. "Don't get me started. Damn police are all hicks. People think where we come from in Mississippi it's so prejudiced. Maybe deep in the woods. But this"—she swept her arms around her—"this is the worse place there is."

In the backseat Q-Mac nodded in agreement. "I think if the police hadn't beaten us like they had all them years, we would still be stupid and killing each other. A lot of gang banging has slagged down. Happened right after Rodney King—we all decided to get together in South Park. Bloods and Crips from all different hoods reunited. Tied the blue and red rags together, drank together, Crips and Bloods played football together. It was good to see some old friends, kids I knew in elementary school before I claimed Crip."

"In my hood, Watts, they still peacing it," said Coco.

"Not my homeboys. Uh-uh." Q-Mac rocked her head slowly back and forth. "Eventually they went back to saying, 'They killed so-and-so.' Bloods felt the same way. Too bad it couldn't last. It's weird 'cause some of the Bloods that we grew up with asked me that day in the park, 'We known you all your life, why you gotta turn Crip? Why couldn't you turn Blood?' "

She checked the nails on each stubby finger. "Red just ain't my color. Blue always been my favorite color. There is something about Crips that just turns me on."

Q-Mac shifted in the backseat, the leather groaning. Almost five-ten, she weighed more than two hundred pounds. Her skin was pitted from acne, yet the expression on her moon face was disquietingly gentle. When I first met her in Coco's living room, she said nothing, but I kept catching her looking at me before she quickly averted her eyes. Later she told me she didn't know any white people. But it was her voice that threw me off-guard, a faint baby's murmur, as if a small timid girl were trapped deep inside that cumbersome body.

Coco finished her joint and we went inside. They slid into one of the big coral-colored booths, ignoring the table of uniformed cops behind them. The two women had known each other since they were little girls in South Central. Both their families had moved to L.A. from Mississippi. One day, going through Coco's photo album, Q-Mac had recognized a picture of Coco's father. He was her uncle. Q-Mac and Coco, it turned out, were cousins.

Q-Mac joined the same Crip set as Coco's nieces Jade and Wanda, when she was fifteen. Now twenty-three, Q-Mac was the teenage girls' "big homey."

"Jade, she's crazy," she told Coco. "She moves too fast. She'll get hurt. She and Wanda, they young. They always trying to fight some bitches, to prove something. Me, I just chill—but if you ask me where I'm from, I'll tell you."

Coco took a sip of beer and gave a dismissive toss of her head. "It's them new booties." She explained for me. "A new booty is a person who has been gang banging for a year or two. Jade wants to earn her stripes."

While they ate, she and Q-Mac sized up other women in the restaurant—"ho," "bitch," "hoochie," "hood rat"—they had as many derogatory names for bad women as Eskimos do for snow. To me, it seemed a form of self-loathing. Q-Mac thought about this and defended her gender. "It's like how the homeboys say that by being a woman we scared, that we snitch. When my ex-boyfriend killed someone, I didn't tell the cops I saw it. They took me down to a holding cell, I was only fifteen. They harassed me all night. I looked them cops dead in the eye and said, 'I don't know what you talking about.' They tapped my mama's phone line and everything, said they were gonna arrest me. They waited for me to break down and cry. My own homeboys threatened to kill me if I talked. After that, I was getting ran home from school every day, boys and girls shooting at me." She turned quiet for a moment, remembering. Then, "Guys cry, too. They get scared and crack up under pressure."

"I had a homeboy last year that snitched," Coco said, her voice falling and rising from one beer, "snitched on all his homeys. He hung himself in jail."

They looked at one another with understanding. "Men are the ones who are stupid," Coco snorted, " 'cause they blast someone in a sunny spot or go and tell somebody the next day."

"Girls, we more sneaky." Q-Mac launched into a story about how she and her homegirls staked out card clubs to roll men. One would disguise herself in a wig, so that she couldn't be identified later. "I only played that part once, 'cause those men like the petite type of female." The girls searched for marks in the casino near the Hollywood Park Race Track or the Normandie Casino. "She rubs against his leg, gets him to invite her back to his room, 'cause there's motels at these places." Q-Mac and another girl would wait outside in the parking lot until the man's room light went out, then charge inside with guns. "If a man's half-naked with three girls and a gun on him, he's gonna give it up. We got Rolexes, diamond rings, money. The one thing you look for when you choose the man is a wedding ring—a big one. You want to know that he got money and you definitely want someone who's married. Married man's not gonna press charges. We'd go back out and look through their wallet"—disgust filled her baby-girl voice—"and they always got pictures of their wife and kids."

This started Q-Mac thinking about her own man. Like Bird, he was in the L.A. County Jail. "He called last night. Wants me to get an apartment for him when he gets out. I told him I can't do that." She turned to me. "See, I get two hundred dollars a month from the county, and that really just helps me get personal items like underwear, buy an outfit. But it don't help me live, 'cause you can't find no place for two hundred dollars. Got to have kids to get low-income housing."

She reached out and slapped Coco's hand for emphasis, "Like, my man was asking me, 'Where were you last night?' I told him I went to get my hair done. He said, 'How much your hair cost? Why you spending all this money? Why you not taking care of business?' That made me mad. I'm not used to nobody asking me questions, 'cause I've been single all my life. You know, like, ever since I started having sex, I've never really been with a guy. I kick it with my girls and just have, you know, one-night stands. Never really *loooove*"—she stretched the word—"or any-thing. I loved a man once, but he was married to someone else. So last night I told him, 'If you would have put me in house with all them things before you went to jail, you wouldn't have to worry about any-thing now.' I said, 'If that's the way you feel about our relationship, then you can go about your business, 'cause I can do bad by my damn self. I don't need nobody to do bad with me.' I'm doing bad already."

Q-Mac lived with an older married sister and her children in a well-furnished neatly kept house, but her status as a rent-free boarder seemed demeaning. She considered herself homeless. "See, I've never had any-thing of my own." She broke off eye contact, examining a ketchup splotch on the tabletop. "My mom had thirteen kids. She wasn't that motherly to me. Just smoked crack. I never had a room of my own. I just put all my clothes in a bag. If she would have given me my own room, just my own privacy, I wouldn't be involved with the stuff that I am today."

She cut herself off. There was a customer survey card on the table and Q-Mac began filling it out. I asked if she ever thought about leaving her gang. "I tried it. I stayed with my dad for a year in Long Beach. I didn't like it. I missed my homeys and the hood." The waiter stopped by to pick up our dishes. Q-Mac shyly handed him her survey; she'd checked GOOD in every category. In the space for comments about the service she'd written in uneven capital letters: I THINK THIS WAS NICE.

"Seems like the older I'm getting, the wiser I'm getting," Q-Mac said wistfully. "I'm realizing that gang banging isn't going to get me nowhere. But I can't get out of it."

"I've been gang banging since 1981, okay?" said Coco, now slightly drunk from one beer. "You ask any bitch from Watts and they'll tell you who's O.G. 'Cause I've been around."

"Uh-huh," said Q-Mac. She waited a respectful moment to allow Coco her reverie. "When you got to get home to your kids?"

Coco slumped a little. "I guess soon. I hope that girl who's sittin' remembered not to give Tasha any sugar. Give her candy, it's just like cocaine. Tasha gives me the most headache of any of them." Neither woman seemed to know what she wanted to do, as if both felt a night out with the girls should be more fun. They looked to each other for confirmation of the good time they were having. "We better go home," Coco said finally. "I just got too many children. *Damn.*"

SOMETIME around seven o'clock Monday morning, Coco called me, hysterical. "They've taken away Tasha! They've taken our baby."

Coco burst out with a volley of details. Bird's ex-wife Janet brought the police with her to take Tasha away while the little girl was visiting her grandparents. Janet had apparently told the cops that Tasha was in danger because Bird was in jail and Coco was a gang banger. Coco begged me to help. Bird, on the line from jail on a three-way call, wanted to appeal to the judge for his temporary release to find Tasha and bring her home.

After Bird hung up, Coco called the public defender's office, keeping me on the line to make the actual inquiries. I didn't understand—she knew her way around the legal system better than she did the corner grocery store. Then it dawned on me that she needed my voice, my *white* voice.

I spoke with a public defender who sounded young and white and, as she listened to Bird's plight, sympathetic. Perhaps she was struck by the unending commitment of this young father, barely out of his teens, for his daughter. She agreed to meet Coco at the courthouse, where she would make an appeal for Bird's temporary release.

Coco stood waiting at her front door in the red sleeveless dress she had worn to visit Bird in jail. Scratch marks crawled up her forearms like ivy, and yellow bruises circled her throat in a gruesome necklace. Upon finding Tasha missing, she had hit Bird's cousin in the mouth, busting her lip. A fight broke out. One woman held her down while six of the women in Bird's family bit and scratched her. The men just watched—until Coco managed to punch one of their wives. Then they jumped in, too.

Coco's house was immaculate. There was no evidence that small children lived here; the usual toys and CDs were nowhere in sight. Coco must have cleaned all night, trying to calm the turmoil in her mind.

"Janet's always so fucked up on sherm," she said, collapsing on the sofa. "That's why the court awarded Tasha to Bird, even though he'd been in the pen. When we got her, she was only six months old. Janet never changed her diapers. Her little rear end was bleeding!" She paused, trying to gain control of the catch in her voice. "Tasha used to cry in her sleep. She'd cower, like you were going to hit her. It's not Janet so much. It's her boyfriend. I think he hits all her kids."

She pressed her fingers to her temples to keep her thoughts from colliding. She now viewed everyone as a potential enemy. Even Roylene. Never know, Coco said. Next Roylene might start stealing her kids.

She handed me Li'l Chick while she put on gold earrings. The baby playfully grabbed at my face. "See him? The little ho will go with anyone," Coco mumbled under her breath, then allowed herself a small chuckle. "Just like his father."

She glanced at her oldest son. "You gonna be a gang banger when you grow up, Phil?"

He shook his curls vigorously. "*Noooo!* I'm gonna be a lawyer, so I can get my pop out of jail anytime."

In Court 83, under gloomy fluorescent lights, prisoners filed into a glassed-in cage on which hung the sign: COMMUNICATION WITH CUSTODIES IS FORBIDDEN BY LAW. Coco scanned the row of inmates, all of whom were black or Mexican and, except for one young girl in cornrow braids, all men. No Bird.

The judge droned his way through the cases. A few were charged with drug possession or parole violation, but most were here for beating their lover or wife. Two hours passed. Coco scratched at the nail marks on her arms, rocking herself back and forth. Trembling, she shoved Bird's custody papers at me to give to the lawyer. She promised me—as though I held some kind of authority—if she could only have Tasha back, she and Bird would stop gang banging forever.

At last Bird marched into the glass cage. Like the other inmates, his expression betrayed nothing until his eyes found Coco's and then the mask cracked. He smiled, almost imperceptibly. Immediately the bailiff approached Coco, ordering her to sit up, studying her hands for secret signals. Then he returned to the glass box, deliberately blocking Bird.

When the judge called Bird's name, Coco sobbed and shook so badly that she could barely speak. While Bird's public defender huddled with the D.A., quietly conferring, Coco crossed her fingers and ankles and, too scared to rely on luck alone, prayed in a hoarse whisper.

The public defender announced that they had come up with a deal—the D.A. would allow Bird to be released for one week to retrieve his child and resume his sentence upon his return. If he failed to show up after the week, his sentence would increase from forty-five days to six months.

The judge shook his head. "Won't work."

The emotion coiled up inside her sprang loose and Coco leaped from her seat. "Oh, please, please, I swear he'll show up! Please, just let me get my baby!"

The bailiff looked at her but, perhaps out of pity, said nothing. The judge demanded to know how the lawyer could ensure Bird's return. The young woman replied that she would personally accept any legal punishment the court doled out if her client failed to show up. "You sure you want to do this?" the judge asked. The lawyer nodded. "Starting tomorrow," he said to Bird, "you have one week to find your daughter."

Coco broke down and wept with relief. "Thank you, Jesus!" she shouted over and over. "We're gonna change," she promised me and Bird's attorney as much as Jesus. "Turn our lives around."

TASHA'S abduction gave Coco something to focus on, a center for her hard life. Overnight her ambivalence toward raising four children transformed into determination to bring Tasha home. The talk ceased about moving back to Watts to hang out with her fellow Crip girls. "I'm going to stay right here. Bird and I spoke about it. He want me to stay. Soon as we're on our feet, we're moving out of L.A."

Over the next several days, Coco and Bird failed to get Tasha back. Janet refused to open her door to Bird and finally Bird and Coco went to the police, hoping for help. They waited in the Long Beach precinct for two and a half hours for assistance, watching as a white woman came in and met with an officer after only ten minutes. At last an officer glanced at Bird's custody papers and dismissed them curtly. They weren't certified. "We want you to come with us, Gini," Coco said on the telephone.

But my presence at the precinct the next night failed to produce the desired effect. With his officers investigating a homicide and a bank robbery, the watch commander had no one to spare. He instructed Bird and Coco to park outside Janet's house. When he could, he'd send over a patrol car.

So we waited in the blackness. Janet lived on the corner of a residential block in a modest two-story yellow brick apartment building near the Rollin' Twenties. "I could do this a lot faster if I'd go in there, whip everyone's ass, and get what's mine," Bird said in the car. "Of course, I'd take one of my homeboys to fuck up Janet's boyfriend."

I asked why he hadn't.

"I'd be in jail and I'm only out right now by a hair. A thin one."

In the backseat Coco went through the pile of papers on her lap from Bird's custody battle. In halting speech, like a child learning to read, she recounted Tasha's life according to the social worker's report. Her parents married while Bird was still in prison for robbing a credit union. They wed while Janet was pregnant and separated a month after Tasha's birth. Janet had two previous children; the whereabouts of both fathers were unknown. Before Tasha was even two months old, Bird initiated custody proceedings. Citing Janet's history of drug use, the court awarded Bird full custody and ordered Janet to seek immediate drug counseling. The man now living with her, the report said, had beaten at least one of her children, a boy, burning him with a cigarette above the eye.

Coco's bottom lip trembled. She looked over at the darkened apartment. "Something done happened that we do not know about in that house. Something terrible that have that girl waking up out of her sleep, crying, 'Daddy.'"

Bird lifted up his Adidas cap, rubbed the sweat off his freshly shaved head, then pulled the cap back down. "Once we get Tasha, I'm gonna finish up my time, get out of gangs, then we're moving to Oklahoma. I'm gonna go to a black college."

Thirty minutes passed and Coco's leg was pumping nervously, like a jackhammer, shaking the custody papers she gripped in her hand. Suddenly she slammed her fist into the car door. "Call 911! The cops aren't coming. I'm telling them I'm gonna sue their ass if something happens to that little girl."

Bird started the engine, making a U-turn to look for a phone booth. At the corner a patrol car passed, the driver waving Bird over. The blond officer addressed Bird politely, explaining that he'd looked up Janet's case and learned that she had gone to the Long Beach municipal court, where a judge gave her papers allowing her to take Tasha. He studied Bird closely. "I don't know what she told the judge or the L.A. police, but she must have told them something about you."

Coco and Bird fell silent. I waited to see if either would explain that Bird had been in jail when Janet took the girl, but they said nothing. The cop advised Bird to take his custody papers to the Long Beach judge the next day: the Los Angeles superior court held jurisdiction over the Long Beach municipal court. Then the police could help him.

Later, at home, Coco and I sat on the bed, sorting through more papers to take to the judge in the morning. She confided that she had dreamed of Tasha the night before. "Lord, I don't like when I dream. When I was eighteen, I dreamed my daddy died of respiratory problems. My mother called me the next morning to tell me he died. And I had visions of my homegirl being killed by a man. Two weeks later her man killed her."

She crept to the door to peek out at Bird watching TV on the sofa, then returned to the bed. "I hate to say this," she whispered, "but last night I dreamed there were ambulances in front of Janet's house. Then they brought out a body bag." Coco sucked in her breath and clutched at her blouse. "Sticking out of the bag was this little yellow hand. And the fingernails looked just like Tasha's."

IT took Bird's ex-girlfriend Roylene a long time to answer the door when I visited her the next day. At last she peered sleepily through the torn screen, wearing a short cotton bathrobe that was ripped under the arm. At first she didn't want to talk about Tasha, unsure how much I knew, but she eased up after learning I'd gone to Long Beach with Bird and Coco. "Janet's a bad mother. A *bad* mother. Bird was a hard gang banger in his day when he still lived in Long Beach. But, see, he and Coco got these kids and that's slowing them both down. They know they got something to live for. But that broad is gonna say he and Coco bragging about being gang bangers, carrying guns around. They might lose Tasha, 'cause no judge is gonna like that."

Moments later Bird's mother strode in. "My son's not talking to me," she announced. "I told him it was his father's side of the family that gave Tasha to Janet. I'm not in that mess. He's mad. Told that girl, Coco, to tell me don't even come up to their house no more. I told her, 'I don't play that.'"

She laughed, snorting, and nodded toward Roylene. "What do you think of my son and his situation with Coco and Roylene?" she asked me. "Pretty strange, huh? You know, if it was me, I'd avoid the kind of trouble my son is in. That's why I live by myself. Don't have to stay home, don't have to cook for someone. Only one I worry about is me."

She displayed her toothless grin. "But my son is a family man. Yeah, he got involved in gangs. But when Bird robbed that credit union, what you think he spent the money on? All on Janet. He bought her all-new furniture, bought bunk beds for her kids—'cause she got two other kids by other men. Bird cared for all of them. Then he got in the pen. I went over to visit Tasha one day, just busted on in there, and Janet was in bed, digging this other nigger. One month after Bird went to the pen!" She flicked imagined crumbs off her shirt. "Bird still married to her, too."

The phone interrupted her. "It's Bird," Roylene said, pushing the phone toward me.

His mother grabbed it away from her.

"Bird, go buy me some new shoes!" she shouted into the receiver. "I took my shoes off at my friend's house. When I woke up, they'd walked away. Well, look, I don't want to hear it. I have problems of my own. When you gotta go back to jail? Well, you need some money? 'Cause I got some money now. But I gotta go."

She shoved the phone at me and I heard Coco yell, "We got her, Gini! We got Tasha back! The Long Beach judge saw our papers and we went with the police to her house and she's here now."

The battle for Tasha, it turned out, was only beginning. Janet's accusations about Bird and Coco's gang activities had led the judge to reopen the custody hearing. "But you'll help us win, won't you?"

I hung up and Roylene walked me to her front porch. She told me she went to the emergency room the night before. She had been throwing up, vomit coming out her nose. "Gini, I'm three weeks pregnant."

She didn't know what to do. She'd only known the father, Ducky, for a month. Just as Bird had demanded of Coco, Ducky insisted that Roylene keep the baby. "I already got one son without a father. Soon as he's seven or eight years old, I'm gonna tell him I was a Crip, gonna explain it all to him. 'Cause I lived here all my life and when my boy gets to be a man he's gonna be up against the same thing." Her fingers found their way to her belly, absently caressing herself, soothing the infinitesimal creature inside. "Don't need another little kid stuck facing . . ." She did not finish the thought.

GOOD-BYE

The woman in the front house was used to me by now and no longer stepped out on her porch to say hi or ask for money when I pulled up. It was my the last day in L.A. and I had come to say good-bye to Coco and Bird. I headed toward the back. As I rounded the corner of the house, I saw Tasha in Coco's doorway. She held a coloring book against the door frame, her tongue sticking out the side of her mouth in concentration. Her thick hair fell into three braids, each fixed with a white rose clasp. She felt my eyes upon her, then turned around to smile and yell my name, suddenly frowning dramatically. "Philip won't share his coloring book with me!" Philip immediately let out a cry of protest from inside the living room and she recanted.

Inside Coco welcomed me affectionately, hugging me with one arm, the other hand clutching a can of green beans for the kids' lunch. She looked toward Tasha. "Did you tell Gini what Janet did to you?"

"Of course not," the little girl replied. She turned toward me to recite: "Janet hit me in the chest and Leon hit me in the back 'cause I misbehaved." She crawled up on the couch next to her father, who hugged her close to him. Bird felt blessed, he said. Everything would be okay.

Tasha snatched at the plastic blue rosary beads dangling from his neck. "Daddy, is this against the law?"

"No. That's God."

Tasha let go of the rosary and picked up her foot. "When you were in jail"—she studied her soft toes—"did you do things that were against the law?"

"No, baby," Bird answered evenly.

I hadn't seen the rosary before and Bird told me it was from Victory

Outreach. I was incredulous. Back when he first mentioned Victory Outreach to me, a church housed in a converted movie theater that worked with ex-gang members right across from the corner where Bird hustled food stamps, he'd spoken with derision. I had wondered if he or Coco ever attended meetings. "No. We're not ex-gang members," he had replied. But tonight, when I half-seriously asked him if he planned to join the church, his voice was solemn. "Yeah. Me and my girl been talking about it. There's just been too much shit going on."

Tasha wanted her father to draw her a picture of a sports car. While she watched him, I reached from behind her to hug her. At my touch, she jumped and spun around with an angry glare I had never seen before. When she realized who it was, she caught herself and smiled. She displayed the jumpiness Coco talked about whenever the child returned from Janet's. Tasha took my hand and led me into the kids' bedroom, where she settled down on the bottom bunk, her feet dangling beneath her. I sat next to her.

"Want to talk about Janet?"

"Ummm, I don't care."

"Do you want to go back there?"

She shook her head.

"Do you love Janet?"

"I love Janet," Tasha said, tilting her head in a jarring adult gesture, "but I don't like Janet."

From the living room Bird called to her and Philip. He was taking them to the store for new shoes. Li'l Chick crawled behind the older children into the living room, whimpering for attention. Bird picked up the infant, pressing him against his cheek. "In a week I have to go back to the white man's jail," he said sadly to his baby son.

After they left, Coco seemed at a rare moment of peace with herself and spoke gently. "I don't believe Janet doesn't love Tasha. I'm a woman—I know she loves her child. She has some goodness about her. I told her I wouldn't fight her. How would it make Tasha feel to be around me, knowing that I beat up her mother? I told Tasha I never want to hear her say she hates her mama. I don't want her growing up thinking her mother doesn't love her or that she shouldn't love her mom. When I see her hurt, it hurts me."

She picked up the custody papers from the couch and stacked them in a neat pile. "When Bird gets out of jail and we get this Tasha business settled, we want to move to Oklahoma for college. He wants to get married. I haven't thought about it. If I think about it, it would make my head hurt."

Did she still think about going back to Watts, about becoming an O.G.?

"With Roylene out of the picture, I have to take care of my kids full-time. Which is fine. I have no desire to go back to Watts." Her eyes narrowed. "My friend just got killed there day before yesterday. Big Snipe. He was trippin' with some crazy Crips. He was trying to deal with this nigger and he got shot. Q-Mac called me in the middle of the night to tell me. Motherfucker who killed him was from the hood, too."

"There ain't shit to do now in my gang. I learned my lesson when Tasha got snatched." She hugged me and kissed me on the cheek. "Not ever gonna leave my kids."

IT was time to leave. I pulled out of Coco's driveway, waving good-bye. At the light on the corner of Manchester, the same corner where the remains of a child cast in concrete were discovered in a Dumpster, I read signs hanging from a chicken wire fence, hawking the necessities of life in South Central: ROOMS $100!; a flier reading REWARD: MY MOTHER NEEDS A WITNESS, offering money for information connected to the shooting of an elderly woman; a handwritten sign with a telephone number advertising car rides to Chino Prison for ten dollars. I turned onto Manchester, passing the black and brown faces waiting at bus stops or standing on corners, and headed west toward the airport. Eventually the storefronts with their hand-painted signs segued into outdated postmodern mini-marts, the Fabulous Forum, home to the L.A. Lakers and the L.A. Kings, then a coffee shop in the shape of a gigantic donut, pitched precariously to roll in the street. After Inglewood the faces faded to white until there were no faces, only glittering Mercedes and BMWs with tinted windows and planes roaring overhead. There was no sign of what I left behind until I passed a wall near Santa Monica with a message scrawled in red: BURN L.A.

PART II
San Antonio

Texan Roulette

THE setting July sun radiated into my car, defying the air conditioner and cooking the interior as I drove into San Antonio's West Side to pick up Alicia, a seventeen-year-old member of the Lady Eights, the female branch of the Eight Ball Posse. Modest brick homes cast late-day shadows on small tidy lawns on one side of the street, the last remnants of urban development money that dried up before HUD could pump life into the street's other side, where rows of faded shacks deteriorated like terminally ill patients.

I crossed the bridge over Apache Creek, which was little more than a dirty brown trickle. An upright pitchfork, painted on one side of the concrete embankment, loomed several yards high, like a monstrous corporate logo or some satanic signpost to the gateways of hell. Which, if you belonged to the wrong gang, it was. The pitchfork was the symbol of the BCs and the LA Boyz. On the other side, where I was headed, was painted an identical pitchfork, only with its prongs pointed down, the markings of their enemy, the Eight Ball Posse.

The sidewalks were nearly empty, except for a few young mothers and small children, and the stray dogs which, like the teenagers, roamed the neighborhood in packs, fighting over turf. I turned down a narrow side street as two frantic dogs, jaws locked together in combat, suddenly appeared in front of my car. One was a deep-brown pit bull; its opponent a snow-white mongrel, chest splattered with blood, a piece of flesh dangling from its muzzle. I slammed on the brakes. The dogs jumped away in tandem, neither releasing its grip.

A young man darted across the street toward the animals and I shouted to find a water hose. Circling the dogs, he glared at me. "Man, I'm not going to spray them. They're not my dogs."

Children and their mothers gathered, others peered out from behind curtains, silently watching the brown and white dogs' deadly dance. When another car turned down the street, almost hitting the animals, they let go of each other. The white dog disappeared around the corner, trailing blood. I followed it in my car, driving over gigantic graffiti scratched in the cement in the middle of the street: TERRITORY OF EIGHT BALL.

I again spotted the young man and called out to him, "Why all the stray dogs in this neighborhood?"

For a moment he stared sullenly, saying nothing. At last he asked, "Why all the stray people?"

THROUGHOUT the 1980s San Antonio's stray and misplaced children began to find each other, forming secret tribes, developing their own language, writing their legends on walls: THE STOMPERS, THE TOWN FREAKS, THA FELLAS. If this graffiti was the extent of teenage terror, the city had light-years to go before reaching the level of gang war raging in Los Angeles. San Antonio is a Mecca of Spanish-American culture, a retirement paradise that is home to the Alamo, rodeos, and debutantes, with the tourism industry second only to the military. In 1988 its sheriff's department listed only one shooting officially classified as a drive-by.

Yet the same year the *San Antonio Express News* Sunday magazine ran the cover story S.A. GANGS: A PROBLEM WAITING TO EXPLODE. The article described several gangs in the city's downtown, ragtag armies of brawlers, drug dealers, and paint sniffers who police dismissed as disorganized street punks, although they'd murdered two homeless people and beaten a newspaper employee to death. Social workers and others on the front lines insisted that many more gangs existed than the paper reported. "When gangs first began surfacing, police would tell us we didn't have a gang problem," Tanji Patton, an anchorwoman for local KMOL news, recalled. "We heard that line so often it became a joke in the news room."

Gangs represented a threat to tourism the city could ill afford in the 1980s. As the rest of the country rode high on the Reagan illusion of prosperity, Texas was slammed hard by the oil crisis, spinning into a recession throughout the latter half of the decade. San Antonio's economy collapsed. Major banking institutions were bought out or went bankrupt, and the largest NCNB became known as "No Cash for Nobody." "Real estate and development became worthless. Construction jobs just stopped," recalled Mike Beldon, president of the Chamber of Commerce, who heads his own roofing company. "Ultimately a lot of people lost jobs and if they found another one it was at a much lower wage."

Amid economic failure, the local and federal governments slashed some $6 million from youth activities, closing down or limiting the hours of parks and libraries and eliminating job programs targeting at-risk youth, the kids most likely to join gangs. Some school systems instated a policy banning failing students from all after-school activities, including sports, music, drama, and field trips. Kids dropped out or were pushed out of school in droves: 810 were expelled in one year.

Faced with poor schools that didn't want them and few recreational options, kids had little to do. Left to their own devices, they banded together according to neighborhood. Although San Antonio is 54 percent Latino, most residents will tell you that Mexicans live on the West Side, blacks on the East Side, whites on the North Side, and a mix on the South Side. The kids possess an acute sense of these invisible boundaries, wearing T-shirts that display the four points of a compass and proclaim in large block letters WEST SIDE or EAST SIDE. On the East Side, poor black kids, mimicking L.A., called themselves the Crips and Bloods. On the West Side, Chicanos formed the Kings and their female counterpart, the Queens, which eventually exploded into the city's largest gang. The Kings' adopted symbol was Mickey Mouse, who both boys and girls tattooed on their backs and chests, flashing the K with his gloved hand or brandishing a pistol. Disney's all-American icon eventually became so identified with the Kings that a middle school in the wealthy northeast district booted out students who wore "Mouse ensembles."

In time other gangs formed: Suicidal Locos, Hispanics Causing Panic, Big-Time Criminals. Some just went by the crimes they specialized in: ATM Robbery, Church Burglars, Burglary Rape Crew. They hyped themselves up for violence by snorting coke and watching gang movies. Whenever I asked cops about the genesis of San Antonio's gang wars, their opinion could be summed up in one word: *Colors*. Although it seemed absurdly simplistic to blame a city crisis on Dennis Hopper's 1988 movie about L.A.'s Crips and Bloods, I heard this from kids, too, who'd seen it fourteen and fifteen times. Though *Colors* is ultimately a morality tale, the children most influenced by it chose to identify with the power of the shooters.

Despite public skepticism in 1989, the sheriff's department initiated a gang unit as the San Antonio school district armed itself with a special police unit to patrol campuses. Less than a year later, with the new safeguards in place, three students at Sam Houston High School were gunned down during a shoot-out at lunch. As paramedics carried one of the wounded boys past TV cameras, he flashed his gang sign. The gesture was most likely intended to inflame his rivals, but outraged citizens saw the youth thumbing his nose at authority, the cops, their city. In response to the outrage over the shooting, the police department finally launched its own gang unit, though its chief suggested that the measure was temporary.

Throughout 1991 San Antonio's kids continued to shoot each other, until by year's end, the *Express News* declared it THE YEAR OF MAKING WAR. Most residents now believed that the city faced a gang problem, according to a newspaper poll, but not in their neighborhood. Those polled who said they felt the effects of violence were mostly minorities. Only 6 percent were white.

Then Rachel Grant was killed.

WOMAN SLAIN IN GANG SHOOT-OUT OUTSIDE MALL screamed the banner headline. Waiting for a bus outside a Toys "R" Us at a North Side mall, the sixty-four-year-old grandmother was caught in the crossfire between two warring gangs and shot dead. A color photo on the front page of the January 5, 1992, *Express News* showed police standing over her body, the popcorn she had been holding strewn on the ground. Although Grant and her killer were both black, the message to the public was clear: if old ladies could be killed outside the mall, everyone was at jeopardy. Soon afterward the paper published a pull-out map describing thirty-five gangs by name, clothing, and ethnic makeup, along with a warning list for tourists, businesses, and parents on how to escape gang violence. In the days after the tip sheet appeared, the paper received eleven thousand requests for copies.

In April 1992, as news of the Los Angeles riots spread around the world, the San Antonio City Council nervously boosted the DARE drug program, a kids' graffiti cleanup, and the federally funded Summer Youth Employment program. But it may have been too little too late. While juvenile violent crime had soared to unprecedented levels throughout the country, murder, rape, and robbery had increased almost three times as fast in Texas. As "family values" became the buzzwords of the 1992 presidential campaign, two gun-toting gang members were arrested among the crowd at Bill Clinton's whistle-stop in San Antonio on the cobblestoned walkway along the San Antonio River. Every Sunday night Military Drive turned into a local war strip, with kids cruising past the three miles of shopping malls and fast-food outlets in a pageant of gang colors, insignia, and display of weapons. And almost every Sunday night someone was shot.

By the summer of 1993, the San Antonio school district, the county's largest, with 60,000 students and ninety-three campuses, had stationed two armed officers at each high school campus and one at each middle school. Its headquarters at Alamo Stadium housed seventy-five officers with twenty-four-hour dispatches and crime data computers. San Antonio was starting to seem like a town under siege. But whether the cops or gangs were in charge of the takeover was unclear.

A HAZING IN A DEADLY SORORITY

In this chaotic environment, girl gang members became gang victims in a way unique to their gender. For several years the newspapers had reported incidents of sexual abuse connected to gangs: *Aug. 21, 1992 . . . Ten-year-old girl raped in gang rite on East Side . . . Boys bragged to the police that she chose to be gang-raped over being beaten up by the female auxiliary . . . Sept. 11, 1992 . . . Parents hold meeting . . . sparked by growing phenomenon in which officials said gangs are using rape, including sodomy . . . April 7, 1993 . . . Fifteen-year-old girl who moved out of parents' home three weeks earlier found stabbed numerous times to head, chest, and neck and sexually assaulted . . . believed to be gang-related . . .*

Rumors spread of a practice among some gangs called "roll-ins." A new female recruit rolled a pair of dice and whatever number appeared determined how many guys would have sex with her. A twelve-year-old girl now sat in the juvenile detention center on charges she lured her thirteen-year-old friend to a party in a trailer, so that nine male gang members, ranging in age from fourteen to thirty-one, could brutally rape her. During her indictment, the girl showed no remorse—the same had been done to her. In detention she'd received dozens of fan letters from gang boys who admired her nerve.

Then, in April 1993, a firestorm of national publicity fell on San Antonio's girl gangs in response to an item in the local Planned Parenthood's newsletter. Three fourteen- and fifteen-year-old girls walked into a West Side Planned Parenthood, saying they needed HIV tests because they had submitted to a local gang's initiation rite: each willingly had sex with a boy who said he was infected with AIDS.

The HIV initiation titillated and mortified the world as San Antonio made headlines from the *London Times* to *Newsweek*. One girl, though not among the infamous initiates, admitted to having sex with four boys to join her gang. "You're showing how much you're willing to give up for the guys, 'cause they're willing to die for you and I'd rather get laid than get shot."

But no one spoke to the girls who claimed to have had sex with the AIDS-infected boy; they vanished among the city's thousands of teenage gang members. The Planned Parenthood clinic, protecting the girls' confidentiality, refused to release their names, saying only that their test results were negative.

The official police view on the alleged AIDS incident was that it never happened. The girls lied about the initiation, submitted themselves to HIV tests, learned the results, all for an elaborate hoax. "They were probably bragging about it," speculated a police spokesperson.

As the papers had documented for several years, sexual initiations were only one of the ways girls in gangs were used, or abused, sexually. When I asked the police for statistics on gang-related rape, however, the figures were unavailable. The San Antonio police could provide the approximate number of gang members on file in 1993—some 5,000—and the exact number of reported drive-by shootings from January to June— 642—but had yet to compile statistics on gang rape.

Those who worked with the victims of gang rape filled in some of the missing gaps. "In war, men rape women and children to demoralize their enemy. The gangs are doing that here," said psychiatrist Dr. Robert

Jimenez, who counseled gang girls at Charter Real Hospital." A young girl—and usually they're very young—has second thoughts about joining or staying with the gang and starts to waver. To get her to behave properly, you have to soil her. Then you can build her from scratch."

Of the hundreds of gang girls Dr. Jimenez has seen, only fifteen were gang-raped as part of a ritual initiation. "Most often this isn't premeditated abusive rape but tremendous psychological coercion. A girl wouldn't have sex if she had a choice, but if it means being left out, she'll do it—giving in to her boyfriend for as much sex as he wants, when he wants it, and how he wants it—sodomy or whatever." More common was the spontaneous act of gang sex: "pulling a train" on a drunken girl at a party—the boy's rank in the gang determined whether he was the engine, the caboose, or somewhere in between—a form of entertainment familiar in college frat houses. Any unknown young girl who showed up at a gang party was presumed by the male gang members to be fair game. The girl who drank too much (or had her soda spiked with Visine, or her bubble gum soaked in vodka, or one of the dozens of covert schemes kids concocted to make someone intoxicated) could expect the worst, anything from having her jewelry stolen to waking up with a strange boy on top of her and a trail of others waiting their turn.

In the aftermath of the alleged AIDS incident, I went to San Antonio, though not because I was searching for something especially sinister lurking in the city. Quite the contrary. It was precisely San Antonio's resemblance to other places and occurrences—Tailhook, the Spur Posse, Anita Hill's hazing by Congress—that made events there so awesome and so threatening. "Gangs mirror society, what society teaches them," said Cynthia Test, a gang counselor. "Society doesn't want to look inside its dark soul. Children always come forward with the truth, whether it's ugly or beautiful. And we've become an ugly society. Our kids are mirroring that and no one wants to take the blame."

ALICIA answered the door, her long red ringlets still wet, smelling faintly of strawberry shampoo. She hurried out to meet me before her boyfriend came home. Normally Robert, who at fourteen was three years younger than Alicia, expected her to be at his mother's house when he returned from hanging out with the Eight Ball Posse. But tonight, in a rare act of defiance, Alicia had agreed to introduce me to a few of her fellow Lady Eights, the Posse's ladies' auxiliary. Her toothpick legs stuck out of wide-cut shorts, tapering down to black combat boots. She climbed into my car; beneath the ceiling light, her lower lip appeared oddly puffy.

She scanned Guadalupe, the main drag, for signs of Robert but saw only one or two lone women standing listlessly in the twilight. "Whores and junkies," Alicia muttered. Reassured, she sank back into the seat. She seemed wistful, almost beaten down and unhealthily thin. She spoke only in response to my questions, and then so softly, with the barest trace of a Spanish accent, that despite the fierce heat outside, I had to turn off the air-conditioning to hear her.

She directed me to the Cassiano Homes to hunt down her friends. Few of them owned phones. She spent most of her time at these housing projects when she wasn't with Robert. The kids called them "the Courts": row upon row of identical twin-story yellow buildings strung together across patchy lawns with clotheslines full of shirts and sheets, waving in the breeze like pastel-colored flags. Built in the 1950s by the federal government, the Cassianos were one of thousands of housing projects that sprang up across the country for low-income families, the elderly, the physically and mentally handicapped. San Antonio's local housing authorities operated fifty-four projects and boasted the nation's oldest. Fifty years later the projects had become merely warehouses for the city's poor. In San Antonio 23 percent of the population live below the national poverty line, although that figure rose to 47 percent—nearly all Mexican-American—on the West Side. Even so, the Cassianos were not the worst projects in the city. With 499 apartments for some 1,323 people, they were decidedly more livable than the notorious downtown Victoria Courts, which made headlines in 1992 when a gang of teenage girls set upon a rival girl who was strolling her baby and stabbed her twenty times.

For the last three years the Cassianos had been ruled not by the housing authorities or the residents, but by the sons and daughters of the people who lived there. Kids peddled cocaine out of vacant apartments and practiced target shooting at streetlights. In this foreshortened universe, enemies lived two houses away, with a river of bad blood between them. Members from three warring gangs—the Eight Ball Posse, the LA Boyz, and the BCs—lived in the complex and sniped at each other across neighbors' yards. Five months earlier, an Eight Ball leader was gunned down in front of his girlfriend's door. The night he died he'd gone on a seven-drive-by shooting spree.

Alicia instructed me to pull up between two apartment buildings, and instantly a throng of teenagers clad in black T-shirts, the Eight Ball uniform, edged toward us across the lawn. "They're coming to check out your car," Alicia told me. People in the Courts made it their business to know every car in the neighborhood, as a matter of survival. San Antonio holds the distinction of being the drive-by capital of Texas, averaging 3.5 shootings a day. Any car out of sync with the rhythm of the street— traveling too fast or too slow—transported potential tragedy. My rental car stuck out because it was new. Hardly anyone here owned a car; drive-bys almost always went down in hot cars or, at the very least, ones with stolen plates.

As we stepped outside the car, the mob surrounded us. Along the edges of the crowd, young women with baby strollers craned their necks to watch. A tall husky boy with a wedge haircut and a raw pockmarked face asked what I was doing, not, I noted, without civility.

When I explained why I was there, the boy nodded knowingly. "Want to know what gang life is about? It's all about kill or be killed."

His friends chortled. "Hey, Miss! Miss!" one yelled. "Wanna get initiated into the Eight Ball? You gotta beat me in basketball!"

"Eight Ball are the best lovers!" another announced.

Their chest beating went on for a couple minutes, the guys making wisecracks in a hybrid of street Spanish and English—gangly boys in baseball caps and shorts several sizes too big. They were surprisingly unthreatening; I hadn't expected them to be so playful.

The husky boy called Blimpy wanted to set the record straight. "We don't disrespect our girls. They grew up here in the hood. We know them all." He jutted his chin toward Alicia, who said nothing.

I asked if guys passed girls around. "Well, yeah. But that's the girls' choice."

The other boys snooped around my car. A sunburned kid peered inside, then popped his head up. Barely in his teens, the boy was doing a poor job of hiding his desire to steal the car. What did you need to rent a car like this—a license? A credit card? Was my name on file? Blimpy quizzed me about life beyond the Cassianos, wondering if New York was worse than San Antonio. When it became evident that I was there to talk to Alicia, the boys grew bored. Abruptly Blimpy excused himself and the lot of them trotted down the sidewalk.

When the boys had gone, Alicia dashed into the complex. "I'll be right back!"

She returned with two teenage girls in tow, hips swaying in self-conscious synchronicity. One was skinny with a pale pretty face. The other, Scariella, was sunny-haired, with golden irises the same color as her skin, so beautiful I struggled not to stare—a barefoot teenager with a dove in flight tattooed above her ankle, a rose in bloom over her breast. When the skinny girl realized why I was there, she denied her gang affiliation and turned back to the apartments. Scariella remained with us, bold and charming, wearing only thigh-cropped shorts and a see-though crochet bra. She had lived her entire seventeen years in the Cassianos and had known the Eight Ball Posse since they were toddlers—her oldest sister was a Lady Eight, or an Eight Ball Chick, as most in the Courts knew her. Yet Scariella herself refused to join the Lady Eights. Not because she disapproved of their lifestyle. The Eight Ball had a reputation, when they could afford it, as rapacious cocaine users (an "eight ball" is slang for 3.5 grams of coke, although the gang's name actually referred to the eight ball in pool) and Scariella's own mother sold them coke out of their apartment. Scariella's reason for not joining was loyalty to her twelve-year-old-brother, who had been murdered by his own gang.

Earlier, driving through the maze of the Cassianos, Alicia had told me Scariella's story. The man who killed Scariella's brother, a twenty-one-year-old three-time loser on parole from state prison and a widely disliked renegade Eight Ball member, had sought to cement his hold on a gang of adolescent boys called the Eight Ball Juniors. Scariella's little brother tried to leave the gang, and the guy made an example of him, shooting him dead in front of the other kids. A local Chicano artist had painted the youngster's portrait among the murals of Our Lady of Guadalupe and Aztec warriors that decorated the Cassianos' walls. He has his sister's golden-brown eyes. In the lower corner of the painting, Eight Ball homeboys surround his casket with bowed heads. In the wake of his death, the city made extravagant promises, including more money to prevent gang violence. But nothing had changed. It was near this memorial wall that the Eight Ball still congregated.

• • •

In the end, rather than wander alone in this town of tribes, Scariella compromised and joined the Queens, the female adjunct of the Kings. She and Alicia were among hundreds of girls on the West Side who claimed gang allegiance.

The current generation of girls began joining gangs in the late eighties and early nineties. Some were, of course, the steady girlfriends, or "wives," of gang members. (Almost any pair of kids who stuck together for more than six months informed me they had a "common-law marriage.") These were the "good girls," who stayed home watching kids or washing their boyfriend's underwear, all the while denying his gang activity with the false ignorance of a Mafia wife. Presumed to be spoken for, such girls were left alone by other gang members. So, too, did their boyfriends at times, who banned them from gang parties because their girls might cramp their style.

Among the girls who were invited to parties were the wanna-bes, who, in another environment, would have hung around rock groups but in the barrio thrived on the celebrity of local gangs. Considered "gang hoppers," they partied with the male gangs, switching loyalties among the most powerful members like hairstyles in the quest for status. Boys routinely courted fresh young girls, showering them with booze, drugs, and attention. But once the girl became classified as common property—if she changed her mind once too often or maybe only once—she was taken for granted in the extreme. These were the girls who were made available any time in any way to any gang member, individually or as a group. They were easily talked into stealing money or a car from their parents for the boys, perhaps believing if they did so, they'd be part of the family and find love. Other gang girls, who viewed the wanna-bes as an irritating fact of life, like menstrual cramps or cockroaches, watched them come and go with disdain, secure in the knowledge that they were just skanks, bitches, sleazes, easy lays. Hos.

The truly "down" girls formed their own gang or were initiated into a coed gang. The most common was a ladies' auxiliary. That the names of the girls' cliques—the Lady Eights, the BC Chicks, the LA Girlz—were extensions of the male gangs' names was symbolic of the sexual hierarchy. Each female gang boasted its own leaders but often took orders from guys. These adjuncts tended to develop only after the male gang had become firmly established, as a female entourage was one of the fringe benefits of power.

Now, with the Eight Ball Posse in a shambles as a result of the drive-by death of its leader, the Lady Eights' role had become diminished. Even so they remained needed, if only as party favors.

This limbo status offered pros and cons to the Lady Eights. On the one hand, it freed them somewhat to date whomever they chose. Scariella, for example, suggested Alicia check out boys from Klik, a rival gang from the more upscale North Side. Klik boys were older, Scariella said, and didn't try to put the moves on you by smacking you. Such social mobility, however, tended to operate more in theory than in practice. In fact, a girl could still be beaten for dating a rival gang member. She could be beaten by her boyfriend for any number of infractions: not showing up when she was supposed to, mouthing off, refusing to give in to sex. Cheating.

Excited by the possibilities my car offered away from the dreariness of the Courts, the girls volunteered to show me their neighborhood. As we started to pull away, a young kid, naked from the waist up, raced toward Alicia's window, his concave chest heaving rapidly. "Hey, Alicia! Robert's looking for you," he hollered, his features sliding into a goofy grin. "He's gonna bust that lip bigger than it is now."

Involuntarily, Alicia reached for her mouth, her fingers delicately tracing her swollen bottom lip.

"He asked where you were and I didn't tell him." He pressed his groin against her window, his knobby pelvic bones peeking out above his trousers. "Now you owe me something."

Laughing, Alicia shoved on his stomach with her hands, sending him stumbling backward. "Get going," she ordered me, and as I hit the gas I felt her anxiety ebb into excitement; for now, at least, the novelty of the night dwarfed her fears. As we drove, she quizzed Scariella about last night's party.

"The LA Boyz shot one of the guys from GTA." Scariella pointed out a darkened house. "They shot at him right there."

"What they shoot him with?"

"First they shot with, um, a nine. Then they came back with"—Scariella's forehead wrinkled—"I don't know. It was a big gun." They chattered on about firearms like other teenagers discussed stereos. Scariella added as an afterthought, "They didn't kill him."

"I think I heard about that on TV. Is that the guy they shot in the eye?"

"They shot him in the shoulder."

"Oh."

I asked if they liked guys who kill other guys. "It's not that," Scariella insisted. "It's because they're in a gang. It's the way they dress, the way they wear the same caps and hang out with each other."

When I asked whether, in their neighborhood, it's possible to date a boy who isn't in a gang, they looked at me as if I were crazy. "*Everywhere* you go, guys are in gangs," Alicia said. "You go to school, gang members. You go to teen clubs, gang members. Our friend works at Pizza Hut on the South Side and all she sees are LA Boyz and Ambros. They're everywhere. You don't have a choice about the guys you go out with."

SCARIELLA'S friends lived across the street from a cemetery. In front of a tiny house, a mousy-haired girl sat on a rock in a dirt front yard next to two dusty Siamese cats. "That's Marie," Alicia muttered. "She used to be the leader of the Queens." Next to Marie a tall sloe-eyed girl combed her wet blonde hair—her sister Lynn, another ex-Queen. Both Lynn and Marie left the Queens when they became mothers. Lynn, seventeen, has one boy; Marie, sixteen, has two children and she is pregnant with a third.

Marie poked a stick around in the dirt, saying little. Lynn, although smiling, informed us she needed cheering up because she'd lost her job at Pizza Hut when she didn't show up because her baby was sick. Then she brightened, suddenly remembering some gossip about the BCs, who, she insisted, were all HIV-positive. "My friend works at the Good Samaritan Center and she overheard them talking. The BCs went there for tests." I took Lynn's accusation with a good deal of salt. The BCs were the Eight Balls' enemies and gang members typically attributed the most horrible traits to their rivals. "They beat up the girl that gave it to them," Lynn went on, "kicked her ass bad."

With little prodding, she admitted her own gang, the Queens, existed primarily to beat up other girls. When I asked them why, Lynn and Scariella cried out in chorus, "For fun!"

"The Kings would tell us to beat up girls from other gangs or to steal their purses, and we would," Lynn explained. "When we first formed the Queens, the Kings were real nice. They would protect us. When we went to clubs and wanted to talk to other guys, they wouldn't let us." She spoke as though this restriction were a good thing.

Alicia, though, saw the negatives of this arrangement. If you didn't want to beat someone up, because you liked her or didn't even know her, you could be beaten yourself for insubordination.

Lynn flipped her wet hair back over her shoulders. "You don't always have to do what they say. Like, this guy wanted me to get photos of his enemies, so he could make sure he shot the right guy. He had a whole album full of pictures. On the back of each he wrote the name of the girl who got it for him. But I said no. See"—she glanced over her shoulder at the screen door, to check if her parents were eavesdropping—"we were our own gang. We set the rules. Some of us carried guns. My mother bought me mine." She shrugged. "It all depends how you got initiated."

There are many ways to be initiated into a gang, none of them pleasant. In one ritual, a girl is beaten by other gang members. Members are forbidden to hit in the face or below the belt; they punch solidly in the chest, sometimes up to a hundred times. This is more painful than it sounds—as anyone who locates their sternum and thumps it with their finger for a minute or two will discover. "Jump ins," another initiation rite, are a rib-kicking, nose-busting free-for-all that the initiate endures for a specified amount of time. Other young gang members are required to commit a crime, a burglary, an assault. All of these initiation rites apply to both male and female recruits. Only "trains," sex with multiple partners in succession, are reserved for girls alone. It's considered the coward's way in—after all, gang logic goes, all the girl does is lie down and spread her legs.

Scariella offered to take me to her sister's house to show me a video-tape of some of the Lady Eights' initiations so that I could see for myself what happened.

At the apartment, two blocks away in the Alazan Apache housing projects, where tattooed teenage warriors guzzled beers outside, a young woman cradling an infant sat mesmerized before the lunar glow of a computer game on the room's centerpiece, a colossal color TV. I could pick up a TV just like it on the street for thirty dollars, Scariella informed me as she stuck in the videotape and sat down on the sofa.

I recognized the backyard of one of the Cassianos. It is dusk, the sky the color of a deep bruise. Two girls, one lean and muscular, the other stocky, face each other inside a ring of onlookers, among them young children. The two girls circle each other, eyes fixed on one another's face, until the muscular girl abruptly seizes her opponent's shoulders and they both begin swinging, slugging each other in the stomach. The muscular one kicks the stocky girl hard above her crotch. Off-camera, someone counts out loud, ". . . fifty-seven, fifty-eight, fifty-nine . . ." At "sixty" he yells, "Stop!" The girls, breathless and sweating, hug each other.

Suddenly on-screen a pair of bright red lips abloom in a pale moon face crashes into the lens. "Teaser!" the girls cried. Teaser was the leader of the Lady Eights. Everyone had a Teaser story. "She shot a girl, a bystander, and paralyzed her from the waist down for life," Alicia recalled, tucking her leg up beneath her on the couch. "Before she left for prison, she put me in charge of the Lady Eights. But then I got demoted for talking to this guy from another gang."

Had anyone visited or written Teaser? I asked. No one had. And though they racked their brains, no one could remember which prison she was in or even her last name. But they all missed her.

The videotape cut to a party of drunk and stoned teenagers, all dressed in black, making out on couches or smoking joints, flicking their middle fingers at the camera. The walls behind them are covered with spray-painted declarations of the Eight Balls' rule.

Scariella provided thumbnail profiles of the partygoers: "That guy's in jail, that boy next to him in the White Sox hat is my cousin, he died last month."

The camera rests on a dark-eyed boy, his upper lip sprouting just the slightest suggestion of whiskers, not yet worth shaving. "Oh, look, there's Tommy!" Scariella cooed. "He looks so young!" Her eyes drank in the image. "It's nice to see them when they were . . ." She didn't finish the sentence. She meant, simply, "alive."

WHEN at last she spoke, Marie told me she planned to name her baby after her boyfriend. Both her other children had taken their fathers' names. "My oldest one's dad is a King; he got paid to shoot someone, I think, and panicked and fled town. The other is GTA." She patted her stomach. "This one's GTA."

The girls didn't really believe in abortion. The Pill, too, carried a stigma—too much forethought. Alicia's older sister was kicked out of the house after her aunt found her birth control pills. Nor did the girls ask their boyfriends to wear condoms, at least not every night. They just drifted into making love without contraception, as if in a dream. Some boys flat-out refused to wear a condom, leaving the girls pleading to God for their periods. After God failed Marie the first time, she dropped out of middle school, which didn't allow pregnant girls. She was still fighting and jumping girls in to the Queens when she was five months pregnant.

Back at the sisters' house, a diapered baby opened the iron-gated door. His tiny elfin ears were misshapen, his eyes sloped downward. Whimpering dirty face streaked with tears, he tottered to Lynn, who took him in her arms and kissed his wet eyes. He didn't have Down's syndrome, she explained, but something like it. Alice said that Lynn fell while she was pregnant.

Scariella announced that the Klik were throwing a party and asked for a ride. Marie decided to stay home—she had a job interview at McDonald's in the morning. But the prospect of a party excited her sister Lynn, who sauntered toward my car. Her baby, sensing his impending abandonment, began breathing hard, his face darkening. He stared intently after Lynn as she locked the gate behind her. When he saw her open the car door, it became too much for him. He threw himself at the wire fence, desperately reaching for his departing mother. Lynn poked her head out the window to shout good-bye to him and we drove off. I could still hear screaming half a block away.

When I dropped Scariella and Lynn off, Alicia remained behind in the car with me. "I know what happens at those parties. It's too ugly. Everyone does a lot of coke. A lot. The boys get all hyper and that's when they go do drive-bys. You hear what she said about that guy getting shot? My boyfriend doesn't want me getting shot. He's in the Eight Ball, yeah, but right now he's not hanging out a lot." She paused, listening. In the distance someone set off firecrackers. "But sometimes when he goes out, I sneak out anyway with Lynn and Scariella."

She held her knees, fanning them in and out. "I always thought, 'I'm the one who's gonna graduate.' I was real good in school. I was in an advanced chemistry program and everything. Until I joined the Eight Ball. I don't know why we got in. We just walked by when they were having a meeting. After I joined, everything got messed up." She worked for one of the Lady Eights selling coke. Alicia's teenage boss paid the Mexican Mafia 10 percent off the top in exchange for a two-block area in which to deal. She'd give Alicia five bags to sell, adding a sixth for either Alicia's own profit or to snort—Alicia usually preferred to snort her paycheck. "I've gotten into so much trouble with my mom. I had to be transferred to another school, so I just stopped going." Her probation officer—she was on probation for beating a rival gang girl on the bus with an umbrella—urged her to finish her GED and apply to college, but Alicia thought that would take too long. "I want to be a court reporter. I love to type—" She stopped. The rearview mirror glowed red . . . then blue.

"Cops!" Alicia warned. I heard the snap of metal. "Seat belt! They're probably stopping us 'cause they noticed a new car." Alicia took a deep breath, then slowly exhaled, her expression vanishing like air from a balloon as her face deflated into neutral.

Behind us two uniformed officers climbed out of a cruiser. One stuck a flashlight in my face. "What are you-all doing?"

When I explained, he said, "We're on the violent crime task force. That's what we're doing." He looked at the card I'd handed him. "Just be careful. It's hot out here. A lot's happening tonight." Already, he said, they'd reported three drive-bys. While the officer spoke, the other shone his flashlight on Alicia, who stared straight ahead. After they left, the life returned to her face. "They heard some shots. That's why they stopped us." She read my confusion. "Didn't you hear them just now? It sounded like fireworks? When we were leaving Scariella's—*bang, bang, bang.*"

"How come you didn't say anything?"

"I don't jump up anymore. It's like, 'Oh, gunshots.'" She glanced behind us. "The cops are following us. Let me off at Robert's."

She was living with Robert's family because she and her mother weren't talking. A few days ago she'd called home for the first time in four months, but thinking about that encounter made her jittery. Twice she asked me the time, anxious to make it back before Robert. When I pulled up, the house was dark. From the blackness her voice called out, "Y'all be careful!"

ON my way home, I passed the Cassianos. Blimpy and some Eight Balls had already memorized my rental car and now waved me over. Alicia's skinny girlfriend who had refused to speak with me earlier appeared at my window, informing me that their new leader, Doomsday, wanted to see me. The boys wanted their say.

The Eight Ball Posse hovered around a beat-up green Plymouth, so low to the ground that it looked like it was missing wheels. Someone opened the door for me and I took a seat on the ripped leather. Around me teenage boys lounged on the grass, jostling each other for my attention; one wanted to know if I smoked weed, others showed me their bullet wounds. A husky teenager, shorter than I, with arms that bore lesions from self-inflicted cigarette burns, turned his bare back to display a gaping red hole. An AK-47, he said; the bullet was still inside him. This was Doomsday. Beneath his playful roughness there seemed a steely, meditative quality about him, a deep-seated self-control that led outsiders to feel they could reason with him—I knew this because counselors told me they held more hope for Doomsday than many of the lost boys in the neighborhood. But I sensed a quiet menace, too, a prerequisite for anyone lasting four years as the second-in-command of a handful of outcasts. If he were drunk, I was warned, he could become dangerously unpredictable.

Doomsday wanted to know if I thought he initiated his girls sexually. "We don't do that to the girls. If they want to be down with us, we let the other girls handle it. Beat them up." He paused to scrutinize a decrepit Datsun cruising by. "I'm not trying to make us look good, but the Eight Ball used to be big-time when we started. We had drugs. Girls. Then the girls started hanging out with GTA. Klik. Those guys talked about the girls real bad. Said the Eight Ball Chicks were whores. So we cut the girls off, 'cause they were putting a bad name on us."

"Scariella's a Klik Chick!" one boy yelled.

"Is that why the Eight Ball Chicks disbanded, or because their leader went to prison?" I asked.

Doomsday raised an eyebrow. "What leader? Teaser?" He dropped his head, letting out a laugh that sounded like a snort. "She was a *crazy* girl. Now she's a crazy *guy*—in jail, if you know what I mean." He waited a beat while his boys laughed. "We didn't really cut the girls off, they just don't hang out with us so much." He nodded toward the skinny girl. "She's still in, 'cause no one ever jumped her out. So she's like a guy. She carries the Eight Ball name and can come to the meetings. Unless it's something serious. Then we don't let the girls come."

"Girls get scared real fast," said a lanky kid.

Doomsday clarified for me. "The cops might say to them, 'If you don't tell us, we're gonna hurt you.' Girls are real weak, you know?"

The skinny girl, who was listening, made no argument. I asked her if she spied for the Eight Ball. "Sometimes I overhear things and I tell them, 'cause they're my friends," she responded weakly.

The Eight Ball Posse wanted to know if I'd talked to the BCs. Doomsday pointed out the major differences between the two gangs: "We hit girls when we're drunk only. Not like the BCs. They hit them all the time. They train their girls"—he raised his hand before I could interrupt—"not everybody, just the leaders. Two or three guys."

In the middle of our conversation, a big-nosed kid broke from the circle, hitting the ground behind some bushes. I looked toward the others for clues, but no one else moved. Blimpy explained that the kid was fifteen and out after curfew, which made it illegal for individuals under seventeen to walk, stand, drive, or ride in a public place between midnight and 6 A.M. Critics felt San Antonio slipped in a "rich white suburban kids clause" that made it okay to pass through the curfew zone if you're on the way to or from another city, allowing wealthier Olmos Park and Alamo Heights teenagers to legally drive to and from parties, no matter what hour. Teenagers on the West Side and the East Side racked up minor records for behavior that was legal or inoffensive in the suburbs.

Doomsday watched a patrol car pass by, then gestured to the younger boy to come back. "It's quiet now. We have no money for guns. Every day there's three cops driving or walking around the the Courts. It's hard to do anything."

"So do you feel safer now?"

"You're never safe here. But this is the longest time it's taken us to get shot at. I was last to take a hit."

"Once we had cross fire that lasted thirty minutes." The lanky kid pointed to a nearby lawn. "Right there. They just kept reloading."

"The last Super Bowl, they drove by here and shot this old man. Her grandpa." Doomsday tossed a look at the skinny girl. "Someone was outside with a camera. We got the drive-by on videotape."

Blimpy, who so far had said little, broke in. "Excuse me, miss," he said softly. "I don't know how to say it, but when you go to different neighborhoods like this, do you get scared?"

"No," I said, answering before I'd made up my mind. "I'm too busy thinking about what you're saying."

"You're not scared right now?" Doomsday asked, his lips curling into a thin smile. "Say we were drinking right now—I'm not saying *we* would do this—but if we were drunk, there are gang members, like the BCs, if they were drunk, that would—" He struggled with his words.

I helped him out. "Do something to me?"

"Yeah. 'Cause we've already talked to other gangs tonight. They've told their girls that if you do something wrong, they're gonna go hit you up, take your car, your money."

Although I wasn't lying when I said I wasn't scared, I didn't know these boys and there were a lot of them. I decided not to press my luck. A few minutes later I walked back to my car. Blimpy's head appeared at my window, leaning toward me with a serious expression. "I'm warning you, miss, and you can ask Scariella and Alicia if you don't believe me. Be careful if you're with the BC. They *will* rape you. If they don't rape you, they'll take your car. They'll do something. Have someone go with you."

Doomsday stood behind him. "You could get shot," he said as he waved to Blimpy to follow him away from my car. "I never thought *I* would."

SLUMMIN'

Tricky seemed unpredictable, a little unhinged. The goateed teenager was one of the heads of the LOs, which, he informed me, might *look* like a gang but was, in fact, not. It was an "organization." (LO stood for "Latino Organization.") The LOs were organized to sell and distribute cocaine, which brought Tricky power (men tried to sell him their daughters for twenty dollars' worth of coke, he said) but not security. He'd scaled back operations after his seventeenth birthday, when he received five shots from a Mac 10 loaded with exploding hollow-point bullets. Tricky had not been expected to live, much less walk. In the end he lived up to his nickname and did both, landing himself a legitimate job while keeping his hand in coke. Just a few days earlier, Tricky boasted, a star player of the San Antonio Spurs scored two ounces from him for $2,200.

When I explained that I was investigating the lives of girl gang members, he said, "I flush girls down the toilet. Kick them to the curb. But we have them in the organization. Anyone messes with us, we send the girls to talk to them, start a relationship, and set them up so we can take over." The girls were known as POLOs: "Property Of Latino Organization."

Tricky offered to introduce me to a couple of white LO girls from the North Side, the affluent point on the city's compass, later in the week. He mentioned their father's name, a prominent executive I recognized from the newspapers. Although I was worried that Tricky might be a couple bottles short of a six-pack, I decided to rely on him. Since I'd arrived in San Antonio, people kept telling me in conspiratorial tones about the children of cops, politicians, and teachers who were involved in gangs, but warned me that none of them would ever talk. "They're like their parents," one gang counselor said. "They hide their dirty secrets because they've got the most to lose." Tricky, while not privileged himself, was my best hope of penetrating that wall of silence.

A week later I arrived at his house in downtown San Antonio, where he lived with an assortment of siblings, parents, grandparents, and any out-of-sorts teenagers Tricky's good-hearted mother let crash. I pushed open the door, banging into the TV console, then squeezed past it into the living room, dominated by a large crib holding a sleeping infant. On one couch a muscular teenage boy gazed at a Salt-N-Pepa video, on the other a pair of girls huddled, looking slight and delicate and punishingly shy. They appeared to be about eleven or twelve, but were, I learned, eighteen. One was named Canary, who, when I asked about her role in the "organization," said she cooked and cleaned. The LOs, Tricky had explained, set up a girl in the houses where they made drug deals, figuring cops would be less likely to suspect or bust a girl. Her name was put on the lease, and she took care of the guys' needs, serving as a front if police came.

The other girl was dark-skinned, with a nose ring. I took her for Tricky's little sister; in fact, she was the mother of his baby boy.

Tricky plopped down on the couch and yawned, then extended his middle finger in the dark-skinned girl's direction. "*Fuuuck* you, ugly."

He'd slept with the girl during a one-night stand in a motel, Tricky said. "Worst mistake of my life. My mother has her stay with me. She pays more attention to her than me. I don't want to talk about it." He was up, headed toward the door, tapping the guy watching TV on the knee. "Let's go to the North Side."

The boys piled into my car and we headed toward Highway 281, which connects downtown San Antonio with subdivisions on the North Side, where home owners boast swimming pools and jealously manicured lawns. It was also a breeding ground for some of the first significant gangs of the current generation. Because the teenagers were middle- or upper-class, cops and parents tended to attribute their delinquent tendencies to contact with kids who lived in Section Eight, or government-subsidized housing, in their neighborhoods, as though dysfunction were a disease from the lower classes. Others viewed upscale gang banging as a fad brought on by too much TV, the inevitable next step after consuming rap music, gangsta videos, and overpriced knockoffs of "ghetto wear." These middle-class gangs had started innocently enough in the early eighties as competitive break-dance cliques in junior high. By high school, one group split into two, becoming known as the Klik and the Klan (no relation to the white supremacists), and began crashing each other's parties, sometimes armed with baseball bats, until their rift evolved into a full-fledged war. The kids now went to battle in sixty-dollar Polo shirts, hundred-dollar Nikes or Red Wing boots, and Girbaud jeans. At the moment Tommy Hilfiger was the designer of choice, with preppy yacht clothes roomy enough to pack a pistol.

Despite the manifestations of ghetto violence in their suburban homes, many parents denied the problem. In 1992 a deputy sheriff's Chevy truck disappeared out of his driveway. The crime was more critical than a routine auto theft and more potentially embarrassing to the sheriffs' department, because the back of the truck held a small arsenal: a dozen semiautomatic weapons on loan to replace the department's outdated revolvers, along with two shotguns and a thousand rounds of ammunition. During the subsequent manhunt, sheriffs traced the weapons to gang members all over the county, including the sons and daughters of the elite. "A police official's kid, a lawyer's kid," a sheriff remembered. "We told their parents, 'You can make your kids give them up or you can play dumb and we can return to your house with a search warrant and the media.' "

All the guns were recovered.

As we passed a luxury office building, Tricky said, "That's where their father works," referring to the North Side girls we were going to visit. "We never initiated them in, but they know more about the LOs than any other girls."

Suddenly Tricky's beeper went off. He had to make a detour to connect with a regular customer, a woman who would, after scoring cocaine to shoot up, pick up some Happy Meals from McDonald's, along with her "surprise for Daddy," and drive the thirty miles home to the rural farm community where they raised their children to keep them away from "this environment."

The guy in the backseat was a member of the Klik. Klikster, as I came to think of him, was athletic and handsome. While Tricky dropped out in the eighth grade and was functionally illiterate, Klikster had graduated from high school, served as president of the student council, played on the football, baseball, and track teams, and joined the ROTC. For all his accomplishments, his life had been no less hard. His father was arrested for murder and died in jail, his older brother was shot and killed on Military Drive, the gangs' main cruise strip. Nevertheless I could see how Klikster might appeal to the kind of girls I imagined we were about to meet. As for Tricky? What they saw in Tricky I would have to wait and see.

We turned into a subdivision called something like Sunshine View or Happy Valley, a string of pale blue townhouses. Tricky forgot the code to the electronic security gate, making us wait until someone else came along and we could pull in quickly behind them.

"Tricky!" the young woman cried at the front door, hopping up to hug his neck. With no makeup, her brown hair pulled in a loose ponytail, and wearing glasses, jeans, and a flannel shirt, she looked like a typical college student. She shook my hand, introducing herself as Barbara, and invited us inside. The apartment was decorated in cream and sky blue with a plush new carpet. A young girl with a head of curls the color of homemade taffy danced across the room, her flowered dress twirling around her bare legs. She punched Klikster flirtatiously on the arm. This was Sandy, Barbara's little sister.

With everyone gathered around the dining room table, Tricky's mood improved until he was almost polite, as though proud of his associations with the two. The sisters were bright and articulate, with an uncanny habit of answering in unison. Barbara was a twenty-year-old college sophomore. Sandy, only fifteen, was the bolder of the two; it was she who, hanging around downtown on Commerce Street after school, had first met Canary, one of the girls I'd seen at Tricky's house, who introduced her to the LOs.

"As a result, a lot of our friends are criminals," Sandy chirped.

Barbara agreed, "We have wonderful criminal friends . . ."

". . . which makes our dad crazy. Basically my dad doesn't like anybody we know, and he thinks it's their fault that we are the way we are."

"Tell her who your father is," Tricky prodded.

Sandy leaned over her pale freckled forearms folded on the dining room table. "My dad knows a lot of people in this city. There was one cop downtown who'd call out to me whenever I walked by, 'Oh, Miss Gangster, you're nothing but *shit*. Your dad is nothing but *shit*.' With all the other cops around. What was I going to do? Go 'Fuck you!' and get arrested?" She exhaled, sending a blonde wisp flying off her forehead. "I told my dad, and I don't know who he talked to, but he got that cop demoted from bike patrol to foot patrol. Afterward, that cop couldn't even look at me. That's how much power my dad has."

It was a power he used on occasion to threaten his daughters. Her father told Sandy he would have her thrown in jail if he could pin anything on her. "One time he was reading in the paper about a gang crime, and they listed their gang names. Dad grabbed me by the arm and said, 'Who's Evil? Who's B-Boy? Who's Ace?' I said, 'Fine. You want to know? Evil, that's Teddy, he set me up with the Kings about two years ago. B-Boy, he's a good friend of mine. Ace, he's an LO, my ex-boyfriend, his real name is Ronnie.' My father was real nasty. He thinks they should just be killed. But the reason we got involved is not—"

Barbara finished her sentence. "Because they're bad people. They're not always saying, 'Let's go shoot somebody.' It's that 10 percent of the time that everyone seems to focus on."

"The 10 percent of the time that your life is in danger," I offered.

The girls responded in chorus: "One percent of the time your life is in danger!"

They had experienced that life-threatening 1 percent just months earlier. Stuck in the back room of a house, guarding a drunk girl against

Tricky's advances, Barbara was safely out of the way when a speeding car sprayed the front lawn with bullets at Tricky's birthday party—all five teenagers outside were hit. Instead of scaring the girls away, however, the incident brought them closer to the LOs. "I won't kill somebody," Sandy declared. "But if Tricky has a beef with somebody, I can't condone it. I don't like it, but I understand it because he's still my friend."

Barbara looked around the table. "We brought them into our little world. They've cooked for us, they've brought groceries for us. They just have to call me and I'll be there," Barbara said. "After Tricky got shot, another guy was in charge and one night he said, 'Listen, Barbara, I want you to tell me if I'm fucking up. I want your advice.' I told them to lay low, go to school, get a job. The police were too hot on them, just then. And they listened."

A woman entered the dining room, dressed in a conservative pastel sweater and skirt at odds with the others' casual clothes. She studied me suspiciously before introducing herself as Grace, Barbara's roommate. Behind her a little boy peered at us from between the rails of the stairway. Her son, she explained, shooing him up to bed before joining us at the table.

The discussion veered to a story in the news about a thirteen-year-old raped in a trailer by nine gang members. The teenagers thought the victim was a liar. "I saw that girl downtown"—Sandy bounced up and down in her seat—"and I went up to her and I asked her to her face if that really happened and she told me no. Denied the whole thing. Said it wasn't her."

Klikster waved one hand in front of his face in a gesture of disgust. "She wasn't raped, that pig. I was there. Nobody raped her, man. The girl who brought her there kicked her ass and the only one that raped her was her boyfriend. The rest is bullshit."

Barbara thought the girl wanted to endure sex with nine boys and men because they possessed power, unlike herself who considered sex with gang boys "just a fuck, just mutual sexual pleasure." She spoke with self-conscious cockiness, as if trying an attitude on for size.

Her sister made a clucking noise with her tongue. "Listen to her! 'Mutual sexual pleasure.'"

"It was!" Barbara squeaked, having trouble with her voice. "It was a kick. Kind of thrilling."

I pointed out that she spoke in the past tense.

"I got pregnant. It made me pull back." Tricky looked at her with a hound dog grin. She returned his stare. "Yes. I got an abortion. What was I going to do, keep it at your house?"

"Why not? Everybody else does."

"When I found out Barbara needed an abortion, I offered her some money," the older woman Grace volunteered. "Afterward, I would go over to her house and take care of her." Grace, who, it turned out, was thirty-two, explained that she met Barbara and Sandy through her teenage niece, who had stayed at Grace's apartment during her parents' divorce. "I guess through the girls I got pretty heavily involved three and a half years ago."

She dug her wallet out of her purse and handed me a studio portrait photo of a young kid with deep-set eyes and sparse bristles on his upper lip. Her son, I figured.

"This is my future husband Ben. He's fifteen. He's in jail for murder. I'm going to marry him as soon as he gets out."

I did my best to keep my face neutral. "Really?"

Grace had Ben's letters ready to show me. She dreamed of appearing on *Oprah* to raise sympathy for her boyfriend's case. She read aloud his touchingly juvenile attempts at poetry, of love that others said was never meant to be and of his desire to gaze endlessly into her eyes to ease the flames that burned, eternally, inside him.

BEN first noticed Grace when his mother and stepfather moved into the apartment complex. When he was nine, he would plant himself near her door, watching her, undetected, as she came and went. He didn't meet her until he returned home from the Texas Youth Commission, the highest level of incarceration in Texas for a juvenile. He shot her son with a BB gun, apologizing afterward, and eventually started baby-sitting for her. Grace was twice divorced; her first husband beat her; the second, an engineer from MIT, was brutally controlling. "I was tired of that, sick and tired, lonely all the time. When I met Ben, I thought he was seventeen or eighteen because he'd been to jail. We were buddies. I didn't know he had a fixation on me. It developed into something else and got out of hand."

The first time they'd slept together he was thirteen.

She'd moved away from San Antonio to escape him, but once she returned, they'd resumed their strange affair. Since his arrest she'd become consumed with his upcoming trial. Grace told a convoluted story: a teenager in the neighborhood was shot to death and an eyewitness pointed to Ben. The D.A. was determined to prove that Ben, a member of a rival gang, had committed the crime.

Grace believed Ben was framed, but you could talk to a random dozen women in love with inmates and hear the same thing. Now the gang of the murdered boy called her house at all hours, hissing just before the phone went dead, "Bitch, you're hanging with the wrong crowd." Fearful she would be the target of a drive-by, Grace went to the police, who staked out her apartment the first weekend after the murder. Until a few days ago, she'd covered all the front windows with blankets. Sandy, too, received threats. As she walked out of an ice cream store one afternoon, a guy pulled up around the corner, asking if she knew Ben. When she didn't respond, he stuck a gun in her face. "Don't play dumb with me." She didn't plead with him—if you asked for compassion, she told me, you'd be shot. It was always better to make them think about what would happen to them if they were caught—not by the police, but by your homeboys. Finally the boy put the gun away. It wasn't Sandy the gang wanted. They wanted her to take a warning to her friends.

For Grace, the worst was learning that fifteen-year-old Ben would be prosecuted as an adult. The thought of him in adult prison, where the Mexican Mafia ruled, terrified her. The court set bail at $100,000 and she'd been in and out of every bond joint around. She'd managed to scrape together $6,500. If she coughed up $10,000 more and found something to use as collateral, she could buy Ben's release. But she'd run out of money.

When she visited him after his first eighteen hours in adult jail, "it was like he was someone else. They removed the person and left me the shell. His eyes, his face, his mouth—it looked ugly." She fell silent. "I don't know what happened in there."

Now her ex-husband threatened to take away their son because the D.A. planned to bring statutory rape charges against her for sleeping with Ben. It also could ruin her career.

It occurred to me that I didn't know what she did for a living. "You'll never believe it," Grace said dryly. "I'm a substitute teacher."

• • •

In Grace, Barbara, and Sandy, I confronted startling contradictions to gang life as it is commonly known. These young women had so many things going for them—education, intelligence, and more money than most of the girls I'd met. What motivated them? I couldn't trace the girls' criminal roots to any sort of abuse or deprivation.

Some of the sisters' actions were clearly standard-issue adolescent rebellion, as I witnessed a few days later when the two sat doing lines of cocaine over their mother's kitchen table in the three-bedroom where fifteen-year-old Sandy still lived. While Barbara poured me a soda, Sandy chopped up rocks of cocaine with a razor. Barbara had once dealt drugs, a short-lived enterprise that she and her roommate Grace undertook to pay their rent. They'd displayed dangerous naïveté, cutting cocaine with Ritalin, a drug prescribed for children with attention deficit disorder—a combination that could potentially cause a heart attack. Tricky sold this junk for them to a girl who mainlined it. She lived, but word went around that the girls were mixing bad stuff, putting an end to their experiment.

I understood this rebellious flirtation with drugs—my own generation had been as heavily into drugs as the one I now encountered—but I hadn't known anyone who got even with their parents by firing rounds of live ammunition at someone or by hanging around guys who did. But then, when I was growing up, few middle-class students brought guns to school or allowed themselves to have their ribs or noses broken in a ritual beating. Middle-class kids were typically sheltered from such violence. But perhaps Barbara and Sandy's protection and privileges served to enhance the violence, making it all the more titillating and unreal.

The girls cultivated a disconcerting casualness to the brutality. They seemed to have taken a turn toward darkness simply out of personal choice; they certainly had the ability to reflect about what they and their friends were doing. Yet they went ahead anyway. At one point they denigrated their older friend Grace, saying she really didn't know anything about gangs, as though she were lacking a fundamental character trait. "She never did shit for a gang," said Sandy. "She never got shot at."

While they snorted coke at the kitchen table, the phone rang. Two LOs were in need of a ride. Though the truck belonged to Barbara, she checked with her younger sister. "Well, shit, they can wait," Sandy said, not looking up from the mirror. "What are we, their personal taxi? I mean, we have a guest. Did you tell them that?" She licked her finger, dabbing up the remaining powder, then rubbed it on her gums. "Tell them we'll pick them up later."

This was a switch. Ordinarily, the girls jumped whenever the LOs called. The other night, after a similar request for a ride, Barbara had posed as a boy's aunt in order to convince his friend's parents, where he was spending the night, to let him go out with her. The girls then chauffeured the boys to score weed, singing gangsta rap songs on the way, personalizing the lyrics to refer to killing their particular rivals. Barbara's reward was a five-minute make-out session against the truck's hood with a gang member just released from twenty-four-hour observation in a psychiatric ward. Why he had been there, he didn't know.

"I think the boys began liking me because of my truck," she said when she hung up from today's call. "The only bad thing is I like to make out and that's kind of hard to do when I'm driving. Maybe we'll hold hands, but I'm sorry, I'm getting into my sexual peak and I want more." She rested her chin on her palm and sighed. "The main reason I started hanging with gangs was because there were cute guys."

Her choice of cute guys was determined by Tricky, the head of the LOs. She recounted the night she wanted to sleep with an LO. "A pity fuck, really. He was being dissed by all the chicks and I felt sorry for him and said I'd fuck him." Gang etiquette required that the boy ask Tricky's permission because previously Barbara had slept with another LO. Since that guy wasn't at the party, Tricky gave the other boy the go-ahead. "Their thinking is that it prevents fights," Barbara explained.

Barbara cleared the kitchen table as Sandy hid the razor and bag of coke in a cigar box decorated with paper flowers. This was her "memory box." Along with drug paraphernalia and a rosary, it held a shell from the time Evil shot at the Ambros, a bullet from Sandy's own .380—a semiautomatic with fifteen bullets to a clip—a .357 from B-Boy's gun, three hollow-point bullets and a shell from a .45 automatic, just whose gun it was she couldn't remember. "When guys have guns, I always ask for a bullet. For memories."

The girls finished their cleanup just before their mother arrived home from the elementary school where she taught. They both hugged the pleasant-faced woman with soft brown eyes, and unburdened her of her books, asking about her day in voices girlish and sweet. They clearly adored her.

Later, in Sandy's bedroom, they spoke admiringly about how their mother had divorced their father and gone back to school to receive her degree in education. They claimed she disciplined them, not letting them get away with anything—at least anything she knew about. Wouldn't it break her heart if she learned how her daughters spent their days? "Well, yeah," said Sandy. "That's how come we've never told her the truth."

Barbara was nervous about her friends knowing too much about her family. "When people first meet us, the guys are like, 'Ask them who their father is.' It scares me. And it pisses me off. It's not that I'm not proud of my dad. I'm proud of his success, but it's not something I want a lot of people to know. They make assumptions about my background. First of all, they think that because I'm white I don't know what's up, that I'm stupid. That people can take advantage of me. We have to prove ourselves more."

Fair-skinned, with light hair and eyes, the sisters were of mixed parentage; their father of German and Dutch ancestry, their mother half-Mexican. The girls chose to claim only their Mexican roots. Mexicans are the majority in San Antonio, and Latinos are on their way to becoming this country's largest minority, outnumbering African Americans. "I consider myself Mexican, even though I don't speak Spanish," Barbara said. "The guys make fun of us because we don't understand. They'll say shit about us to our face. Tricky gave me shit. He's part white, but he's from the West Side. He got on my case because I'm educated and I use big words and it scared him or something."

Barbara removed her glasses, blew on them, then wiped them with the corner of her flannel shirt. "It's hard being half. You take shit from both. At college I was at a meeting and some guy stood up and said minorities were getting all the scholarships and how hard it was for him to be a white male. I told him, 'They don't give us scholarships just because we're minorities, but because we get good grades and need to be given a break.' Like, if you're Mexican, you can't think.

"After my mother's divorce, we had to struggle. We didn't always live in a good neighborhood. Maybe I did this to fit in."

How far would they go to fit in? They had hidden guns for the LOs. Once the boys borrowed Barbara's truck, returning it with the interior reeking of gunpowder. Another time Sandy, partying outdoors with friends, watched two black-clad figures walk up and open fire. She'd dived behind a car, rolling into a tight ball, until the boy next to her screamed for her to start shooting: "Shoot!" Finally she just fired blindly, hitting a kid in the knee.

AT some point I tracked down the guy who had impregnated Barbara. We met at his house, where he sat cuddling his infant daughter on the porch steps. He was a personable man in his twenties, who admitted he had dealt heroin long enough to put his young family on its feet. Now he had quit the LOs and worked two minimum-wage jobs.

He spoke highly of Barbara, out of his wife's earshot. "Most of the guys tell a girl, 'I'm your boyfriend,' but they're just playing with their mind, just using them to get laid. Pulling a train is very common. Me and Tricky wouldn't let that happen to Barbara and Sandy. They would let us use their car and everything. So we would take care of them.

"There are some girls who steal cars, shoot, rob. They're more like guys. But there are barely any girls tough enough to give orders or become leaders. Barbara and Sandy are respected because they're smart, and their house is there for us to hide. Sandy's more down, more likely to do something criminal. At first Barbara hung around to make sure her little sister was okay, then she got sucked in."

"How can they be so violent?" I asked. "They don't seem that different from people I grew up with, and I could never pull a gun on someone."

"That's what you say right now. Everyone says that. But the time comes when you will. Maybe you won't have a choice. Because I used to say that. You just get trigger-happy. You just start shooting."

A TALE OF TWO GIRLS

Alicia's family lived in a ramshackle yellow house, one side ablaze with red azaleas, the last on the block before the paved street crumbled into a dirt road. The Eight Ball Chick had moved back home from her boyfriend Robert's. When I knocked, two or three broken locks rattled on a dented side door, which looked like it'd been kicked open on more than one occasion. At last it swung open, revealing a small man in an undershirt with a graying mustache who glared at me from behind the screen. I resisted the urge to look at my watch. Alicia had asked me to come over around three, as her stepfather would be at work and we could be alone. I moved to go inside, but the man blocked me with his hand, gruffly calling Alicia.

Behind him she gestured me inside. I stepped past him, but Alicia didn't introduce me—the two didn't speak at all—and a moment later he slipped down a darkened back hallway, leaving us in a large open living room with paneled walls and a TV turned to cartoons with the sound off. Alicia picked up a bowl of soup from the linoleum floor. Above her head a black-velvet Jesus raised his eyes heavenward, forgetting her. "I was alone all the time at Robert's. He was never there and the rest of the family was so loud. Here, it's weird. I haven't talked to my mother in months. I never talk to him." She tilted her chin toward the back. "I'm alone all the time, but it's quiet." Out of a corner came a small coo from a white dove huddled on the bottom of a neglected cage. Today was the first time she'd eaten, Alicia announced listlessly, since she moved back three days ago.

She absently picked up a library card off the end table. "God," she whispered, tracing her sister's name in raised letters with her finger, "I wish I had a library card."

On a shelf, among a confusion of fake flowers, a statue of the Virgin Mary, and an ashtray overflowing with pennies, stood two plastic gold trophies of triumphant winged women above the declaration: BEST READER, THIRD GRADE. As a child, Alicia racked up so many fines for overdue library books that she was frightened to go back. When I offered to take her to a bookstore, she looked up incredulously, as if she'd won a trip to Disneyland. But, a moment later, she quickly reined in her excitement rather than risk being disappointed.

She took me back into her bedroom. Nearly everything in the room— a pair of white bedspreaded twin beds, the posters of Madonna and Marilyn Monroe, a basket brimming with free samples of Clinique compacts and lipsticks—belonged to Ellen, her sister, who was in college. Alicia had run away so much that most of her possessions had either disappeared or were stored in the garage.

She perched on the bed, frowning. "Robert's friends tell him I'm a bitch 'cause I like to go out," she said suddenly, "but I'm not like Scariella." Alicia constantly found some way to bring up Robert in the course of conversation, repeating his name like a mantra. From beneath the bed she slid out a photo album with ALICIA in large letters on the cover. On the back childish loopy handwriting, big circles dotting the *i*'s, declared: ALICIA LOVES ROBERT!

She flipped through the pages of her past: she and her mother in front of the Christmas tree, her mother caressing her tiny daughter's face, wet with tears; young Ellen and Alicia, giggling and naked, bathing in a yellow tub; Alicia grinning from the center of a cluster of kids in birthday hats. Later in the book, the pictures abruptly change. Alicia cuddles with girls on a bed in a dingy room that looks abandoned, graffiti covering the walls. "That's Scariella's bedroom. Her mom wants to be with her boyfriend, so she doesn't live there, and her grandmother never goes upstairs. We do a lot of coke there."

Another photo shows Alicia hugging her nine-year-old nephew, who she's dressed in an Eight Ball black bandanna and baggy trousers. Cradling a stuffed frog in one hand, he holds the other hand clawlike, his fingers pointed down in the symbol of a pitchfork—the Eight Ball sign. There is a newspaper clipping about Robert's arrest for firing into an elementary school yard during recess and, next to this, the picture Alicia sent him in juvenile detention of herself in black, throwing the Eight Ball sign, I LOVE YOU DICK HEAD scrawled on the back. There is a letter from Robert saying how scared he is, how he hates detention and wants to quit the Eight Ball forever after his release. He had promised they'd run away to Houston together and go straight, and at the time it had given her adolescent hope, but he'd been released and here they still were.

There are the photos of boyfriends before Robert, as well. Most of them are dead.

Then there were the omnipresent newspaper clippings found in every gang girl's photo album: the obituaries. One recounted the death of Tommy, the Eight Ball leader murdered a few months earlier, shot with an AK-47 outside the Cassiano Homes. Days before his death, the paper reported, he'd told police he was in danger. He'd received phone calls from girls in a rival gang, warning he would be shot.

One article she'd saved, however, confused me. It was about the murder of a teenager named Nick, a leader of the BCs, a rival gang.

"I thought he was your enemy."

"He was," she replied evenly. "But we were friends in middle school. All the Eight Ball and BCs were friends. Doomsday, Blimpy, and Nick were good, good friends." Every time one of them died, she said, the killer was someone close to him, often someone who knew him all his life.

"Nick died over a girl. There was a BC party, everyone coked up, and he was sitting on the floor with this BC Chick, Patty. Another BC came over to her, grabbing her ass, kicking her, saying she was a bitch and that everybody fucked her, why couldn't he? Nick and him started yelling and ran into the street. The guy shot Nick five times. In the jaw, the arm, the hip . . ."

Back in middle school, they'd all hung around together. Nick and Doomsday staged dog fights, pitting stolen rottweilers and pit bulls against each other. They drank beer, smoked cigarettes, did coke, anything to break up the grind of poverty.

Nick and Doomsday originally formed their separate gangs, the BCs and the Eight Ball Posse, as counters to the Kings, the biggest gang in town, to avoid becoming easy targets. Kids on the West Side who didn't claim Kings joined one of five newly formed gangs: the Eight Ball Posse; the BCs (for "Bad Company"); Damage Inc.; GTA (for "Grand Theft Auto," their area of expertise); or the LA Boyz (started by Lanier High School football players who took the Lanier Athletics logo for their name). Soon afterward, many of the gangs formed female cliques, inviting the neighborhood girls to join. Then, sometime in 1990, the stakes rose when the BCs announced their plan to do a drive-by on a rival gang that Doomsday's brother belonged to. Doomsday warned his brother of the BCs' attack and together they launched a preemptive strike. During the ensuing shoot-out between the Eight Ball and the BCs, an Eight Ball was shot in his leg. That night a blood feud was born, with best friends taking sides against one another.

Though the hostility started for a specific reason, it rapidly escalated to include perceived slights and insults. Soon the LA Boyz, GTA, and Damage entered the fray, choosing sides. As kids carried stories from one side to the other, words became as lethal as bullets and were often answered with the real thing. An old man was killed in the crossfire when two boys sharing the same last name opened fire on each other over the right to claim it.

The war had gone on for four years now. Yet sometimes when they'd run into each other on the street, they'd remember their past lives. One night as Alicia walked home from the Cassianos, her pockets full of cash from selling coke, a BC named Freeze stepped out of the shadows, pointing a gun at her face like a shiny black finger. Freeze and Alicia had played together as little kids, but he'd heard she was with the Eight Ball now. Alicia denied it—she only knew the Eight Ball because she hung around the Cassianos. Freeze just shrugged and asked if Alicia wanted to buy his gun. She pulled out a hundred-dollar bill. His eyes lit up. He insisted that she go with him to a BC hangout. "Freeze and some BCs brought all these guns for me to see," Alicia remembered. "Uzis, TEC-9s, all these fucking guns. I'm freaking out, thinking, 'They're gonna kill me.' I told them I'd buy one the next day. All the time I'm acting like I'm ready to party and inside I'm thinking, 'If the Eight Ball find out, *they'll* kill me.' We spent the whole night doing coke, Freeze asking me who I think is better, the BCs or the Eight Ball? 'Who do you hear about more?' I said, 'I hear about both of them.'

"I wound up spending the morning just hanging out with the BCs, doing errands for Freeze's mom. I was scared someone was going to see me, but I started feeling comfortable with them. Sometime during that day I told Freeze I was in the Eight Ball and told him the truth of why I got in—that it was just something to do. And he said he wouldn't do anything, 'cause I was cool. He dropped me off at Scariella's. She started yelling, 'What are you doing with them? You'll get killed if anyone in the Eight Ball sees you!' I was shaking from all the coke the night before. I was sick after that for two weeks. I still see Freeze on the street, but we never smile or talk to each other."

Looking through her memory book, even Alicia seemed dumbfounded by all the children she'd known who now lay in the neighborhood cemetery. "Tommy died last spring. Nick died only a month later. In four months, four friends have died. Sometimes I wish nothing had happened, 'cause we'd all still be here, the way we were in the beginning. Everyone feels that way. When they get drunk, Doomsday and Blimpy still talk about the good ol' days with Nick." She closed the photo album and slid it beneath her bed. "But you can't think that way too long." The past was a dangerous place, a place to get stuck.

She led me outside to my car. As she looked toward the chain-link gate surrounding her yard, a long breath escaped her lips. "*Shit,*" she said quietly. "He always does this. My stepfather locks the gate. He locks me in, so I have to climb over it. Sometimes he'll see me coming home down the sidewalk and lock it before I can get here." Her words were angry, but her voice flat and uninspired.

She helped me over the gate. For a moment we looked at each other from opposite sides, her hands gripping the fence of her small wire prison, until she turned her gaze down the dirt road. "I've been staying away from the Eight Ball 'cause of Robert, but sometimes, you know, I miss it. I miss the pain. Because pain makes me forget my anger. And I have a lot of anger."

"DOOMSDAY, that's my cousin," the girl told me. "When Nick was alive, I was stuck in the middle between the BCs and Eight Ball. Doomsday used to tell me, 'Why you with a BC? Break up with him!' Nick would be like, 'I'm gonna shoot your cousin if you leave me.' One time the BCs were gonna shoot up my grandma's—'cause Doomsday was over there—but I yelled at Nick, 'If you shoot my grandma's house, I'll never talk to you again.' 'Cause my grandma had nothing to do with it."

Wicked moved easily through the maze of tombstones in the flower-studded wasteland of the cemetery, leading me to Nick's grave. Wicked and Alicia were enemies or, rather, the boys they'd liked were enemies. The girls hardly knew each other. Wicked was a BC Chick. "Alicia's a good fighter, I'll say that. She won't back down. People are intimidated just by the look on her face. I don't know, me and her, we're alike. If we ever fought, I don't know who would win."

Since the boys had disbanded the BC Chicks after Nick's death, Wicked spent much of her time keeping Nick's memory alive. He was always a part of her day. She visited his grave regularly, telling friends she was "going to see Nick," leaving little presents for him, flowers, notes, photos. She'd grown obsessed with death, the cost of caskets, floral arrangements, burial plots, superstitions. "If you shoot someone and they fall facedown? That means they're going to come back to haunt you and your conscience will overcome you." She pointed to a tilting stone. "That means he's coming back for someone, like his wife or the one he loved most." She made a wide arc around the grave. "Later on, if you want, I could find you the little girl they accuse my friend Gat Man of killing."

Then she was standing at Nick's plot. "Look, he's sprung little flowers!" she squealed before bending down to discover they were fake.

"When Nick was alive, we never talked about when we would die. Even though everyone was out shooting. He spoke about 'when we get married' or 'when we buy a house' or 'when we have kids.' But after Nick's death, everyone in the BCs changed. No one cared anymore. One of the guys said, 'Fuck it, we're all gang members, we're all gonna have to die. Let's just go out like villains.' He was Nick's pallbearer. He died in June." Wicked turned away from the wind, brushing a blonde strand out of her eyes, revealing a lost expression. She looked thin and frail, as if the wind might send her skittering across the cemetery lawn like a leaf. "I can show you his grave, but they scratched his picture on his tombstone all up."

One time when she came to visit Nick she found the boy who had killed him kneeling at his grave. Nick had been his best friend. "His nickname's Right Hand. Nick gave him that name."

Right Hand was a sullen-faced boy with wire glasses who rode his bicycle around in mad circles, like a dog with its tail broken. From all accounts, he was a disturbed kid. Before he shot his friend, he'd once offered to shoot Wicked when she and Nick were fighting. Because of overcrowding, he'd spent only three months in juvenile detention for Nick's murder before being released.

"I pulled up at the cemetery and there he was, all scrunched into a little ball on top of Nick. He was crying, 'Bro, forgive me.'" Wicked wrapped her arms around herself, rocking gently in imitation.

The real culprit in Nick's death, in Wicked's mind, was Patty, the BC Chick over whom Nick and the boy were arguing. Wicked and Gat Man shot up Patty's apartment one afternoon to scare her. "In my heart I want to kill Patty. I won't rest until she's dead."

Sixteen years old, Wicked possessed the intelligence and bravado to command her homeboys' respect. They felt she was the only one of them who could make it out of the barrio and urged her to stay in school—no mean feat, considering how few gangsters made it beyond the ninth grade. Wicked had been kicked out of the San Antonio school district for carrying a Mac 11 into her classroom. Nick had neglected to tell her that he'd hidden it in her backpack for safekeeping.

For the last two years she'd attended an alternative school, a sort of last chance for troubled kids. I visited her there once, going into the library to look for her. Students are barred from wearing gang attire or tossing signs, but their swagger, their tattoos, the way they slouched in their chairs, the aggressive way the boys and girls flirted, as though issuing a challenge, spoke as loudly as if they had all pulled out semiautomatics and fired as I entered.

"SINCE Nick died, I don't party with the BCs much," Wicked said as she helped me navigate through her West Side neighborhood. "They don't want me to be with nobody, they just want me to be single. I'm with the LA Boyz now."

She turned up the car radio until it was blasting *"If he's your boyfriend, he wasn't last night,"* a female rapper taunted.

Wicked was taking me into BC turf. Remembering Blimpy's warning about the gang's penchant for rape, I asked if what I heard about the BCs was true.

"Oh yeah, some of them," she said in her high-pitched voice that reminded me of Minnie Mouse. "They sell girls or beat them up and rape them. But the girls always come back. Me, there was total respect, 'cause I was Nick's lady. I knew he had other skanks. I mean, all the gang members have skanks. I didn't know that before he died, 'cause Nick made sure I never found out. He would fuck a girl and then beat her up and tell her, 'If Wicked finds out that I was with you, I'm gonna kill you or kick your ass or all the boys are gonna rape you.' Everything came as a shock to me afterward, all the girls that Nick was with. The boys kept saying he loved me and never wanted me to find out. I mean, it was the girls who told me after he died. Patty and others—"

She stopped suddenly, cursing me in Spanish. "Girl! You're not supposed to do that!"

I had been staring at some boys posing on the sidewalk.

"Don't keep looking at them! They'll think you're interested or else they'll probably shoot you."

Rattled, I made a wrong turn, then slammed on the brakes. Wicked swung around to look at the car behind us. "Girl! I'm getting nervous! People round here will kick your ass for driving like this."

Somehow we made it into BC territory. Every other stop sign on the narrow streets had BC scrawled across it in blue, the gang's color. A corner store was decorated with a memorial mural to Nick.

"We'll go to Tony and Dirty Dog's house. They're BCs, but my friend Gat Man, an LA Boy, is staying there. They're my boys."

Gat Man, she said, wanted to replace Nick in her life. I was intrigued to learn what kind of guy Wicked would choose after losing her first boyfriend to a gang member's gun. "Gat Man doesn't care about anybody. He's already killed a lady. He has no wish to live, so nothing really matters." She sighed. "Stupid Gat Man. He doesn't learn. I don't think he's gonna have that long to live. You say his name to other gang members and they hate him or are scared of him. I don't know. He's my friend and everything, and I love him—"

"You think he loves you?"

"He says he does. I don't think he knows what love is."

Gat Man was known as a ruthless killer. Eighteen years old, he had already piled up a long and ugly police record, from grand theft auto to assault to a capital murder charge for his role in a drive-by that killed an innocent woman and a little girl.

One day I'd watched him from my car as he spoke in Spanish to a counselor. Like a lot of male gang members, he exuded sexual energy, a combination of threat, lewdness, allure, and genuine distrust of everything that moved. It was a potent mixture that thrilled some women and one of the reasons boys so easily wrestled away the attention of counselors, social workers, and journalists from girls. Meeting Gat Man was a chance to meet the devil. If I, an adult reporter, could sense his power, how seductive must he be to a sixteen-year-old girl like Wicked? Especially one growing up in a world that denied her any real power or opportunity of her own.

Wicked and I parked in front of a pale pink clapboard house, where a pregnant rottweiler limped near the chain-link fence. Wicked shoved it out of her way, edging toward a garage in back, hollering Gat Man's name. A moment later two teenagers swaggered out. One of them, a bulky guy with a mustache, wore a baseball cap that read DIRTY DOG and a T-shirt in BC baby blue. Behind him I recognized Gat Man's hard, handsome face. He regarded me strangely with sleepy, hooded eyes. I followed his gaze to my car, where a black bandanna flapped from the antenna. An Eight Ball boy must have tied it there, at the same time writing his gang name in the dust of my bumper, like a cat marking its territory. It was a little joke that I'd somehow missed and one that could have resulted in my car being shot, since the LA Boyz and BCs belong to the Blue Circle, symbolized by a blue bandanna. Gat Man tore off the black rag and tossed it in a trash can. He then hoisted himself onto the back of a pickup truck, staring at me with a lopsided grin. Clearly he was a showoff, yet the impression stubbornly lingered that the wrong word could spark disaster.

For a few minutes he dodged and circled my questions before ducking inside the garage and reappearing with a bulge beneath his striped Polo shirt. He pulled out a boxy slate-gray gun—something Arnold Schwarzenegger might carry—and placed it in my arms, which drooped from its unexpected weight.

"That's a Mac 11!" Wicked squealed. "Gat Man taught me how to shoot it."

Apparently, I was the only one who felt uncomfortable holding such a thing in broad daylight and suggested we go inside the garage. There they produced two shotguns, one sawed-off. Wicked explained that the guns favored by gangs used to be AK-47s and other large assault weapons—but today the guns of choice were machine pistols like the Mac 11 and TEC-9s, easier to handle and to conceal.

Gat Man had been the first in his crowd to shoot someone. He was fourteen. "We had beat the shit out of some King, spray-painted his face, and he came back with his brothers. Some lady was yelling at us to stop fighting. I got tired of her, just held the gun up, didn't know what I was doing"—Gat Man raised his arms in the air, extending his finger like the barrel of a gun—"closed my eyes, and shot." He opened his eyes and smiled. "A lousy aim. As I got older, I didn't do drugs. I didn't drink that much. I shot at people. When I got angry, I'd go out and light someone up and get my release. It was my high."

From what did he require so great a release? Gat Man thought about it. He assured me he didn't come from a bad family. In fact, his father gave him anything he wanted. "My mother is in the military, so she's always gone. Her career was more important than me. My dad, he's like my best friend."

Dirty Dog agreed. "Our dads partied with us, did coke, got us guns. My dad gave my little brother a 9-millimeter for his fourteenth birthday. He'd go along on shootings with us."

In jail, when Gat Man found himself among rival gangs out to kill him, he'd phoned his father for protection. "They had to put me in lockdown. I called him and said, 'Get me out of here. Whatever it takes.'" What it took was an expensive, well-connected lawyer who was able to put a capital murder suspect back on the streets without a monitor.

I glanced around Gat Man's makeshift apartment. Water blossomed like dark Rorschach blots on the concrete floor near a rusted sink in the corner. A bedspread serving as a curtain blocked the entrance to an inner room just big enough for a mattress. The garage was his fifth hideout in months. He could never afford to become too comfortable, in case his enemies tracked him down. And Gat Man had a lot of enemies.

I asked if he had anyone else, other than his father. He looked at me silently for a moment. "I have a little boy. He's two. But the mother of my child won't let me see him." Gat Man's face clouded over before he let out a forced little laugh. "I tried to go over there today, but . . ."

Wicked cut in. "Girls are afraid of Gat Man. When they find out who he is, they don't want to get near him."

His trial was coming up in a few weeks. I gently asked if he understood what would happen if he were found guilty of a capital murder charge in Texas.

Gat Man looked me squarely in the eye and mimed sticking a needle into his arm. The method of capital punishment in Texas is lethal injection. "But if I'm found guilty, I'm not waiting around. I'll run."

The devil I'd encountered, instead of evil, sounded wounded, hollow. Having failed to die a gangster's death in a hail of bullets, he now seemed to be fading away, emotion leaking out of him like air.

We headed outside as a shiny maroon Corvette sped up and out climbed a muscular teenager, a chubby blonde girl following awkwardly behind. Wicked snickered. The girl, she said, was rich and let this gang banger drive her father's car in exchange for his company. Gat Man called out to the guy, telling him to take me on a drive-by.

I said I wasn't interested. Gat Man looked confused. "What, you afraid you'll get arrested?"

When I tried to explain that I couldn't contribute to someone's death or injury, that my being in the car would transgress an ethical line I couldn't cross, they gazed, blank-faced, unable to comprehend my point. In the end I offered to take Wicked home.

On the way back, a battered pickup truck, its bed loaded with bare-chested boys, cut us off at an intersection. The driver did a double take when he saw Wicked, then hit his brakes, blocking the road.

The driver, a short red-faced man with eyelids like broken shades, climbed out and staggered toward us. He stuck his head inside Wicked's window, saying nothing. He exhaled deeply, as if about to nod off, when his whole body spasmed, jerking his head backward. The sickening odor of stale beer wafted through the car.

"Wicked!" He coughed. "Come party with us."

Wicked gave a little toss of her hair, laughing. "No, Mick."

Sweat and dirt rode the deep ravines of his face. He pressed himself closer to her. "Come here." He grabbed her thigh with one hand as he opened the car door.

Wicked, surprisingly vulnerable, looked alarmed. "No, Mick." She sounded very young. "I'm going home."

He clasped her forearm, half-pulling her from the car. One of the teenagers jumped off the truck and was at his side. "Mick, let's go. Wicked's gotta go home."

Grunting, Mick flung the kid's hand off his shoulder. He whirled back around, seemingly unable to remember where he was.

"Get away from me!" Wicked shrieked.

Another kid leaped from the pickup. The two boys yanked Mick off Wicked, wrestling him away.

I pulled her inside, backed up, and made a U-turn before turning to her for an explanation. "God *damn*. Gat Man's dad, he's a pervert!" she yelled, her green eyes moving in all directions. "Mick the Pervert, that's his nickname. His girlfriends are little girls. He's a forty-year-old man who fucks fourteen-year-olds! Gat Man's got to control his fuckin' dad!"

So this sorry drunk was Gat Man's father.

Wicked tried to ease the shakiness of her breath. "I mean, they all know *me*. I'm not like that. They're not supposed to treat *me* like that."

ALICIA'S older sister Ellen, when I met her, appeared so different from Alicia that the two could have been raised in separate families. In contrast to Alicia's thin drawn face, Ellen possessed a peach complexion, perfect white teeth, and shiny brown hair pulled back in a neat ponytail. She attended college, majoring in elementary education, with no financial help from her family, shelling out $4,000 a semester. She worked part-time and received student loans and a scholarship that required she teach in a poor school after graduation, an experience she eagerly anticipated. Despite these accomplishments, Ellen was self-effacing. "I see myself as weak. I couldn't deal with the things Alicia has. I think of my sister as a survivor."

It was hard to glean a sense of survival from Alicia's drained demeanor, her words easing out like a tired joke. Because I suspected there was much Alicia could not talk about, I'd asked her if I could speak with her sister. She'd shrugged her tacit permission.

Alicia, Ellen remembered, had started out with everyone on her side. Their mother enrolled in a parenting program after she'd given birth to Alicia, the youngest of three daughters by three different men. Her mother flourished in the program, also attending night school to become a nurse's aide, while the man she lived with, the girls' stepfather, brought in a second income. The director of the parenting program took special interest in Alicia, who thrived under the attention, doing well in elementary school and making captain of the softball team.

It was when Alicia was eleven that she began running away from home. Ellen recalled she was never gone long, but her behavior grew stranger with each disappearance. During one of these times, at fourteen, Alicia met a gang member called Psycho, a spindly kid around her age. Before then gangs had seemed just another clique at school to Alicia, like jocks or preppies, as much about fashion as anything; after the first time she and Psycho hung out, Alicia showed up at home with her eyebrows shaved off. Ellen believed everything fell apart because of Psycho.

Alicia and Psycho spoke a few times on the phone and one night made plans to go out. Waiting for Psycho on a corner, Alicia noticed a neighborhood kid at a pay phone. He offered to stay with her until her ride came; it wasn't safe. Her instincts told her to turn down his offer—he was decked out in gangster dress, and Alicia was worried that he might be from a rival gang—but the boy refused to leave her there alone.

Moments later Psycho arrived in a low-rider packed with gang bangers. Alicia took one look at his face, contorted in an ugly sneer, and realized that he had recognized an enemy. Once she was next to him in the backseat, Psycho ordered the driver to pull up alongside the kid. Who, Psycho wanted to know, was he down with?—derogatory street slang for "What gang are you in?"

"No one," the boy replied.

His refusal to claim his gang infuriated Psycho even more. "Fuck this shit," he'd hissed, quickly grabbing something from beneath the car seat. "I hear you're from—"

Alicia didn't hear the gang name before Psycho fired. Her ears burning from the explosion, she felt the car jerk as it propelled forward.

"You killed him! You killed him!" she heard herself scream, unable to look back.

"Shut up!" Psycho shouted. "Why you talking to him? I should have shot you, bitch!"

While his homeboy drove, Psycho beat her until her screams stopped. Afterward, the boys went on a shooting spree, firing into home after home as Alicia slumped, half-unconscious, in the backseat, hands covering her ears and eyes against the flash of gunfire, the shattering glass. "She never knew if they killed anyone or not, which I guess was Psycho's plan," Ellen said. "They didn't even know *who* they shot. It could have been some deaf guy Psycho thought was throwing up an enemy gang sign. He told Alicia that she was just as guilty as they were. She never said so, but I think he forced her to shoot, as well. She used to cry when she talked about it, and she had nightmares. She found it very, very hard to live with herself."

But Psycho wasn't finished with her. He embarked on a campaign of terror to ensure her silence. "One night she left with my little nephew to sell shotguns at a pawnshop," Ellen told me. "I came home, was getting out of my car, when a silver mini-truck screeched up with a bunch of guys in back. I heard someone behind me say, 'Well, if you're going to shoot her, shoot her now!' And I just froze. My mom was too scared to open the door."

That night the truck peeled past the house again and again, the boys firing into the air, screaming, "Alicia, you're ours!" Ellen and her mother huddled on the floor of a back bedroom, shaking with each shot.

After the incident, the director from the parenting program contacted a woman who worked with gang members, asking her to intervene. The counselor helped Alicia transfer out of her school and began taking her to Victory Outreach, a national church organization based in gang neighborhoods. The woman's trump card was her friendship with a powerful ex-gang head, whom she begged to talk to Psycho on Alicia's behalf. But the ex-leader was leery. He suspected that Alicia was more involved in gang activity than she let on, doing drugs, probably selling. He didn't believe she truly wanted out.

For now, the counselor put aside the question of Alicia's involvement with drugs; until the death threat was removed, she saw no hope for Alicia. At last the gang leader agreed to meet with Psycho. He told him that Alicia planned to become a born-again Christian and Psycho agreed that if she was in church, he'd let her go. But he warned if he ever saw Alicia with another gang, she was his. And if he were arrested for the night of the shooting spree, he'd not only go after her but those who intervened for her.

Her freedom negotiated, Alicia attended Victory Outreach for a while. But when school let out and the days passed into summer she started running away again, only to return a day or two later, high as a kite, unable to speak or focus her eyes. Ellen feared she had joined the Eight Ball. "They're known as sprayheads. You fill a soda can with gold or silver paint, put a pop-top in the bottom, or a piece of glass or a rock, and shake it around to keep the paint from drying up, then suck it in. You trip. I'd come home and my mom would be yelling at Alicia about being high. And Alicia would say no, even though there was gold paint dripping out of her mouth."

Finally, believing her daughter on the verge of suicide, her mother committed Alicia to the mental health ward of a hospital. During the first few days, she threw temper tantrums, swearing, biting the attendants. Then, after six months of therapy and antidepressants, Alicia began to reveal her secret. She told her sister that their stepfather was the first guy she'd ever kissed.

SEVERAL weeks later Wicked reached me by phone, her usual high spirits at low ebb. She had just come home early from a party off Guadalupe, where gang members peddled heroin and cocaine to prostitutes. All evening Wicked stared at one of the women, slumped in a thread-worn chair, barely able to keep her head up, her cheeks sunken, gazing into space with hollow eyes, the tell-tale sign of heroin addiction. She looked vaguely familiar. Finally Wicked asked one of the boys if he knew the woman's name. It was the answer she'd been dreading. The woman was Wicked's aunt.

"Ah, Wicked, you don't got to be ashamed," the boy told her. "My aunt's a prostitute, too. Look at my uncle, he's a dealer. We're all the same. We have to stick together."

The night before, her father had threatened to kick her out without her clothes or break her legs if she continued to run around. She knew if it came down to that, she'd make it; she knew the streets. Her uncle had been one of the founders of a notorius adult criminal gang. Every Saturday the family visited him in the San Antonio jail. In six weeks he would be transferred to a maximum-security prison. The newspaper covering his trial called Wicked's uncle the "top assassin" for his gang, whose trademark retribution for drug deals gone bad involved binding the offenders' hands and feet with duct tape before shooting them in the head. "When they sentenced him for thirty-five years, he stood there like he didn't give a damn. And that made me want to be more like him. He's my role model."

But Wicked was no good at concealing the conflicts inside her. After boasting about her uncle, she revealed her fears about her father's possible crimes. "When I started getting in trouble, he started talking to the BCs to find out what I was getting into. He became their friend. He helps them out, they help him out. My mom can't leave him. She won't."

"Did your father ever hit your mother?" I asked.

"No. He's never hit her, 'cause she doesn't deserve to be hit. I mean, my mom, she's loyal, she's obedient. I was like my mom with my boyfriend Nick. I'd stay home, I never smoked weed or did coke. He didn't believe it was right for girls to do that. I was always watching my back. Once he died, it was like freedom. I went crazy, experimented with everything. I wouldn't think of him as much and could do it without any fear that he'd come after me. No way he could hurt me more than he did by dying."

As for the future, Wicked could see herself like her aunt in ten years, strung out and selling her body. Or she could find herself, like so many older BC Chicks, raising a baby alone.

I reminded her of the college scholarship a counselor at school had encouraged her to pursue, and the seminar for exceptional high school students that she was slated to attend. But Wicked was wary. "Those people are all poindexters; I can't relate to them. They all want to be engineers or lawyers or jobs I've never heard of. I don't know. I'll probably just get married."

Those who tried to help her, she believed, knew nothing of how she lived. "I tried to talk to a priest after Nick died, to straighten things out, but he was so outdated. His vocabulary was like the old English Bible. Like, when I was telling him how things were, he went into shock. He freaked out. He couldn't believe what it was like. I said, 'Well, Father, I hope you recover. Later.' "

IN a Hooters at the River Center Mall, where buxom young waitresses in uniforms of hot pants and cropped tops served burgers to the families around us, Alicia sat across from me, a too-skinny teenager staring at nothing, wearing an expression that might be mistaken for boredom. "I remember waking up one night—the bathroom is next to my room—and the light was on and he was standing there naked. I closed my eyes 'cause I thought I was dreaming and when I opened them again, he was on top of me, touching me. It would be like every Sunday. Or when Mom was going to school at night, he'd kiss me in the car while we waited for her. He'd tell me, 'If you tell your mom, she'll leave us and get rid of you' "— she waved her hand limply—"you know how those stories go."

When she was eleven, Alicia did tell her mother. "I was trying to say that he touched me, but she didn't want to hear it. She kept telling me to kill her; she had a knife in her hand, and she grabbed my hand in hers, trying to make me stab her."

Afterward, Alicia ran away for the first time. Unsure where to go, she wandered around until she ended up at the house of a friend, who let her spend the night. The next day she arrived at school in the same clothes she'd worn the day before. The counselor called Alicia into her office; her mother and stepfather were there, along with a translator for her stepfather. The counselor asked why she ran away. Frightened at first, she replied because her stepfather hated her cat. The counselor insisted something else must be wrong. And so finally Alicia told them.

"My mom just freaked out. She was crying and crying. She promised me, 'He ain't gonna be there when you get home tonight.' And I listened to her. All that day I was acting big, doing whatever I wanted. But when I got home, he was still there."

In the almost six years that followed, she and her stepfather barely spoke. The bedroom visits ceased, although he never admitted to fondling her. Trapped in the house with her stepfather, she'd grown angry at her mother. Sometimes it boiled over into hatred, and she'd lash out, running away to the Eight Ball, returning home high, spitting out expletives. At times she hoped, deep down, that her mother would conquer her terrible neediness, throw out her stepfather, and scoop up her youngest daughter in her arms like a little girl.

All around her the people she dreamed might save her instead deserted her. The hospital's drug program turned her away when her mother's insurance ran out. The parenting program failed to find a sponsor to send her to a boarding school where she would be free of gangs. Back home, she sought the only way she knew to ease the pain, heading out at night to party with the Eight Ball at the Courts. By the time her mother finally did kick out her stepfather, it was too late; the fights between Alicia and her mother only escalated.

Four months before I'd met her, Alicia had attacked her mother, throwing boiling water on her, knocking her to the ground, kicking her furiously in the head and stomach. Afterward, she wrote a hasty note to her sister Ellen, begging her not to turn her into the police. Then she fled to Robert's.

Now she was back with her mother, who in Alicia's absence had broken down and allowed her stepfather to return. "I needed someone to talk to and I called my mom, saying I was sorry. I wanted to see her, but I was scared."

To prepare for the move back home, her counselor took Alicia to a *curandero*, a traditional Mexican healer, who performed a cleansing rite. Alicia sought the cleansing because she was afraid to let her mother see her as she was. Soiled. "See, two weeks ago, Robert beat me up real ugly 'cause I didn't want to have sex with him." While she spoke, Alicia refused to look at me, her eyes trailing the mariachi band that played in the mall outside the restaurant. "I had two black eyes, a broken lip. Afterward I asked him if I could go to Scariella's 'cause I wanted to take a bath. He was afraid that I wasn't gonna come back. Finally he said I could go, but if I wasn't back in, like, fifteen minutes, he was gonna look for me and kick my ass again."

On her return, she took 18th, a residential street that sliced through BC territory, the only shortcut to Robert's. At Tampico she noticed a group of four or five boys beneath a streetlight. BCs. One yelled to her as she passed. She stopped to talk with them. If they were in the right mood, gang members would give you a break, she explained, especially if you were a girl. But if she ignored them and kept walking, they would almost certainly hurt her.

The boy who'd called out to her was Freeze, the only one of the group she recognized. They'd been friends in middle school, before Freeze became a BC. During daylight hours, Freeze was easy enough to joke with, but by sundown he began drinking and snorting coke. By night, his eyes glazed over, his mood turned mean, and he prowled the neighborhood, searching for prey.

He stared at her beneath the streetlight, wondering what happened to her swollen face. She lied. "I said I was upset because my mom died. I wanted him to feel sorry for me."

But Freeze didn't believe her or didn't care. When she turned away, the mob surrounded her, herding her into an empty lot next to a corner house. Laying on a bed of overgrown crabgrass and weeds, she gazed up at the broken light dancing through the canopy of tree branches, the cold barrel of a gun pressing against her forehead. The boys taunted her for forty-five minutes, calling her an Eight Ball bitch, a skinny, dirty sprayhead.

She was going to have to pay, they told her.

Freeze ordered her to take a deep breath, to smell the world one last time before he shot her. Instead one of the boys gripped her arms and another spread her legs while Freeze raped her. Her mouth covered with a sweaty palm, Alicia followed Robert's truck with her eyes as it circled the block, searching for her. Once he yelled her name.

ALICIA hadn't reported the rape to the police nor had she seen a doctor. Her mother instructed her to be examined at a clinic but to tell no one. Freeze warned if she told anyone, if he went to jail, his gang would hunt her down. Put a gun up her ass and pull the trigger.

She was terrified that her rapist had AIDS. Rumors spread like the disease in this West Side neighborhood. "A lot of my friends have been raped by gang members," she said suddenly, as though to justify her experience. She tugged at a long red ringlet. "That's just the way life is around here."

Sex as a Weapon

"Sex," a gap-toothed guy from another San Antonio gang was telling me, "is about unity. Some guys might joke before the orgy, saying, 'Let's bring the bitch to the altar.' And the altar is the bed. It's a group setting. See"—he wiped sweat from beneath the rim of his baseball cap, as he contemplated in philosophical terms the finer points of pulling a train—"this is what guys do: they hang together, drink together, get high together, do drive-bys together, and fuck together. It takes another man to bring out the man in you. It's like a homosexual that is not a homosexual."

When it came down to it, I didn't meet a gang in San Antonio that didn't share girls. Not every member had a taste for this kind of activity—less than half the guys in a room might walk to the back to slam whatever body was available and some might even go home in protest—but every gang had at least one or two aficionados. One day, after I'd come to know them better, I asked Blimpy and Doomsday why they didn't pull trains like the BCs. Since I first met them they'd tried to convince me that they treated Eight Ball Chicks with respect, albeit within the boundaries of conventional gang mores. Doomsday was quiet.

"Who hears this?" he said at last, eyeing my tape recorder. "I just don't want Scariella to tell Lea any shit." Lea was Doomsday's common-law wife and the mother of his son. "But we've pulled trains a bunch of times. I'm always first. I ain't taking sloppy seconds."

WHEN I finally met several of the BCs, expecting angry, fierce teenagers, I was startled to find two ordinary-looking stoned boys, Tony, green-eyed and sandy-haired, cute in a Matthew Broderick sort of way (nicknamed Lover Boy for fathering four kids by four girls), and Fred, lanky and awkward. Both called me "miss" and laughed nervously at questions they found embarrassing. Unlike some L.A. gang members who demanded cash for conversation, then talked anyway when none was forthcoming, Fred and Tony seemed surprised that anyone cared about what they thought. I found them gathered at Ray's Drive-In, one of the BCs' unofficial meeting places, along with Patty, the BC Chick they'd once blamed for their leader Nick's death. Patty, it seemed, was forgiven.

They were discussing Nancy, a BC Chick legendary in the neighborhood for the number of boys she'd taken on and for her tolerance for abuse.

"Nancy looked up to us, would do whatever we told her," Tony explained. "At first she was like a tomboy. But then she started getting older"—he worked this around in his mind for a moment—"getting guys' attention. She got BCs' attention. We pulled a train on her lots of times."

Patty burst into giggles.

"Other gangs would come to us and want to party, bringing beer and drugs and say, 'Give us that girl!' And we would."

Tony paused to take a noisy sip from his Big Red cream soda. "Drunk or sober, she'd do what we said. She'd take on ten guys. I don't know if she enjoyed it. She never complained. There were times she had a good time and times she had a bad time." He took another slurp. "The BCs had this shack with a bed. And a couch. And a floor. Girls had sex—"

"It wasn't sex, it was *looove!*" insisted Fred, who gazed at me through a marijuana-induced stupor, his voice thick, as if his tongue decided to take a nap.

Tony laughed, spraying cream soda through squeezed lips. "We all wound up at the Good Samaritan health clinic! Syphilis, gonorrhea, herpes, chlamydia"—he rattled off diseases as if names of old friends— "Nancy had them all. And she gave them to us."

Patty laughed again. "Chicks are crazies!"

"They all kicked her ass after we got the clap," Fred said, grinning at the memory. "First the guys, then the leader of the BC Chicks kicked her ass, yelling, 'You gave my boys diseases!'"

Among those rumored to have had sex with Nancy were Tony's father and other men who provided their sons with drugs and guns in exchange for young girls. Nancy usually agreed to have sex with whomever the boys presented; if she refused, they pleaded or, worse, ignored her until she felt bad and gave in. One time Nancy didn't give in. An older man tried to have sex with her on the floor of the BCs' shack. When she cried out, he began to beat her. Several boys came to her rescue, but wanted sex in return for protecting her. In the morning they discovered her rib was broken.

But now as Tony joked about Nancy, affection warmed his voice, along with awe for this survivor. "*Everyone* used to beat her up. She was always doing something wrong. We'd send her out to do burglaries, she'd fuck it up." He shook his head, smiling. "But Nancy was *down.*"

From their own experiences, the kids could pretty much piece together Nancy's story: raised poor, dropped out of school before eighth grade, abusive father. But such details didn't make a difference. Friendship was easily uprooted by the tug of economic or psychological self-interest—the guys wanted sex and Nancy was willing to provide it for them. "Nancy never had a relationship, never fell for anybody," Patty said. Then, perhaps acknowledging the loneliness that gripped each kid at the table, even if no one dared say so, she added, "But Nancy always wanted to be around. She always came back for more."

As the BCs stood up to leave, I asked them how old Nancy was.

Tony looked skyward, thinking. "Hmmm. Fifteen?"

The BCs had existed for at least four years. "So you were having sex with her and knocking her about when she was—"

Tony filled in the blank. "Eleven. But she had the developed body of a woman." He half-closed his eyes, his voice lowered, and he held his hands in front of him, as though wrapped around an invisible waist.

"Nancy looked real old for her age," Fred agreed. "Like, seventeen. She'd run away from home. She'd been around."

WHAT happened to those girls who admitted to making it with two or three gang members and then tried to stop?

"The girls don't report rape. They don't consider it a crime. The persons who did this to them were their friends," my contact at the police department told me. "I know it's not clean-cut. I also know that the reason she's with these guys is her home life is worse. Her stepfather is raping her. People don't want to know there are guys out there who want to have sex with their children. *I* don't like to hear that. I know there are nights I can't sleep because of them. And there's gang rape."

Yet, by the end of 1993, the SAPD's sex crime unit would have only six reported cases of gang rape on file. Of these, only two victims pressed charges; one later recanted. She was the thirteen-year-old girl allegedly beaten and raped by nine gang members in a trailer. In an about-face after testifying, she announced that the D.A. had forced her to lie, even though one of her attackers confessed to the rape as part of his plea bargain. The judge dismissed the charges against the others. The officer I spoke to was convinced that her assailants intimidated their victim into silence, but there was nothing he could do.

"And that AIDS initiation?" he went on. "I'm sure there was a guy who said he had AIDS. I'm sure there were some girls who believed him. We live in a community where kids play Russian roulette with guns. It's entirely possible it happened just as the girls described."

At the sheriff's department Sergeant Kyle Coleman of the gang unit discussed with me how little law enforcement could ever really know about the situations teenage girls faced. The gang unit had seven members to cover the 1,297 square miles of Bexar County—and none of the deputies were female. Occasionally, the gang unit visited troubled boys at home to form some impression of their family life, but neglected the girls. "The problem with an all-male office is that we can't get close to the female members," Coleman admitted. "Can you imagine doing a home visit to a fourteen-year-old girl and finding her alone? You'd open yourself up to all kinds of allegations."

Before I left another officer held up a mug shot from his desk. "See this guy? He's wanted for ten rapes, all gang-related. We hauled him in here, but someone upstairs mistakenly released him. He stole one of the cars out of the lot. So he's back on the streets. He's believed to have AIDS."

The sheriffs were also investigating the murder of a young gang girl by another gang member. Among her personal effects was a handwritten list of boys she had slept with. It included 75 names.

IN sharp contrast to the numbers of rapes reported to police, the Rape Crisis Center documented 5,000 incidents of sexual assault during 1993; 60 percent involved teenage girls under eighteen.

Its then-director, Martha Moses, attacked the issue of denial head-on. "San Antonio is 54 percent Hispanic and it's a military-based economy. Both traditional Hispanic culture and the military are patriarchal; often gender roles are stereotyped. Spanish women typically don't speak out about abuse. People joining the army now are not drafted. Many enlist to get a life and many come from homes where the boys are being physically abused. It's not surprising if the cycle of violence continues with their girlfriends, wives, or daughters."

Spousal exemption, Moses pointed out, "didn't come into effect in Texas until 1991. In other words, before the change in law, when a man married a woman, he had the right to do anything he wanted to her sexually. Legally there was no such thing as 'raping' your wife. This is the type of environment that gang kids come from."

She played a tape of a gang leader who had volunteered to describe the role girls played in his gang and to settle once and for all, he said, "this issue of rape." All he asked was to be left alone with a recorder: "When it comes to gangs, there is no such thing as raping. Most gangs do not rape chicks." His voice was low, cocky. "I'll tell you straight right now, the girls have a *choice* of initiations: (A) fighting one-on-one with a guy for two minutes, (B) get shot in the leg with a Glock, (C) get jumped in by six chicks for a minute and a half, or (D) they can roll the dice and hope that they get two at the most.

"Most of the time the girls will take the dice, 'cause to them it's probably the easiest of anything. There are two dice. If they roll eleven or twelve, fine, they're going to get fucked by at least twelve of us. That's what they want, that's what they get.

"Most guys do not use protection. They'll go in, fuck the shit out of her, then let the next one come in. Now, suppose somebody gets pregnant and shit? We don't give a fuck—afterward some of us refer to them as our bitches or our hos. But that's what they are. They're the bitches of the gang. They proved it, right?"

Barely taking a breath, the kid droned on about how easy it was to attract girls. "Gangsters are main targets for girls. They like our rough mentality, how we have no mercy for other people . . . When your gang is dominating it's like a vacuum cleaner—girls just want to be part of your group. It's a pressure thing. I'll tell you right now, girls are so stupid. They just like the excitement: we get in fights downtown, the parties, the music thumping, all the cool people are there . . . Especially if they've never smoked or drank before, they like the way they feel, all high, buzzing, and tripping out. And they know that shit don't come for free. If you wanna hang with us, you better be down for your shit. That's why we fuck them in.

"It's gonna come a day when she thinks in her mind that she loves a guy and he's going to tell her, 'Why don't you get in the gang, if you love me . . . I'll get you in.' Sometimes girls will join just for that, just to prove that she loves her boyfriend. She'll let more than just her boyfriend fuck her. Then most likely he'll break up with her, but then she doesn't have a choice. It's done, she got fucked, she's in.

"Sex used to be a thing of love and now it's just a thing that we use, a tool, a thing that we want. We use people for it. It's just a simple pleasure that we do when we want to.

"Don't mistake me, now. There are some girls that will pull guns on you and shoot you or some that will try and kick your ass. Hell, there are some guys that do give respect and do not believe in beating up chicks. That's why we have our girls' cliques to kick other girls' asses, so we don't have to worry about it . . . After a while the girls can start initiating chicks their own way. Ain't no problem. That's a girl thing, so we don't have to worry about fucking them all the time . . . But the girls' gang is under the guys' gang, and that's the way it's gonna have to be, and that's the way it's gonna have to stay, and as quick as we brought them in, we can take them out. We got more guns, more connections, more people, and that's why the girls won't ever take us over. That's why the girls will always be under us and that's why we can always make sure the girls will get fucked in, if that's what we want.

"Most girls will want to get out of it within no more than four months. After they see someone drop . . . There really isn't much of a way to get out . . . You just have to take it the hard way, you have to get shot out; if we don't respect you, then we might rape you and kick your ass out. But rape is not a big thing around here, assault isn't a big thing around here. I'm here to explain to you that there is no gang rape here. Only on rare occasions do we put a gun to their head and say, 'Give it up.' That happens about 5 percent or less in San Antonio. The rest of the girls are stupid and naive."

ONE evening a girl described just how frightening it was to be female. "Girls are scared of guys," she said. "I am. You know, even though they're my friends and stuff, I'm scared of them. Especially when they're drinking. If they get a little girl drunk, that's it for her. They'll train her. Their first question about a new girl: 'Is she a ho?' I knew what would happen to me if I got drunk. I was nothing special, I was a girl, too. Unless you're somebody's sister, you have no protection. Shit happens."

Shortly after she turned thirteen, two gang members dragged her by the hair into an alley, where they tied her hands to a gate with wire, then lifted up her legs above her head and tied her ankles. One of the attackers was a friend from school. Her ex-boyfriend, himself a gang member, paid them to rape her after she'd broken up with him because she'd caught him in bed with another girl. "No one could hear me screaming, and finally they put a sock in my mouth. First one got on, then the second one, and that was the most painful one for me because it didn't just go through the front, it went through the back, too. They raped me over and over again, they would switch off. They were calling me a bitch and telling me they'd kill me or my mom if I told the cops. Just before they cut me down, I saw a knife going in my back. Then I just felt this sting. My ex-boyfriend was watching me the whole time, laughing.

"I got pregnant, so I took morning-after pills and got rid of it. I was real popular, but I had to change schools just like that, because everyone knew within a day. They weren't picked up for about a month. When I rode the bus, the oldest one would follow me, telling me they were going to kill my mom.

"After two weeks, I lost it. I tried to commit suicide. My mom found me. I guess I was unconscious; she told me I was just hanging there. After that, they put me in the state hospital.

"I got one of the guys put away, but he was only in nine months. I couldn't testify against the other guy because he was Mexican Mafia. I still see him around.

"But the bad thing is I could get AIDS from it down the line because one of them shot up coke and used dirty needles. So I have to go get checked every six months. Last time I got checked, they told me that they found something in my blood system, and I panicked. I would kill him if I came down with it. They were wrong this time. I still think about it a lot. If I come down with AIDS, I'm going to go on a wrecking spree."

• • •

HARD-CORE gang girls loathed the back-room girls, the chicks who cried rape, with the contempt the strong hold for the weak. After all, as one named Sweetie told me, when her boyfriend tried to rape her, she had pulled a gun on him. Sweetie weighed nearly three hundred pounds, and though she called herself "a kindhearted gangster," she displayed a terrifying temper, inherited, she said, from a father who broke her jaw and a mother who drove a red convertible with the bumper sticker: 51 PERCENT SWEETHEART/49 PERCENT BITCH: DON'T PUSH IT.

As a leader of a large co-ed gang, Sweetie had forbidden her girls to be trained. (She learned only later that the boys used her fierce reputation to intimidate weaker girls into giving up sex, warning that Sweetie would kick their ass if they refused.) For her own initiation she insisted upon fighting men. There was no girl big enough to challenge her. She went up against five guys; after she broke the nose of one, three others jumped in to take his place. When the melee was over, the injured boy went to the hospital while Sweetie headed out to eat with her new homeboys. Since her gang disbanded, she'd received three offers to lead female cliques, including one from a forty-year-old woman who ran drugs and guns in town and wanted Sweetie's help in starting her own gang.

Unlike a lot of girls in San Antonio, who lacked the sophistication and leadership qualities of girls I'd seen in L.A.—in part because the current generation of gangs was so young—Sweetie took care of business. When a thirteen-year-old friend was shot and killed and her homeboys did nothing, she pursued the gunman into a shopping mall parking lot and fired at him in the middle of a Friday night crowd, blasting out the window of a Chuck E. Cheese's restaurant. When she was nine months pregnant, she beat up another pregnant girl on the bus. "She was down with baby blue," Sweetie explained, meaning that the girl was part of the Blue Circle and a rival. "She came up to my face and said, 'Fuck the black, bitch.' I kicked her in the stomach, her face, her back, and forced her to say she loved the black. She was still saying it when I left her crying on the floor." Both girls lost their babies. Sweetie cried about that.

The day before, during a gang party, she'd burst in on a girl sitting on the toilet, accused her of being a "gang hopper," and pounded her head against the wall until her terrified victim jumped from a two-story bathroom window to escape. A few boys had tried to stop Sweetie from beating the girl "to protect their pussy for later." But she resented such girls and the bad reputation they gave to all gang females, maligning them as sex-crazed, deranged sluts. Nor did she have sympathy for the fact that the girls often came from abusive homes. After all, her own home life was hellish.

"That ho I beat up last night? She's now saying she wants to kill me," Sweetie said as proof the girl deserved no mercy. "But see, everybody says that, all these bitches, and I am still alive."

It didn't matter that Sweetie had led girls, she made it plain she didn't respect them. "I don't trust no girls. No bitch. Too many hos out there."

GIVEN the lack of sympathy among their peers, I wondered what solace adults provided victims of gang assault. The chances of their seeking help on their own seemed slim. The girls I met didn't view themselves as victims; instead they appeared passively in denial or hostile and rebellious. Some, in a survival instinct to halt the abuse, unconsciously tried to render themselves ugly by gaining weight, denying themselves health care or exercise. Others became pregnant, knowing that once they had children the abuse would be curtailed significantly, even as premature motherhood sealed their fate, ensnaring them in a lifetime of poverty.

For those girls who did reach out, well-meaning counselors often offered mixed messages. At Victory Outreach church, I met a thirteen-year-old girl who'd been abducted and held by a gang member for two days, raped repeatedly. Yet when I asked whether the girl had reported it to the police, seen a doctor, or received psychological counseling, a gentle-faced church woman, herself once a victim of rape, shook her head. "She's receiving the word of God. God will handle it."

At Charter Real Hospital I spoke with a psychiatrist who counseled gang girls, among them some of the girls I'd met. Ninety percent of his female patients had been molested, usually by their stepfather or mother's boyfriend, and he described their lives with sorrowful inevitability: "Ultimately, the mother and daughter form some kind of alliance. They don't hold the guy responsible. The mother's attitude is 'This is one of life's tragedies that happens to girls. I feel for you, but it happened to me. It happened to my cousin. To my sister. But count your blessings. He brings some money home. What do you want me to do? Throw him out?' The mother may cry with her daughter because they've all been victimized, but the sad story is men are men."

This doctor, who grew up in a Mexican-American household on the West Side, held great sympathy for his patients, but as we spoke, it became clear he believed that they were responsible for civilizing men. Because of the women's movement and the sexual revolution, he argued, girls no longer viewed their bodies as sanctuaries that boys had to prove themselves worthy to enter. "In the old days, a girl saw sex as a way to develop spiritual intimacy with a guy. When the courting dance began, she used that gift to educate him: 'You want it, you're going to have to work for it. There's a price tag.'" The doctor sighed. "Even if deep down she knew it was bullshit, at least she pretended and tried."

This was the same disquieting view of the female condition—sex as a bargaining chip, dividing girls into "good" versus "bad" on the basis of whether they held out—that I'd heard in my old Catholic school and from gang boys. The doctor believed girls could escape male violence by embodying females' inherent moral superiority.

The girls I met hardly behaved like the sexually liberated decision-makers he described. Both the church and the doctor seemed baffled by teenage girls and, however unintentionally, left the impression that the girls themselves were somehow to blame for their fate.

Most gang kids, though, never received any kind of professional help. Often their parents, if not abusing them, were oblivious to the pain in the daughters' lives. Adults I spoke to, poor and middle-class alike, denied that their children were involved in sex and gangs, brushing off media reports of gang activity and sexual initiations.

Much of the adult community viewed the activity as just sex among teenagers, a combat zone with its own rules, a contained conflict from which it was largely content to look away.

One evening Alicia and Scariella took me to an adult-supervised teen club, which forbade alcohol. With middle-aged bouncers looking on, girls were encouraged to participate in the "Daisy Dukes" Contest, coming onstage to strip before the crowd. The night I was there, six teenage girls stripped down to their panties and bras—to chants of "Take that shit off!"—although Alicia assured me that in the past girls had performed naked. Next came the boys turn. Prohibited from showing genitalia, they pumped against the floor in G-strings as the girls screamed them on. Afterward, the DJ played *Bitch Betta Have My Money*, singing the praises of sodomy, as the dance floor erupted into a pornographic *American Bandstand*. Scariella ground her rear into a Klik boy's pelvis.

Another girl, sandwiched between two Klik members, mimed fellatio on one while security guards looked on. At 1 A.M. the club locked the doors, not allowing anyone to leave until seven the following morning, as a way of getting around the curfew San Antonio had recently passed to protect its young people.

CLEANSING

IF AIDS CAN HAPPEN TO MAGIC JOHNSON, IT CAN HAPPEN TO YOU. TRY HUGS AND CUDDLES INSTEAD. The banner hung above the receptionist's desk at the Las Palmas Planned Parenthood, a tidy pastel-colored office located in a strip mall between a Walgreen's and a Luby's restaurant. A picture of a teenager dreamily hugging her pillow decorated the banner, which had greeted the three girls who claimed to have had sex with a gang member infected with AIDS when they came here last spring for HIV tests.

I'd offered to take Alicia in so that she could be examined after her rape and tested for AIDS. She'd quietly yet eagerly accepted. Waiting for her in the reception area, I watched a little girl waving an AIDS pamphlet in her baby brother's face. Failing to elicit a reaction, she seized the pacifier from the baby's mouth, then snatched away his blanket. The boy burst into tears. A man sitting with the kids, his arms resting upon an ample belly, shook with laughter, egging the girl on while the infant screamed. The mother returned the boy's pacifier against the man's protests. "You're gonna raise him to be a fag."

An hour later Alicia returned. She smiled shyly when she saw me, the first time she had smiled all day. She was clean, as far as they could tell, no evidence of venereal disease; in ten days she'd call for the HIV results. It was a good sign.

WEST SIDE STORY, PART II

The next spring, nearly a year later, I returned to San Antonio for a gang "peace conference" that was sponsored by a local Lutheran church. The effort was the fourth in a series of national gang summits that began with the highly publicized truce between the Crips and Bloods in Los

Angeles after the 1992 uprising. Fueled in part by the shock of the Simi Valley verdicts, the L.A. peace treaty had failed to hold citywide, but it brought much-needed stability to Watts and its housing projects. Other conferences around the country followed suit, each a mixed blessing. The Minneapolis police maligned its city summit as pro-gang propaganda after one organizer, a leader of the Vice Lords, was implicated in the murder of a police officer. (No charges were filed.)

Women staged a protest at the 1993 Kansas City conference, complaining that male gang members pushed aside female concerns. On the summit's opening day, journalists ignored the fifty "sisters," focusing on the male leaders. Marion Stamps, however, a longtime community activist from the Cabrini-Greens Projects in Chicago, refused to allow female gang members and counselors to be reduced to a sexy novelty. Led by Stamps, the women walked out of the summit to form a caucus; they later emerged with a statement for the male gang leaders: "Our place is not behind you, or under you, but beside our brothers in this struggle . . . As women, we have always known violence. It is gang banging and police brutality, but it is also domestic violence, rape, child abuse, and poverty." Stamp, who served as the midwife of a Chicago gang truce, insisted that women be appropriately represented on any advisory board that developed out of the summit. At the closing worship service the male gang bangers apologized to the women in a prayer.

How would the gang summit serve the girls of San Antonio? I wondered. One of the main speakers was Jennifer Ontiveros, a seventeen-year-old gang leader who recently broke away from the Raiders and was now speaking out, eloquently and at grave personal risk. But neither she nor any of the dozen speakers, who included representatives from the Latino grass-roots empowerment movement Barrios Unidos and the National Council of Urban Peace and Justice, formally addressed sexual abuse. From the organizers' perspective, the first order of business was to bring gangs to the table and stop them from killing each other.

While in San Antonio, I had planned to look up the kids I'd met the year before. I drove out to the Cassianos on Thursday evening and ran into Doomsday and Blimpy. They were speaking with organizers who were hoping to persuade the Eight Ball to attend the gang peace summit. Doomsday happened to be at the Cassianos only by chance, to visit his mother. Worried that his activities, coupled with the management's crackdown on drugs and gangs, might lead to his mother's eviction, he'd moved out six months earlier.

Out of the blue, Blimpy mentioned that he had been shot two months ago.

"Show her your scar!" Doomsday suggested gleefully.

Blimpy raised his black T-shirt to reveal the bright red scar, a row of welts on both sides, that screamed from breastbone to navel. He seemed shaken, unable to meet my eye. They'd shot him near the memorial wall for Scariella's brother and he hadn't gone near it since. "I was celebrating that night 'cause I was moving out of state the next day to get away from all this." He gestured around him. "Had the plane ticket and everything. But now . . . what's the point?"

The year had been fraught with gunfire. Another Eight Ball, Doomsday's brother-in-law and Scariella's cousin, was killed a few weeks earlier. Last week the LA Boyz fired on the Eight Ball three times. A teenager came up to us to say he was shot at a couple days ago. During the attack, he saw a BC instructing the tiny kid holding the gun on how to shoot.

When I didn't see any of the girls, I asked Blimpy if he'd heard anything about Alicia. "Didn't you know?" he said. "She had a baby a week ago."

ALICIA sounded unexpectedly perky when I phoned Robert's—she was expecting someone from the business school she'd applied to recently. Then her voice dropped. "Remember when you took me to Planned Parenthood after I got raped? I had a pregnancy test and that's when I found out."

Did she know who the father was?

"I'm not sure. I'm going to have a blood test." She seemed in a hurry to hang up. "I can't talk about it right now."

THE next day, less than twenty-four hours after a gang bullet claimed the life of yet another San Antonio teenager, the summit took its first step toward mediating peace between the city's warring gangs. During the afternoon, I took a break from observing the proceedings to visit

Alicia. A familiar childish voice from inside the house called out, "Gini! Come on in."

Alicia's skin was tan and her auburn hair fell below her shoulders, thick and curly. She looked heavier, but also healthier; her thinness last year due largely to drugs. She led me to a back bedroom, which was cast in amber light from the pulled shades. In the middle of the bed lay a newborn little girl, Jessica Sue. Alicia had heard the name on a soap opera one day while washing dishes. Parting the blanket to reveal a wine-red face, she poked a formula bottle at the baby's minuscule mouth. The doctor had cautioned her not to breast-feed. She had been too angry, too poisonously bitter, while the baby was in her womb.

Lowering my voice, I asked after Robert; she tilted her head to the side door leading out of the bedroom, indicating the boys across the street. "All he does is hang out and get high. Soon as I can figure out something, I'm gonna leave him. He tells me I'm just a piece of scrap he keeps around to cook and clean. He said that when we were in bed. I got upset and put my clothes on the floor so the baby and I could sleep there. He said that's where I belonged.

"He messed behind my back when I was pregnant. I got a disease. Chlamydia. But he only hit me once and then I deserved it, I was acting like a bitch." She laughed sadly. "We used to say we couldn't wait until I had the baby so we could hit each other again."

On a shelf above her head a pink cigar box joyfully declared IT'S A GIRL! After he heard the news, Robert passed out cigars in the street, too stoned to make it to the delivery room. "She looks like him." Alicia gazed at the sleeping infant. "Everyone says so. But he wants me to have a blood test to make sure it's his." Her fingers smoothed the fine black hair. "I finally told him about the BC who raped me. He cried."

The screen door slammed and a skinny teenage boy appeared in the doorway. He nodded in my direction before going over to the bed and lifting up the baby in his brown suntanned arms, which sprouted like twigs from his baggy T-shirt. At fifteen Robert looked much younger than Alicia. He stood silently holding the infant, then awkwardly he placed the bundle down and ran outside. The small circle of boys broke apart to allow Robert in, then closed again.

Alicia yelled to a little boy riding a Stingray near the porch to come inside. "That's Robert's brother, Junior." He entered, smiling shyly. Alicia told him to fix himself something to eat. I introduced myself and asked his age.

His eyes darted to the ceiling. "Eleven? I think"—he looked to Alicia for confirmation—"or am I twelve now?"

"I found out he doesn't know how old he is. He thought he was eight or nine. I dug up his birth certificate. He's actually eleven."

Junior shrugged. "My mom doesn't talk to me about stuff."

He left to scrounge the kitchen for something to eat, came up empty-handed, then jumped on his Stingray to head over to the neighborhood's new McDonald's. As he left, his mother came into the house, cursing in Spanish. Embarrassment crossed her face when she found me in the bedroom and she apologized. "How you like my granddaughter? Looks just like my son."

The three of us sat on the bed, watching the baby's gently undulating breath. "Lynn's pregnant again," Alicia announced, referring to the young Queen mother I'd met last year. "She got pregnant by a Klik guy at a party. She's due any day. Marie had her baby, too, but I heard she gave it up."

Robert's mother shook her head. "I had eight children and I never gave up any of them. That's wrong."

Before I left, Alicia invited me to her baby's shower at her mother's house. I'd try to come, I said, but explained that I was attending the gang summit. She looked at me quizzically. Apparently the efforts of summit organizers had only reached male gang members. Some of the Eight Ball might help negotiate a cease-fire in the neighborhood, I told her. "Uh-huh," she said, busying herself arranging her baby's blanket. Her world, from a few blocks on the West Side, had shrunk even more.

"STOP! Stop! That's my boy right there. We used to go on drive-bys together."

Wicked made me halt in front of a tall skeletal kid, slumped against a fence, clutching his bare stomach. "What's up?" he said, struggling to raise his voice above a whisper. Wicked acted as though nothing about the boy's behavior was out of the ordinary. Finally I asked if he were okay.

"Yeah, yeah," he said. He'd recently come home from the hospital after a six-week stay. He'd been shot with a 12-gauge. "I feel all right. I get tired . . . there's a lot of pain."

I assumed that he was shot by a rival, but the kid corrected me.

"Did it myself. I wanted to die."

"They make you see a psychiatrist, Johnny?" Wicked asked.

"Yeah, but I don't like fucking talking to them. They want me to go to a state hospital and put me in rehab or some shit and I don't want that. Fuck them, I ain't going nowhere. I live with my parents. They have to change my dressing. Nobody else knows how."

He lifted his hands away from his stomach. His trousers drooped, revealing a bandage around his waist, a yellow stain seeping through the gauze. "I lost two ribs, my pancreas. I have a little part left of my intestine, but it's going to grow, so in six months I can get rid of this fucking bag." He jabbed the plastic colostomy bag sticking out of his waistband.

Painfully he exhaled. "Every day I was in the hospital the psychiatrist would ask me, 'Are you planning to kill yourself?' Every fucking day. I hate that question. He looked kind of psycho, too."

He shot himself, he said, because he was addicted to heroin.

Heroin was everywhere, Wicked explained in the car. "The boys are all doing it and they're skinny and ugly." Its comeback in the neighborhood had a devastating effect on the gangs. Coke hyped you up, gave you the courage, if you lacked it, to pull a trigger. Heroin slowed you down. Down to a death crawl.

In a strange way, heroin made life safer for girls. Boys who last year pulled trains or flew into violent rages now substituted smack for sex. The LA Boyz, Wicked said, had formed another female clique of the LA Girlz, jumping in five new girls, but so far the recruits had to do nothing to prove themselves. The boys were too busy trying to score dope.

Tony, a BC I met last year, the handsome kid known as Lover Boy for fathering four children by four different girls, had taken a gun blast to the head. To everyone's amazement, he had survived, only to embark upon a slower route of destruction with heroin. It was rumored that one of his girlfriends shot him. He had called Wicked from the hospital. "He said everything was building up in him—all his kids, his mom, his dad, the gang situation—and he just couldn't take it and shot himself. I told him it wasn't his time. And he said, 'Yeah, I guess God wanted me to suffer some more.'" She examined the ends of her hair. "So now he eases his pain with heroin."

Before the day was over, Wicked and I ran into Fred, another BC I'd met last year. He was all business, driving a new Ford, wearing an expensive watch. The BCs weren't about drive-bys anymore, Fred said, the Eight Balls were too beaten down to waste time on. The BCs were about money. Fred was now a heroin entrepreneur, hiring gangstas as runners. When I asked if he used heroin himself, he shook his head distastefully. But Wicked wasn't convinced. Everyone who started selling was convinced they wouldn't succumb, but eventually they all did. "He'll be popping," she said.

We drove down the street, passing some very small boys, barely nine or ten, who recognized Wicked and threw up their gang signs. Wicked chuckled without humor. "The next generation."

BASSINETS littered Alicia's lawn, which she'd attempted to turn festive with pink balloons and crepe paper. The mediations between gangs had been closed to the press, so I'd been able to make the shower after all. Girls sat on lawn chairs in front of a lean-to serving double duty as a garage and a clothesline, with dozens of doll-sized socks and underwear dangling between its posts. Alicia rocked her child, waving to me with her free hand, beckoning me into the fold. Four of the six partygoers held infants. Girls who last year prowled by night like painted cats now appeared at midday with scrubbed faces and pastel dresses. Gone were the eyeliner, the heavy black boots, the AK-47 pendants, and the TEC-9 rings. None of the rings had been replaced with wedding bands.

"Hey, remember me?" a childless girl called out. I hadn't recognized Scariella. She'd gained weight and allowed her golden hair to grow out to its natural brown. Her flightiness seemed to have faded, too. She told me that she no longer lived in the Cassianos after the police raided her mother for selling coke. "My mom, she's in jail. She's always there. She *lives* there," Scariella said bitterly. Her eyes wandered to the vacant schoolyard across the street. She was leaving in a few days for Houston, she said, to live with her dad.

Inside the house, Alicia told me the real reason Scariella was going to Houston was to have an abortion. The baby's father, a gang member and already a father, didn't want anything to do with her. Alicia felt Scariella could do better than some punk who paid for blow jobs on Guadalupe.

"She's not going to get anywhere with that kind of guy," Alicia said with the insight one reserves for other people's problems.

Alicia's mother brought out a bundle of blankets bearing Disney labels to show the girls. While the girls cooed approvingly at the blankets, Alicia complained to her mother that Robert had still not shown up. "I don't have anything against him. He's always been respectful to me. Never used bad words," Alicia's mother told me. "I don't know what goes on between the two of them. That's their business." She turned the same blind eye to Robert that she did to her own husband.

I tried to bring up the gang summit, but the girls showed little interest. What did they think about the Eight Ball attending? A girl named Tanya, who was jumped in to the Lady Eights with Alicia and lived with Robert's brother—the two girls gave birth the same week—spoke up. "When I was still pregnant, Blimpy and I were in the park, watching the guys play basketball. He asked me, 'What do you think of the Eight Ball?' I told him, 'I don't think of the Eight Ball. There's nothing left of the Eight Ball.' He was looking at me like, why was I saying this? I guess he couldn't hear it from me. I said, 'Nobody talks about it anymore. They messed you all up. I don't know why you all still claim it. You should just be a little group of friends like it was before. Then they started the Eight Ball and look what happened. There's nobody, they're dead.'"

One of the babies let out a muffled cry and his mother hushed him. "As for the girls," Tanya continued matter-of-factly, "most of them who joined since I got in—well, *all* of them—had babies."

By sundown, the girls needed to return home to feed their children and boyfriends. I gave Tanya a ride home to the Cassianos. "It's a shame Robert hits Alicia so much," she said in the car. "His brother doesn't hit me like that." They used to fight, too, before she became pregnant. "But once I got pregnant, he was very nice to me." Tanya was the only mother at the shower without her baby; Orlando had said he would look after their son, provided she didn't stay long.

On the way, I heard a familiar *pop-pop-pop-pop*.

Tanya heard it as well, pleading with me to hurry. At the Cassianos, Orlando wasn't among the group of Eight Balls who had stayed away from the summit and were now flying high on coke. A young glassy-eyed boy, sweat beading on his forehead and his lower lip trembling uncontrollably, thought Orlando might have taken his baby home 'cause he wanted to party.

As we drove around the Courts, I checked Tanya's face in the mirror and it was wet, her mascara running down her cheeks. "What if he decided to walk back to his mom's house? She lives in BC territory." The thought made her shake.

We circled the Courts again. This time my headlights caught a teenager carrying a bassinet. I slowed down and Tanya leaped out while the car was still moving. Orlando, hearing footsteps behind him, swung around. As Tanya reached out for the baby, Orlando shoved her to the concrete with his free hand and kicked her away, "You fucking bitch!" he shouted down at her. "Where were you?"

Tanya stood up, hysterical now, flailing her arms like a sick bird. "What are you doing, running around here with the baby?" She grabbed the infant and whisked it back toward my car.

Orlando raised his middle finger to her retreating figure. "Fuckin' bitch!"

She whirled around. "Faggot!"

Tanya climbed inside my car. "He wanted to go smoke a joint and didn't want me to come," she said, adjusting the quiver in her voice. She pretended to study the passenger mirror, blinking and choking back tears. "He just gets this way around his friends. He wants to act tough."

I drove only a few yards before she made me stop. She wanted out. "I should go with him." She looked up at me as she opened the door. "He really is nice to me," she called softly over her shoulder. Bassinet in hand, she tottered after him.

THAT Saturday night the boys from the Eight Ball and a rival gang called the NDs negotiated a cease-fire of sorts, agreeing to stay out of each other's turf. But by Sunday morning the truce was almost broken when the Eight Ball arrived for the last day of the peace conference decked out in their colors, flashing their sign, angry and defiant. Eventually, however, the boys joined hands in a large circle.

The minister called the gang members to the altar and asked them if they wanted to speak to the congregation. But in front of this crowd of adults, they suddenly reverted to the children they were, shifting from foot to foot or studying their hands. So the minister listed the concerns the boys revealed in closed sessions—for jobs and funds for their neighborhood. Then the members from three rival gangs signed a T-shirt and held it up to the congregation before marching out to shouts and applause. The minister dubbed the dozen gang members "the twelve disciples."

A few days later I picked up Alicia with her baby. Alicia had a purple bruise on the side of her face. Robert had smacked her for looking at some guy from his truck, dumping her on the sidewalk to walk back to her house. I suggested the obvious, that she seek new living arrangements.

On the way to the Battered Women's Shelter, we passed her old high school.

"God, I miss school. I always wanted to go to my prom. My graduation." Alicia sounded prematurely nostalgic for a childhood that at only seventeen she should have still been enjoying. "Too bad." She faked a small laugh. "I could go back, but what am I going to do? I don't know anybody. I'm not going to start all over again."

At the Battered Women's Shelter counselor Eugene Brown greeted Alicia warmly. He introduced her to a female counselor and while they talked, he and I waited in the airy sky-blue lounge, discussing the new program the shelter had launched with the juvenile probation department. It provided twelve weeks of counseling for teenagers with a first-time offense for truancy or running away. The parents were supposed to attend separate counseling sessions, but, Eugene said, "Some don't. They see their children as bad seeds. Not their problem." During the program's first year, they'd worked with twenty-four girls, almost all gang members, many of whom were sexually initiated. One was raped and stabbed seventeen times.

A caseworker with a shy teenage girl at her side interrupted our conversation to update Eugene about the girl's boyfriend, a gang member. "He's telling her friends he'll kill her. He's told her boss," she said. The woman put her arm around the girl's shoulders. "She misses him even now, but she's afraid of him."

Eugene's face fell. The police brought her in after the girl called 911. The Battered Women's Shelter couldn't take her, he explained, because she was sixteen, a minor. For the same reason, the police could not issue a protective order against the man. They could only do so if the minor was married to him or had his child. Even the fact that this girl was pregnant by him was not enough; the law required her to establish paternity. Her mother was in prison. She had nowhere to go.

"Children's Services?" Eugene looked at me. "They have a reunification policy. She is caught between the cracks, too old for Children's Services, too young for adult programs."

The last time the girl came to the shelter Eugene took her to an aunt's. "She was drinking on her porch at ten o'clock in the morning. She sat there and told me how awful this girl was." His thoughts turned inward for a moment. With a small shake of his head, he went on. "I cried all the way home after I left her with that woman."

Eugene excused himself to deal with the problem. A few minutes later Alicia returned. Another girl in the waiting area wandered over to where Alicia rested on the couch cradling her daughter. The girl looked down at the sleeping baby.

"It's hard, huh?"

Alicia glanced up at the stranger and smiled. They didn't need to introduce themselves; their surroundings said it all.

"Looking for shelter?" the girl asked.

"Yeah. My boyfriend." Alicia turned to me. "I'm not planning to go back with Robert this time. I told the woman about him and my situation at home and she said it's best to get out of my house as soon as I can. If anything happens, they'll make room for me here." She clarified for the girl. "My stepfather, too."

"My stepdad was going to be prosecuted for child abuse," the girl said knowingly. "He beat me with a two-by-four across my back, but the social worker said I deserved it 'cause I skipped school. The principal was going to paddle me. Well, she came toward me and I said, 'My father already beat me.' I mean, who is going kick my ass as much as my dad? I told her that she wasn't going to hit me again. I took the paddle away from her and smacked her in the face." She paused, reliving the moment. "Broke it across her face."

She laughed weakly and after a few seconds Alicia joined in, then both girls were laughing at the very notion of being beaten by and having to beat the people who were supposed to help you.

That afternoon we went to see the housing director of the Cassianos with papers from the Battered Women's Shelter that would allow Alicia, as a victim of domestic violence, to bypass the project's waiting list.

Alicia was worried about being assigned an apartment near Laredo Street, BC territory—she'd spotted Robert's "worst enemy" in a BC T-shirt outside on the lawn—or that the manager would recognize her as an Eight Ball Chick. He didn't remember her, but neither did he have any one-bedrooms available. He told her to check back in a few weeks, though. Something was sure to open up.

Afterward, I fulfilled a promise to her and drove her to the bookstore at the River Center Mall. For a few moments she just stood there, gaping at the layout before her, then she crept over to a table of books. "Are you allowed to touch them?" she whispered. Finally she chose three: a true-crime story, a how-to book about child rearing, and one I suggested about ending abusive relationships.

When I dropped Alicia off at home, she seemed more hopeful than I could remember.

LATER that day I went out with Wicked, who invited along an LA Boy. The two planned to introduce me to the head of the LA Boyz, an honor of sorts, since he was older and kept a low profile, leaving the flashy, reputation-building crimes to the youngsters, who, if caught, would serve less time. We found him in a park shooting hoops by himself, a tall clean-cut muscular man in his early twenties. He stared toward the car, brow furrowed. Raising both hands, he began gesturing with his fingers, communicating to the boy in the back seat in sign.

"You stay here," the boy ordered before jumping out of the car and bounding toward the gang leader with his palms opened in submission, like a cowering dog showing its belly. The man glowered in my direction, his fingers moving furiously. After about a minute, the boy crawled back into the car and instructed me to start the engine and pull out. I watched the man pick up his basketball, we locked eyes for a moment, and again his hand flew up. "He's throwing you a sign," I told the kid in back.

"Uh-uh. To you. He wanted to know, 'Who's she claiming?' " the boy interpreted. "I asked, 'Who?' He goes, 'The driver.' "

Some kid had written his gang tag in the dust of my car again.

After we dropped off the LA Boy, Wicked and I drove past the Cassianos and some Eight Ball boys recognized me, yelling at me to stop. I hesitated to pull over, however, because of Wicked. "I should be okay, since Doomsday is my cousin," she said slowly. "Just hurry up. I don't want any BCs or LA Boyz to see me."

A white kid named Squeak with a cheerfully freckled face raced up to the car. "Miss! Miss! Give me a ride to my aunt's?"

Again I looked at Wicked. She nodded, the kid climbed in, and I headed down Guadalupe. As we passed a junkie prostitute wilting in the sun on the side of the road, Squeak sat up. "Hey, you know Cisco?" He directed the question at Wicked. "That lady's Cisco's mom." He shouted out the window, "Hey! Ever suck an Eight Ball's dick before?"

He pulled his head back in. "That's what I always tell those prostitutes." In front, Wicked frowned but said nothing. Squeak gave me directions to an area I recognized as LA Boyz' turf.

"Aren't we going through a bad block for you?" I asked.

"Yeah," he said, glancing around, "but I'm not scared. I'll get a nine and a .38."

"Well, are you safe now?"

Wicked cackled. "No, he's not. My friends in the LA Boyz live right here in these apartments."

We went deeper into LA Boyz territory. Squeak grew fidgety, scrutinizing graffiti that boasted EIGHT BALL KILLER. I suggested he take off his black Eight Ball cap so that he wouldn't be a target in my backseat. He removed it for a second, thought better of losing face, then stuck it back on. I started to argue, but Wicked cut me short. "Never mind his hat, it's his *face* they'll know."

He had me turn down a narrow unmarked dirt road that came to a dead end in front of a small solitary wooden house. Outside stood a massive white guy in a T-shirt that read LEGALIZE MARIJUANA above a cigarette package filled with joints. Two teenagers lazily took hits off a pipe as a diapered baby used their legs for an obstacle course. They were, in all likelihood, LA Boyz selling weed. Squeak studied the scene.

Wicked grinned. "Oh, so you're going to connect? Better hurry up."

"I am going to hurry up. And I'm not going to connect. My aunt lives here."

"Right, Squeak."

"My name's not Squeak. It's Andy."

He jumped out, heading to the door. I realized I'd made a mistake in bringing him here. I might have been starting to see the big picture about gang life, but I'd missed crucial subtleties. And that could cost.

I asked Wicked if she were in any danger.

"A little, if I see any LA Boyz. I mean, my boyfriend lives around here."

"Couldn't you just explain that you were hanging out with Squeak because of me and that I talk to rival gang members?"

"Yeah, but I don't."

Luckily, Squeak reappeared in minutes. Before I could start the ignition, Wicked called to the fat guy in the marijuana T-shirt and he opened the back door and shoved in next to Squeak, the leather seat protesting under his weight. The fat guy was too stoned to notice the Eight Ball rival he crowded up against and Squeak kept quiet, staring dead ahead. Relishing the situation, Wicked engaged her fat friend in pointless conversation, inquiring about prices, telling him to bring some weed to the party that night. Squeak's eyes remained glued to my windshield. With much effort, the hulk at last climbed out, leaving us the view of his trousers slipping down over his large white buttocks.

As we cruised back, Squeak grilled Wicked. "You an LA Girl or a BC Chick?"

"No, but I party with all of them." She twisted her head around to look at him. "*Oooh,* he's all mad."

"You down with them?"

"No. I'm not down with nobody now. I just party with them 'cause I used to be with Nick."

"Nick of the BCs?" Squeak stuck out his jaw impudently. "The guy who got killed? It's good he's dead."

Wicked started as though struck in the face. "Fuck you! It's good Tommy's dead—"

I looked in the rearview mirror. At the mention of the Eight Ball's murdered leader Squeak's face tightened. Wicked rushed on. "I don't mean that it's good Tommy's dead. Tommy was cool. But you shouldn't say that about Nick—"

"Fuck Nick. I hate him." Squeak fell silent, then said under his breath, "Just wait until we get back to the Cassianos."

"You're crazy. How old are you, fifteen? Man, you're dumb. You don't even know me. You just ask around. You'll find out who I am."

I cut in. "Wicked is Doomsday's cousin."

She tossed her head, annoyed, not wanting my help. "So? I don't talk to Doomsday. I don't mean that about Tommy. I just said that 'cause of what you said about Nick."

Squeak looked out the window. "You better take off fast when we get to the Cassianos 'cause we'll shoot up your car."

This is crazy, I thought to myself. I couldn't tell if Squeak was bluffing. All I knew was that there were rules to this game that I still had to learn. Here the wrong word could ignite an explosion. A few weeks ago a boy from the ND gang had gone into Eight Ball territory demanding to know who had scrawled graffiti around the projects where the ND lived. A kid who was high on spray paint lied and boasted he was phantom tagger. The ND shot him in the face, killing him on the spot.

At the Cassianos Squeak jumped out before I stopped, running toward Doomsday, who stood in one of the yards.

"Hurry. Go straight," Wicked ordered.

As we took off, I turned to Wicked. "Are you in trouble?"

She mimicked Squeak's bravado. "It doesn't matter. If anything happens to me, my boys will come back with guns. I'll shoot at them myself."

She was quiet during the drive, lost in her thoughts.

As soon as I dropped her off, I returned to the Cassianos to attempt damage control. The Eight Ball raced toward my car. One of them swung open my door, yelling, "What did she say about Tommy?"

Doomsday put his arm on the roof of the car and leaned over me. "Wicked's nothing to me. I don't care if she's my cousin."

I reached for Squeak's hand, explaining how he had said it was good that Nick died and Wicked had only responded to his cruelty by saying something cruel in turn. I reminded Squeak that she had apologized. Squeak broke away from me, shaking his head. "It *was* good Nick died."

When Doomsday heard the full story, he told me it would blow over. But as I left them half an hour later, after a meal at McDonald's, Squeak hollered, "If you see her, tell her we're gonna cap her." This time he was kidding. How much, however, I couldn't tell.

AFTER a night of fitful sleep, worrying about what might happen to Wicked, I called her house. Her father answered, furious. She had never come home and he demanded to know where I had dropped her off. I wasn't sure. The West Side was a labyrinth to me, but I knew the apartment was within walking distance of her home. "She's involved with gang members!" her father exploded. "She told us it was because we didn't love her enough. We give her everything we can. We gave her two cars. She crashed them. We told her to talk to us. But she keeps doing this. Our tears are dried. Mine are, if not my wife's. When she gets in, I'm going to break her legs."

By six that night, Wicked had still not shown up. I drove back into the West Side, checking where she might be. Finally, in the home of some LA Boyz, she emerged, shuffling from a back room, rubbing her face sleepily. I told her about her father. She sat down on the couch, collecting her thoughts as she accepted a passed-around joint. Well, she said, if she went home now, when she was stoned, she wouldn't care if her parents yelled. I offered to take her, but she raised her hand, cutting me off. At last, because I wasn't leaving, she telephoned her parents. She spoke calmly and directly, informing them that she'd be home later. When she hung up, she looked up at me. "Don't call them anymore, okay?"

I wanted to talk to her about Squeak, but the kids all eyed me oddly. I didn't feel threatened, but it was clear that Wicked planned to handle this in her own way. "I'll go home tomorrow, my dad will be drunk and will give me a big hug, all glad to see me," she said flatly.

"There's nothing you can do here."

POSTSCRIPT TO SAN ANTONIO

After I returned to New York, Wicked called me at regular intervals to relay the downward spiral of her life. Her father threw her out of her family's house and she now lived with other runaways, sneaking home to her mother on those afternoons when she had neither money nor food. Her school expelled her for scrawling her gang tag on school property. Though she blamed the vandalism on her friend, the act of defiance cost her a scholarship to college. Meanwhile her friend Gat Man received life in prison for his role in the fatal drive-by. He wrote suicidal notes to Wicked from lockdown, begging her to wait for him. Hardly anyone visited the once-feared gangster, except for his broken-down father. "Oh, oh, remember Squeak? That guy who said it was good my boyfriend Nick died?" she asked during a call a few days before Christmas 1994, excitement tingeing her high-pitched voice. "The LA Boyz shot him! He's in the hospital." As an afterthought, she added, "The kid he was hanging out with died."

Before she hung up, she mentioned that she was on her way to jail, where she would spend Christmas. She'd been arrested on charges of grand theft auto, a felony.

I heard from many of the other girls, as well. Barbara and Sandy, the business executive's daughters, had broken their ties to the LOs, putting an end to their gangster thrill ride. Sandy was kicked out of a private school for verbally threatening to kill a classmate. She'd broken down, weeping like a little girl, at her expulsion. When she was allowed at last to return to a public school, she surprised everyone by throwing herself into the drama program.

After two LOs were killed, a rumor went around that Tricky gave the orders to murder his own homeboys because they wanted out. "I'm not sure what happened. I didn't want to know," Barbara told me. "When I hung around the LOs, we were having fun. They were nice. At least, they were good actors," she said wryly. "I look back, I allowed this to happen. No one put a gun to my head. At some point I realized kids aren't supposed to die at my age, but it was their choice. They knew the risks. It was easier to fail than to succeed, and most of them don't think they'll succeed anyway." Barbara, with a background that provided economic security, loving parents, and an education, at least could see alternatives. A few months after I met her, she moved away from San Antonio to work with a grass-roots organization to empower Latino women, with the goal of returning to her hometown to continue her efforts.

Grace, now thirty-three, married the fifteen-year-old gang banger, only to lose him to prison; he received a life sentence for first-degree murder. Afterward, she also lost her child in a custody battle with her ex-husband. Grace then divorced the teenager in hopes of regaining her youngest child, although she still visited him in jail.

Alicia received her GED and completed a program to become a nurse's aide. She now worked full-time on the night shift, caring for elderly patients. She spoke with pride about her crippled and wheel-chaired friends, how she helped dress or take them to the bathroom or wipe their chins at dinner and how her patients could not believe this red-haired girl with the wide smile had once been a hard-core gang banger, an Eight Ball Chick. She was proud that with her meager paycheck she did not depend on welfare. But faced with day-care bills, she was forced to live at home with her stepfather, with whom she passed long days in stoical silence. She also continued to see Robert. "He treats me a lot better," she assured me. "I guess he's maturing." Robert's brother Orlando was in jail for stabbing Alicia's friend Tanya in the face.

Six months after I last heard from Wicked, I tried finding her through her mother. The woman couldn't conceal her joy as she told me I could reach her daughter at the dormitory of a community college thirty miles away. "We're so proud. Last year was a rough year."

Wicked's underage partner in the auto theft crime had taken the brunt of the blame for her, secure in the knowledge that it would one day be wiped off her record. Wicked was charged only with vehicular burglary, a misdemeanor. If she stayed straight during her one year of probation, she too would emerge with a clean record.

An officer in San Antonio's school campus police had lobbied for her to be placed in another alternative school, one Wicked dubbed the bottom of the heap, the last resort for kids nobody wants. "That school made the difference," she told me when I called her dorm. "They let us take home computers and video cameras, even though we were all gang members and criminals. They trusted us." In a graduating class of four, she made class valedictorian.

As part of her probation agreement, Wicked performed community service at her neighborhood's Good Samaritan Center, tutoring LA Boyz and BCs in GED preparation. One March evening the Eight Ball's leader Doomsday and his boys strutted into the room with a couple of the counselors. The Eight Balls wanted to hold a war council with the LA Boyz. The threat of violence loomed high.

Wicked waited in the hall, trying to spy through the room's window. At last her cousin Doomsday appeared. He placed his arm around her shoulder. The two gangs, he said, had agreed to a cease-fire. All around her LA Boyz and Eight Balls shook hands or noisily slapped palms. Even Squeak, now recovered from his gun wound, smiled at Wicked, revealing the goofy sixteen-year-old kid still lingering beneath the scowl. Shortly thereafter the BCs joined the truce. The peace, while shaky, lasted, though it was continually threatened by yet another gang, which began launching late-night attacks against the Eight Ball Posse—as soon as one conflict was ironed out, another threat cropped up, like wrinkles in a carpet.

Wicked held her hand over the receiver to conceal a muffled male voice. When she came back on, she giggled sheepishly. She was slangin' coke, she said, to help pay her tuition. She assured me that her dealings had nothing to do with the Mexican Mafia; she'd purposefully cultivated a clientele away from the West Side to avoid paying the 10 percent fee. Then she suddenly mentioned that this year's Day of the Dead had come and gone, the holiday when Mexicans honor their dead loved ones, and for the first time in three years she didn't visit Nick at the graveyard. She saw it as a break of sorts. Then she giggled again and yelped, "I'm getting a tattoo Saturday! On my stomach."

What sentiment was she having tattooed? I wondered. She let out a Minnie Mouse squeal.

"Trust No Man!"

PART III
Milwaukee

O.G.s and Wanna-Bes in the Heartland

THE SHORT, TANGLED LIFE OF
MAMA SHEIK

Mama Sheik had her hair finger-waved and wore her best black-and-white leather pantsuit for the afternoon of her wake. With her fine eye for effect, she would have appreciated the care that went into her appearance. Mama liked flashy clothes; several of those paying their respects recalled the time on a local talk show when she'd switched outfits twice during commercials, reemerging after each break in a different black or flame-red leather jacket. Today seven rings of gold and onyx decorated her blunt fingers that were folded beneath a medallion the size of a large cookie that displayed in gigantic letters one word: SHEIK.

Some mourners compared her funeral, straight-faced, to Elvis Presley's or President Kennedy's, but then exaggeration surrounded everything about Mama Sheik. Even so, her farewell, a few days after Christmas 1993, was the biggest event many folks on Milwaukee's North Side could remember. Eyewitness accounts of the crowd ranged from 500 to 2,000. Inside nearly an entire garden of flowers surrounded her casket.

"Mama was a dreamer," her cousin told the throng packed into the pews and the standing-room-only balcony at the Hephatha Lutheran Church the next morning. "She loved life, and children played a big role in her happiness. She was like a second mother to many." One of Milwaukee's outstanding community activists delivered the eulogy to this congregation of schoolteachers, customers from Mama's tavern and clothing store, glamorous gang bangers in rich leather bomber jackets, and cops in uniform. Some were admirers, others saddened professionals who had failed to save her. At last they shut the coffin lid on Mama, laid to rest in a full-length mink coat and cap in her favorite color: snow white, the color of cocaine.

Outside in the biting cold a police escort waited to lead the glistening white Cadillac hearse to the cemetery. Mama Sheik's enemies would have to be suicidal to crash this funeral. But then one had been crazy enough to kill her, propelling her to an early grave at twenty-five years of age.

In a fast fourteen years, Mama Sheik rose from being a bright, popular seventh grader who organized a neighborhood dance team to the leader of the city's largest girl gang to a bank robber to a businesswoman, and, in her final incarnation, a drug empress. Along the way she wielded the kind of power that eludes most men, scoring $18,000 of coke every other week, often strutting down the sidewalk with a beautiful woman on each arm, all three draped in dazzling white minks. To ghetto kids, who knew her by her first name alone, Mama was proof you could grow up poor in America and fight your way to glory and riches. As the queenpin of the teenage Sheiks, she did the unheard of: she exacted obedience from a male auxiliary—her Sheik Boys answered to Mama alone. "It's just like with Dr. King. They'll never be another Mama. *Never*," recalled a male gang member. "She was queen of the mob."

In my research I'd encountered several girls with ruthless reputations, but none was a shot-caller whose renown reached beyond her hood—no female equivalent of Monster Kody, the celebrity Crip who penned his autobiography from solitary confinement. Then I learned of Mama Sheik.

By the time I arrived in Milwaukee, she'd been dead seven months. Still, I was able to witness her legendary charisma on a video of one of the TV interviews she granted after her release from prison. Leaning over a podium, she speaks in a booming voice with commanding hazel eyes. Her husky build—five-foot-eight and nearly two hundred pounds—is decked out in leather, from the top hat with its brim cockily turned up to the tricolored custom-designed jacket emblazoned with her silver initials. Looking more like a rap star than an ex-con, she describes prison life with a preacher's gift for oratory: "No sunlight. No air. Your skin breaking out, hair falling out. Roaches, rats. You name it, they had it."

The camera pans the faces of her rapt teenage audience, mostly African American girls. If ever they felt the lure of gangs, perhaps it never gripped them so fiercely as the day Mama Sheik marched into their classroom to warn against gang life.

It was ironic that the most powerful female I would find hailed from my home state of Wisconsin, which much of the country knew only from stereotyped images of dairy farms, Polish polkas, and German beer fests. The Christmas Mama was murdered I was in Wisconsin, researching the startling fact that juveniles are arrested there at a rate double the national average. Gangs were cropping up like tumors. On the morning Mama's family buried her in Milwaukee, I visited the state's coed juvenile jail, located in the middle of Wisconsin. Lincoln Hills is the last stop in the juvenile criminal system before adult prison. Mama Sheik had been incarcerated there for two months when she was seventeen. Set on a small hill, Lincoln Hills looks like an idyllic school campus—until you drive closer and catch the gleaming fourteen-foot-high razor wire surrounding the sprawling acreage, set among forests of pine trees and breathtaking vistas. Until recently, twice a week a police van dropped off the most dangerous girls in the state. For many black kids from Milwaukee, Beloit, and Racine, this might have been the first time they'd ever seen the woods. For some white rural inmates, it was the first time they'd ever come face-to-face with a black kid. On this early morning, with the temperature hovering at twenty below, the rising sun sent rays of pink and orange flooding into a slate-blue sky. But many kids didn't appreciate the view. The most dangerous girls in the state—at least those born in the inner city—were terrified of open space, bugs, and bears. Fear kept them from making a run for it.

Built in 1970 for boys, Lincoln Hills opened its doors to girls two years later. In more than two decades, the institution still hadn't quite adjusted to the newcomers, who, at roughly 15 percent of the population, created space problems. Every dormitory-style room in the lone female cottage was filled; downstairs girls crammed into a converted tornado shelter, some in bunks three beds high, separated only by a curtained "door." "This is a predominately male institution that suffers some archaic thinking about girls," the section manager for girls admitted. "The attitude is that the damn girls are nothing but trouble. Because they're a small percentage of the population, they don't receive their fair share of the pie."

Like Mama Sheik, most of the girls labeled gang-affiliated were black and from Milwaukee. (Out of seventy staff members, only three were African American.) A year before I visited, four Lincoln Hills graduates were killed on that city's streets, not counting Mama. Even so, the Milwaukee girls downplayed any danger. A fifteen-year-old Vice Lord, learning I'd been to L.A., gushed about the time she traveled there. "I never thought I'd meet people like that!" she said, referring to the Bloods. "They're heroes to me. In L.A., it's do or die. In Milwaukee, it's just he says/she says." Yet before our conversation ended, the Vice Lord revealed that her cousin was killed for her coat. Her sister was in prison for the death of another gang girl. As she stood to leave, I spotted a scar running from her earlobe to throat. A gash, she explained casually, that required 250 stitches when she was ten years old, the handiwork of another ten-year-old girl hiding a razor in her mouth.

Less than a year after I went there, Lincoln Hills closed its doors to girls because of overcrowding and the state opened an all-female detention center in Union Groves. Originally designed for 50 girls, in months the Southern Oaks Girls' School was jam-packed and needed to build an annex. Clearly, Wisconsin is not immune to the epidemic of misery that has infected our nation's children. No place is.

WISCONSIN'S most famous female gangster first emerged in Milwaukee annals at the age of fifteen. For months a pack of teenage boys terrorized her middle school and others in the city, prowling playgrounds, stomping kids. The mob eluded arrest until the gutsy eighth-grade girl confronted three of them one day. "Don't try anything stupid," she taunted, "or you'll have to fight me." As other students watched in disbelief, Mama, an athletic girl on the track and drill teams, held the boys at bay until school officials and police could be called. Mama received a letter from Mayor Henry Maier, two complimentary tickets to the policemen's ball, and a citizenship award, signed by Police Chief Harold Breier.

The award carried a certain irony coming from Breier. The J. Edgar Hoover of Milwaukee, the chief held a reputation for sweeps and general harassment that created an us-versus-them mentality in the inner-city black community, where under his reign at least 10 black youths were killed by cops under circumstances many residents viewed as suspicious.

The good citizen award was ironic for another reason. From the beginning there were two Mamas and an internal battle waged constantly between them. In middle school she served as student council president, played trombone, and performed in school plays; she boasted a B average in a school system where blacks had the lowest grade-point in the country, averaging a dismal D+. Some teachers loved her because she was outspoken and quick, always ready to help out in the school office, filing papers, answering phones. But others noted in her school file that she frequently seemed frustrated and sought attention by being loud and unruly.

Nor was the citizenship award her first contact with the law. "Mama Sheik came to us when she was very young, must have been eleven. I think she threw six policemen off a bridge," remembered Jeanetta Robinson, the cofounder of Career Youth Development (CYD), which works with at-risk kids. "She was doing something wrong, and the police thought that she was a little girl. Instead they found that they had run into a very serious karate expert." The story, say both police and members of Mama Sheik's family, never happened. Robinson merely spoke with the hyperbole of all Mama's believers.

Even so, Robinson had indeed discovered a rare child, a natural-born leader. "You won't be finding another Mama Sheik in the whole world. She had that kind of charisma. There were long periods of time that, as long as she stuck here at CYD, she stayed out of trouble. She used her talents and gifts to get other kids to do positive things. I had high hopes for Mama Sheik."

Her hometown, though, hardly presented a hopeful outlook for minority kids. "Milwaukee is one of the most segregated cities you'll find," a reporter from the *Milwaukee Journal* told me. Once overwhelmingly German and Polish, in the seventies the city experienced white flight to the suburbs, leaving minorities in isolated pockets: Latinos on the South Side, African Americans on the North Side and in the central downtown area. Some residents used to say that the viaducts connecting working-class Walkers' Point to inner-city downtown separated Poland from Africa.

While Mama was growing up during the early eighties, the quarter of Milwaukee's 600,000 residents who were black experienced the worst ratio of black to white unemployment in the nation. A majority of their kids lived in poverty. When an economic earthquake hit in the eighties, closing countless factories, well-paying blue-collar work all but vanished.

Mama's mother was a nurse's aide, her father a carpenter. They raised five children, Mama the oldest girl. An officer who grew up with Mama's parents remembered her father as plagued by problems of addiction, first alcohol, then rock cocaine. "Her mother was a stocky, surly teenager, a rough girl, even back in the sixties," the cop said. "She met a man just as rough and together they produced four rough-as-hell daughters." Despite their problems, Mama's mother was a strong-willed matriarch, the force in the family, and for some seventeen years the two parents stuck together, raising their kids, sitting down each night to eat family meals.

They lived in the Hillside Projects, a housing project built in the early fifties, the first in Milwaukee that was specifically aimed at African American residents. Squeezed up against a busy highway, minutes from downtown, it is a city-within-a-city of two- and three-story brick and wood frame apartment houses linked together by paved roads and grassy courtyards. The Jones Lutheran Church rests smack in the middle of the complex, along with the Hillside Boys & Girls Club. Mama and her sisters preferred their backyard, where after school they furiously jumped rope double Dutch or practiced break-dance routines, performing the moonwalk, the electric slide, and the worm, treating gravity and anatomy with athletic contempt. When a girl on the sidelines wanted to join in, Mama would dare her to improve on a simple dance step. The impromptu auditions led to Mama's creation of a dance group. She dubbed them the Sheiks, a name she chose after looking it up in the dictionary because it suggested strength.

During the summer, Milwaukee exploded with the rhythms of break dancing. Other kids formed local dance teams like the Time Boys and the Brides of Mac Funk, sparking citywide rivalries. On Saturday nights teenagers headed downtown to the cavernous Palace Skating Rink. At midnight the loudspeakers commanded the skaters to halt their spinning human centrifuge and clear the floor for the main event. Teams lined up to compete, the Sheiks in navy sweatshirts with their name across the back in gigantic letters, others in baggy hip-hop gear, each sporting a gimmick, such as the Traffic Stoppers, who once performed in peek-a-boo lingerie. As the seismic rhythm of Grandmaster Flash or Run-D.M.C. rumbled through the hall, two troupes pounded the wooden floors while male onlookers cheered them on. Like the audience at amateur night at Harlem's Apollo Theatre, the Milwaukee crowd always let losers know who they were by unmerciful boos and hisses. At seven o'clock the following morning, the exhausted winners took home a free pair of skates and cash, everyone else, battered knees and egos. The Sheiks were nearly always a ruling presence. If they didn't claim first prize or if another dancer made the mistake of looking at Mama or one of her girls with something less than admiration, someone had to pay. Usually this meant a stomping in the parking lot.

In short order the Sheiks became known for their fists as well as their feet and metamorphosed into a street gang. Mama added to their ranks based on a number of attributes: physical ability, loyalty, grade-point average (at least 2.0), and a unique initiation. A new girl was required to demonstrate her nerve by jumping a guy forty pounds heavier and two or three inches taller than herself. The Sheiks swelled to more than 50 members.

At the same time, rival dance groups also transformed into gangs, their battles forcing the Palace Skating Rink to close. Other "crews" sprang up during Milwaukee's desegregation of its schools. To circumvent white violence or protests, administrators implemented mandatory busing from minority neighborhoods only. Kids bonded in cliques on school buses as they rolled through unknown or unfriendly neighborhoods. Other gangs took their names, or the police gave them to them, from the streets where they congregated, such as the 2-7s for 27th Street or the 3-4 Mob of 34th Street. Still others formed through ties to Chicago, only an hour away. When a gang kid's family moved to Milwaukee, local teenagers began emulating Chicago gangs, aligning themselves with one of two warring "nations," People or Folks, which possessed a tumultuous history dating back to the sixties, each with its own literature, bylaws, and symbols. Although Milwaukee gangs adopted the symbols and literature, they operated under local rule. By the mid-eighties, the press reported that some 4,000 teenagers claimed gang membership.

As the Sheiks' reputation grew, Mama felt compelled to answer the slightest insult with force. She graduated to frequent fights and suspensions at school and outright defiance when anyone tried to discipline her. Arriving as a new freshman at Bay View High School, she confronted a girl who boasted that she owned the school. "Nobody owns me," Mama shot back. "She was bleeding," Mama recalled later. "Black eyes, split lip, 'cause I had kicked her when her mouth was open." Children's Court placed her on probation for the attack and transferred her to another high school. For a while she did well, keeping her grades high, currying favor by working extra hours in the school office; at the prom she even showed up with a star basketball player. But if anyone crossed her, the dangerous side of Mama surfaced. When some girls tried to jump her little sister, she beat the girls bloody. The school again suspended her for fighting.

But within her own world, the world of the street, Mama could be loving, dependable, courageous. If you loved and respected Mama, she made you one of her own. "Mama's girls dated some of us, even though we were People and she was Folks," said the Terminator, an ex-gang member turned bodyguard for visiting performers like CeCe Peniston and Prince. The hulking Terminator had belonged to the 2-4s, which started out as a bunch of kids stealing dirt bikes and ended with their leader hanging himself in jail (or, as many theorized, was hanged by someone else). We met at the Grand Avenue, a monolithic downtown mall that once banned the Sheiks from its stores for fighting. "Mama was on my kick-boxing team. Didn't matter she was the only woman. She put in her hours training, got her black belt, and took second place in the state finals. She could do anything she put her mind to. I mean, like John Gotti. She was just that powerful."

Because of the respect she generated among men, coupled with the lure of her girls, Mama Sheik attracted men to her ranks. Her Sheik Boys followed her commands, a hierarchy that made her reputation flourish on the street. "A head of the Spanish Cobras told me about her, saying, 'Mama, now she's a down sister,'" remembered Gary Graika, who counsels Latino gangs as manager of the Social Development Commission's Youth Diversion Program. "Here's a guy whose got serious rank in a South Side gang, knowing about this female running things on the North Side. He said she had three hundred people in her group and maybe a hundred and fifty of them were males that followed her lead."

In reality, the Sheiks had closer to 100 followers and hangers-on with a nucleus of perhaps three dozen hard-core members and only a handful of Sheik Boys, an auxiliary that lasted only a few months. "Mama was a black widow spider. She'd grow tired of a man, kick his ass, and he'd leave," remembered a cop. "We never got any complaints—no man is gonna say a woman beat his ass."

This cop, whom I'll call Officer Johnson, gave generously of his time to me, despite the Milwaukee police department's policy of refusing to provide gang statistics, or much else, to the media. On the few occasions that Mama turned herself in to the police, she always asked for Officer Johnson. They met at a funeral after a young girl, Mama's second-in-command, was found murdered in a rusting eighteen-wheel trailer in a weedy junkyard. The news had shattered Mama. Her Sheiks always generated a sense of invincibility, but Mama's lieutenant had been beaten and strangled, her twisted body discarded like a broken doll amid shattered glass and used condoms. The girl's family requested police presence at the funeral to guard against another gang invading the ceremony to dump over the casket. The police had their own reasons for attending. Gang unit intelligence took covert photographs to determine the Sheiks' numbers and their main players. "There were about thirty-five girls, a lot of them on probation for battery, and every one dressed in white," Officer Johnson recalled. Instead of encountering a ruthless criminal, he found a teary-eyed teenage girl mourning her best friend, pain battling with defiance for control over her emotions. "Her girls surrounded Mama in a pew while she sobbed. I sat next to her, telling them to get back in school or the same thing could happen to them."

But Mama fought any feelings of vulnerability. Nothing was more important to her than respect, a word so distorted and mangled in gang neighborhoods that its closest synonym is fear. For Mama Sheik, to be idolized in fear claimed precedence over all else.

Her police record grew like a malignancy. In December 1984 a sheriff's deputy picked her up for resisting arrest after he intervened in a fight between the Sheiks and another girl gang—some 24 girls—and found Mama concealing a stiletto knife. A month later a Sheik Boy held a girl down on the dirty floor of a bus while Mama and four other girls beat her, allegedly for refusing to join in a Sheik chant. Two months later she jumped with both feet on the head of a girl. After eight suspensions from school for fighting and breaking windows, the Children's Court finally sent her to Lincoln Hills during the summer of 1985.

Eager to return home, she lay low at Lincoln Hills, doing her time, charming the staff with her intelligence and ability. She even wrote a letter to the judge describing the pride she felt in learning "to handle my attacking attitude. Lincoln Hills has really helped me to change my ways." She finished by saying she had a job lined up when she returned to Milwaukee. A social worker at the facility wrote in Mama's file: "In her mind there are certain circumstances/situations where resolution by fighting is not only acceptable but needed."

Jeanetta Robinson was well aware of Mama's desire to right wrongs with her fists, but waited for her with a job at CYD. That summer Mama worked hard in the youth program as a peer counselor. She loved helping out younger kids, taking them under her wing. "All of us really wanted to save her," Robinson recalled. "We wanted to harness that part of her that liked counseling kids and help her to control the other part that enjoyed the power she had over them. She got more resources, and more university people at her door wanting to study her. But I think with any human being, when you get that much support and attention, it can do funny things to your head."

Her local fame created pressure within Mama to live up to her image. If the newspaper said she was bad, then she would be bad. After each article, Robinson would sit her down, trying to deprogram her, telling her that her life was not a self-fulfilling prophecy.

THREE SISTERS HAVE A HISTORY OF BEATING GIRLS read the headline of the story in the *Milwaukee Journal* less than a year after Mama's release from Lincoln Hills. Without using names, the article described a trio of girls out of control. Police stopped the oldest sister after a tip that two girl gangs planned a fight. Their search of Mama's car uncovered an ugly arsenal of weapons: tire irons, pipes, chisels, a screwdriver. As usual, Mama impressed the reporter. Six days later the paper ran a feature profile of her, this time describing a B student and former student council president. Mama blamed all her troubles on police attention. "Every time I try to help somebody, I end up in jail. If I come onto a scene, they say, 'That's the leader. We got you.' I can't get a job . . . I can't do nothing. I can be walking down the street and the police will say, 'Hey, sugar baby, how are those girls doing? What kind of weapon do you have today?'

"I constantly get kids coming up, saying, 'I want to be like you. I love you.' I say, 'You don't want to be like me. The police are always after me.' "

Every fight Mama was arrested for she claimed was in self-defense or because she tried to keep the peace. The time she stomped on a girl's head began, she explained, when two girls pulled knives and a chain on her. She publicly denounced gangs. "I'm not involved with that anymore. It's just the police keep making it live on." When the reporter suggested that she invited unwanted attention by going into rival gang turf, Mama bristled. She couldn't stay away or "They think I be scared. . . . If the police harass me, I'll sue them or something. I'm not going to stop my life or slow down because of the police."

What she really needed, she said, was a new life. One that would lead to a job, college, a new reputation.

Two months later, on a sweltering day in mid-July, Mama Sheik and a friend entered the Brewery Credit Union and approached a teller, asking to apply for a job. The credit union wasn't accepting applications, the teller told her. Mama stood silently, her eyes hidden behind sunglasses, then repeated her request. The teller again asserted there were no positions, but Mama didn't budge. At last the woman fetched her supervisor. This time Mama, absently crinkling a plastic bag she held in her hands, demanded change for a twenty. When the supervisor said the bank only made change for those with accounts, Mama and her friend finally left.

"She probably had a gun in that bag," the supervisor joked. But she wasn't really worried. Located on a deserted stretch of warehouses, the credit union was used to strange characters wandering in, such as a homeless man looking for a place to shower or someone wanting change for the bus. She'd returned to her desk for only fifteen minutes when she heard the teller say, "They're back."

She swirled around in time to see the loan officer drop to his knees. Mama's accomplice stood over him, aiming a gun at the back of his head. A moment later Mama Sheik burst through the small swinging half-door, the only barrier between the tellers and customers.

"Get your hands up in the air!" she yelled. "Don't touch anything!"

Mama cast about, seemingly uncertain what to do next. She checked behind her at her companion, then looked back at the terrified tellers. "Put your hands down!" she hollered, contradicting her own order.

One of the tellers stuck her hands in her pocket. Mama lunged toward her and thrust the barrel of her automatic to the woman's forehead.

"Move one more time," she screamed, "I'll blow your motherfucking head off!"

She ordered the three women down on the floor. None uttered a word, believing themselves about to be killed like three pigs in a row. Mama fixed the gun on their backs as her partner rushed behind the counter, emptying the drawers of cash. Mama looked around frantically the whole time, at the street outside, the clock, toward the back hallway.

Then she heard a noise from the back. A little muffled plop. The other woman heard it, too, because she stopped, her hands clasping a fistful of money midair. In the back hallway someone had moved.

"There's someone back there!" Mama cried. Eyes widening with panic, she backed away from her prone captives, the other woman following her. The two raced out the door.

Outside in the alley a getaway car waited. The guy behind the wheel drove only a short distance, out of sight of the credit union, while the women frantically changed their clothes in the car. A man parked in the alley behind a fish store stopped to watch, alarmed—it looked as though the women were ripping out their hair. No, they were wearing wigs, disguises. When they pulled away, he followed their car. He trailed them onto the expressway, all the way to 55th and Lisbon, where the bank robbers pulled over in front of a pawnshop called Doc's. At a nearby phone booth the man called 911.

The cops captured Mama and her accomplice outside the shop. They found gold rings, bracelets, and around $6,000 in cash on her.

Some twenty-five young women crowded into the courtroom for her trial, as five sheriff's deputies, three in plainclothes, warily stood watch. Going to bat for Mama were the director of the Social Development Commission's Youth Diversion Program and CYD's Jeanetta Robinson. They pleaded for leniency during Mama's sentencing, listing her accomplishments, her work at the youth centers, the citizenship service award from the police only three years earlier. The girls packing the spectator benches murmured agreement like a congregation at a storefront church.

The D.A. scoffed. Mama, he argued, sold $250 worth of coke a day that summer and used the drug herself, even while working with youth groups. There was her history of street fighting. She was a true menace to society. Mama and her accomplice apologized, but blamed the organizing of the robbery on the driver of the getaway car, a man with the street name of Slickers, still on the run. They'd planned it over breakfast that morning, then gone to a thrift store for the wigs and clothes. They had been unable to go through with the crime the first time they entered the credit union, but the man forced them to return. Again the D.A. sneered. Mama answered to no man.

Each woman was sentenced to six years for armed robbery. Mama was eighteen years old.

CHARACTERISTICALLY she shot out of prison like gangbusters. She had become a model inmate behind bars at the Taycheedah Correctional Institution in Fond du Lac, Wisconsin, and served only three years. At her parole hearing she came armed with letters of recommendation, including one from the governor's office, opening a special slot at CYD to hire her upon her release. Her new job involved speaking to schoolkids about the dangers of gangs. She'd show up in a mink beret and a blood-red sweatsuit, layers of thick gold-link ropes dripping down her chest. "Now my life has changed. I'm doing better," she told a television reporter. "I'm not involved with any drugs, gang activity, nothing violent. You know I'm out here trying to help the young ladies and the young men. I have little sisters and brothers that are growing up and I don't want them to be nothing like I was."

Gary Graika accompanied Mama on her trips to schools. When she entered a classroom, it vibrated. "There would be all these kids—'There's Mama! There's Mama!'—and when she spoke, it would be hushed. Yet I never sensed an arrogance about her. For a minute I thought she was really making the turn, then I started hearing things."

Barbara Powell heard things, too. Powell was then superintendent at the Women's Correctional Center in Milwaukee, a minimum-security state prison, the last step before inmates are returned to the civilian world. Once freed, Mama visited the superintendent each month to update her on her new life. "See how well I'm doing?" she'd say, wearing the unwavering expression of someone telling the truth—or an extremely practiced liar. Powell would listen politely as Mama assured her she was staying straight. "But I knew she was dealing drugs because I was around a lot of young people. I would ask them what was going on with Mama and they would tell me."

A bemused expression crossed Powell's broad, open face. "She seemed to want to be seen as saintly and bad at the same time. I used to watch her on television; she looked like she was enjoying every minute of it. She wanted the public to believe she had turned over a new leaf. She thought that would keep the law off her. That temper was still there, though, and that was her biggest problem. When you challenged her, the temper would always stir up. I used to tell her, 'You don't change that, we're going to end up burying you.' "

When she lashed out, no one was safe, including women Mama Sheik loved. After prison, she announced to her family that she was gay, but those closest to her had always known she preferred women. "She had the cutest, youngest girls, four at a time," recalled Officer Johnson. "Once she got out, we'd hear about her crimes because girls would get mad at her, jealous, and call in anonymous leads. You know how'd she get a woman? She'd take care of a girl who was battered by her boyfriend. A lot of girls get beaten—male gang members are weak that way—well, Mama would beat the batterer."

She took on the role of the abusive male, beating her own lovers. "She picked women she could knock around and dominate," said Superintendent Powell. "I once said to her that her sexual preference was her business, but why couldn't she do it respectfully? She completely broke down. I thought, 'Oh, I hit home.' "

For a few moments Mama Sheik couldn't talk, just let out loud gulping sobs, her shoulders heaving in a mad shrug. At last she looked up from Powell's tear-splattered desk, forcing the words lodged in her throat. She'd been raped when she was a little girl, she said, by a relative. After that, she made up her mind that no one would ever hurt her again. Perhaps if she had sought help, told someone back then, her habit of fury could have been prevented, but she kept her secret. "She felt, in order to protect herself from rape, she had to be a male," Powell said. "It probably did help her. She was beating people up to demand respect. That was Mama's whole thing. 'Nobody's gonna give it to me, so I'll just take respect.' "

Mama hid the truth from most of the world, allowing few to see through her carefully constructed subterfuge. Despite the persona she presented, she had emerged from prison scarred. Those who know what happened won't say. "Some things she told me that happened there I will never ever repeat," said Robinson, her mentor at CYD. "Before prison she would waver back and forth between going straight or not, but doing that time turned her to Never-Never-Land. She told me she would never go back to prison, she would die first. Or kill somebody. And secondly, she decided the world owed her something and she was going to get it, and get it fast.

Mama Sheik went into prison a smart and talented young woman, teetering on the edge of legitimate success and a life of trouble, and came out committed to a criminal destiny. No longer did she crave the fame that came as a leader of the city's biggest girl gang. Fighting for fighting's sake brought unwanted attention to her entrepreneurial aspirations. And Mama had aspirations. Although she hired former Sheiks for her new operation, they'd moved beyond heavy violence and minor crimes. She now scored two to three kilos of coke a month, an amount, according to Johnson, that can bring $60,000 in Wisconsin. Her sudden wealth needed to be justified. She laundered the money, investing drug profits into a limousine service, a men's clothing shop, a hair salon, and a tavern. An urban Robin Hood, she spread money out in concentric circles that extended from her sisters and mother to include grandmothers, uncles, cousins, and friends. "A lot of people looked to Mama when they couldn't look to their parents," remembered her friend the Terminator. "People who needed money for school, Mama gave it to them. People needed clothes, she bought them."

Unlike other drug dealers, she peddled her product discriminately with regard to the consequences. A woman whose mother was a crack addict and one of Mama's steady customers recalled how, in desperation to save her mother, she confronted her drug connection on the telephone. Mama's salesgirl began cussing, tossing out threats. There was a pause, then Mama Sheik came on the line. She ordered the woman to put her mother on the phone. She made it known that she wasn't coming over anymore to sell her drugs: "You is somebody's mother. That is your daughter. And if you was my mother, I'd kill the bitch who was serving you." The phone went dead. Mama Sheik's crew never returned to the woman's home.

Although Mama herself used cocaine recreationally, she could not tolerate addiction in people she cared about. She fell in love with an addict, coming home to find her with blazing eyes as huge as golf balls. In a rage, Mama would throw her around the room, into the chrome-and-leather furniture she'd bought her that now reeked of burnt cocaine. Afterward she kept watch over her, making sure the woman's two small boys were always safe. When at last Mama lost her lover to crack, she never abandoned the children, lavishing them with clothes and toys.

Her own family worshipped her. I saw evidence of this one afternoon when a counselor for girls at SDC invited me to her office to introduce me to Mama's youngest sister Sharon. She was a striking girl, only five-foot-one, but with a disconcerting way of staring adults dead in the eye. The counselor described meeting Sharon at Bay View High School, where, as the only girl allowed in its program for at-risk boys, Sharon pushed guys out of their chairs if she wanted their seat. "She was running the whole damn school," the woman recalled. "If she didn't like something in the group, she'd get up and say, 'We're going,' and all the kids would leave. I told her I was running this show and she told me Mama was her sister. I told her to get out.

"So that's how I met Mama. I was discussing something with the group when Mama knocked on the door. She said she was Mama Sheik. Which everyone knew. Mama threw the sign for Folks and said, 'What's up, fool? I'm talking to you.' I waited for a minute. I asked if she'd like to speak with me outside. She said, 'No, I want to speak to you in front of these kids, like you dissed my sister in front of these kids.' But after I told her about Sharon's disruptions, the three of us went into the hall. It was clear that Mama didn't want Sharon to turn out like her."

While the counselor and I discussed Sharon, the girl eyed me leerily. Sharon was poised between grief and trying to forge her own reputation. At ten she ran with the Baby Sheiks. She now led a small crew called the Girl Scouts, struggling to match her sister's cult of personality. "Just like Mama made the Sheiks, I made the Scouts what they are today," she told me. "My sister told me before she passed that she could see a lot of me in her."

Sharon insisted that she didn't follow in her sister's footsteps, however. She had her own mind. "I'm gonna do what Sharon wants to do. 'Cause I don't give a fuck about nobody. I'm a self-centered person, that's how I am. I mean, I love, me, I'd die for me. By my conversation and how I look, no one will believe that I'm only seventeen. I know how to talk to old men, sugar daddies, but that's not my style—I have class, I have limits. No older than twenty-four." She draped her arm over the back of the chair and swung around to face me, striking a pose of calculated nonchalance. "I had a little boy a couple of months ago—only seventeen—it was his first time. The only reason I went with that little boy was 'cause he had money. He made like over six g's a day selling dope. And he knew that I was a woman. I gave him a little kiss like he never been kissed before."

Much of this was pure performance for my sake. Two years later I would see another side of Sharon, a soft-spoken young mother who referred to her old self as a "little monster." But back then her self-possession was impressive. Another counselor assured me, however, that Sharon didn't compare to Mama. "She's not even in the same book, let alone the same page. Mama was a legend."

As a mere mortal, Sharon had some hope of surviving her teenage years and flourishing. Legends in the underworld, or on the street, rarely live to middle age. And Mama knew it. "Mama Sheik knew she was beautiful, knew she had charisma," said Robinson. "I think she also knew she would die. The last time she visited the office she was talking along those lines. But you'd think, 'Mama can never die.' She just left that impression."

To ensure that she would never return to prison, Mama Sheik perfected her moves, covering her tracks and keeping her money clean, so that even as she amassed a fortune, no one could prove she hadn't done it legitimately. In 1991 the FBI interrogated her about the robbery of a teachers' credit union. On New Year's Eve in 1992, Milwaukee police questioned her in connection with a restaurant robbery. During a pat-down search, they came up with a small amount of coke and marijuana, a hands-down parole violation that should have placed her behind bars, but Mama pulled off another successful manipulation of the system. None of the charges ever stuck.

In the end it wasn't the police that would get her.

For protection she kept her address a secret to all but her family. Her apartment, in a quiet neighborhood on Milwaukee's West Side, provided sanctuary. Toward Christmas, 1993, she'd filled its rooms with presents for her family. She'd gone a little wild this year, buying winter coats for each of her sisters. Mama's loyalty to her own never faltered; she hired her relatives at her tavern and when her cousin needed a place to stay that December, she opened her door.

One evening before the holidays, while Mama and her cousin worked at the bar, burglars ransacked her home, stealing the coats, the Christmas presents, a VCR, her stereo system. To rob Mama had to be either a spontaneous act of lunatic bravado or a deliberate provocation. Had it been the first, a random break-in, Mama might have been able to tolerate it. But money vanished from hidden places, as if the burglars possessed a layout of the house. The cost to her ego was immeasurable.

Her sister Sharon remembered how Mama withdrew from the family

Christmas festivities, humiliated. Alone at the kitchen table, she stared off into space. "Her house had been robbed and she had no presents for her mother. They say people start acting funny before they die. Christmas Day she kept taking off her coat and putting it back on like she was going to leave the house, but then she wouldn't."

Sometime that day Mama Sheik received a phone call from a local crackhead who said he'd seen her stolen possessions in someone's house. Her own cousin, he revealed, had set her up. On the night of the break-in, her cousin called the burglars from the bar, telling them Mama was out and where to look for cash. "The material stuff didn't make a difference," Sharon said. "But for her to be who she was on the street and someone to come in her house, it just threw her. 'Cause she always told me to think before you react. But that night she didn't. It was just that nobody had ever crossed Mama."

Although her anger could surface at alarming velocity, Mama resisted acting on impulse, especially when it came to business. After she received word of the burglar's identity, she called the police, looking for Officer Johnson. He was off duty that night. Instead the cop who answered informed her that she didn't have enough evidence to merit a search warrant of the man's house. If Mama felt her death coming, perhaps she was too proud to delay it, because after she hung up, she wasted no more time. She made more phone calls, recruiting half a dozen gunmen at fifty bucks a head.

They drove to the burglar's house. Some of the gunmen wore ski masks. Mama planned to surround the house—an ambush. She herself would go to the front door.

Pistol in her hand, she raced toward the porch. Inside the man either heard footsteps or someone had tipped him off. Shots rang out. In the confusion a bullet hit Mama in the stomach, driving through the organs of her lower abdomen.

"It was the longest three nights we ever had. Oh, it was really hard for me." Sharon broke down when she remembered her older sister's final hours. "Her immune system couldn't fight off the infections. And the blood! Blood came out of her nose, her eyes, her ears, her mouth. She was conscious, but she wasn't stable. She couldn't speak, but she could blink or shake her head to tell us she loved us.

"That woman had a hell of a heart. We wouldn't turn off any of those machines. If there is such thing as miracle, I don't know why that miracle didn't come true. Maybe because of the type of person she was. Because when she got out of the hospital, she was planning to go on a rampage. Or maybe our family was going to be in danger or something. Whatever it was, there was a reason for God to take her the way he did."

ON December 29, 1993, at 1:12 P.M., the reign of Mama Sheik came to an end.

"When he killed Mama, it was like killing the President. I nearly snapped when I heard," recalled the Terminator.

"There's only two people in our twenty-five years that came through here like a Mama Sheik," said CYD's Robinson. "She died and the other, a man, will be getting out of prison real soon. With both of them it was understood they could either become a mass murderer or the President of the United States."

The chances of another Mama are slim. One reason Mama lived and died the way she did was she imitated men. If she had gone the route of the majority of female gang members, she would have outgrown her gang, most likely after she had a child. But for emulating violent male behavior she suffered the twin fates of many male gang members: prison and death.

Mama Sheik's short, violent life inspired Robinson to speak out about the need to focus on early prevention programs that target young girls. In the fall of 1994, CYD implemented a new program exclusively for girls arrested for shoplifting and first-time offenses, hoping to reach them before they are lured into gangs. Robinson also argues for exploring alternatives to jail. She holds to her belief that Mama might have been saved had she not gone to prison. When President Clinton was formulating his crime policy, he invited Robinson to the White House. "I told the President we need to intervene with services after the first and second strikes, and even after the third strike we should not give up. Emotionally, it helps a politician to say, 'Lock 'em all up.' But the reality is it comes out of your paycheck and that person will come out of prison worse, they're going to be like a Mama Sheik. Prison should become a place that allows people to change and give them time to learn skills, to transform minds and make people want to come out and contribute, instead of saying, 'I will never go back. I will kill before I go back.'"

When Robinson received the call at night saying Mama Sheik was not expected to last until morning, she phoned Officer Johnson. He was on vacation. Robinson's coworkers suggested that he was unlikely to return to visit the deathbed of a convicted criminal. "I said, 'Oh yes he will.' Because no matter what you must do in your job, you still love Mama Sheik. I mean, you can't *not* love Mama Sheik, even when she's doing wrong."

Johnson did visit her deathbed, as well as attend the funeral. Not out of love, but sympathy for a wasted life. "If I had talked to her that night she called the squad, I would have gone over to the guy's house myself," he said somberly. "I knew this would happen. Every time I arrested her I told her, 'If I can, to keep you alive, I'll put you in federal prison.' "

The man whose house Mama stormed pleaded self-defense. No one pressured the D.A. to prosecute him, perhaps because, as Johnson said, Mama had embarrassed too many counselors in town who had once believed in her. For all the media attention paid to Mama's life, her death was shrouded in silence. Despite the turnout at her funeral, the mention in the *Milwaukee Journal* was terse, six clipped paragraphs under a column called "Metro and State Newswire," beginning "Milwaukee police recorded the city's 163rd homicide of the year . . ."

Nor did anyone step forth to testify against her killer. Johnson thinks that the devotion Mama had inspired in many of her followers had cooled. "She pissed off too many men because she stole their women. One of the guys who robbed her house, a known burglar, a crazy cokehead just out of prison, told me, 'You don't know how big this is. You ain't taking me down for this.' There was more to her death than meets the eye. Some guys were trying to scare her, bring her down. I still think about it, but nothing can be done."

Mama Sheik's family believed the most sinister version of events going around: that Mama had been set up. As they raced to the porch that night, the story went, one of Mama's gunmen turned his weapon on Mama and pulled the trigger. When I asked Sharon why they would kill one of their own, she didn't hesitate. "Jealousy. She was a woman who had gotten too big."

WANNA-BES: THE LOST GIRLS

I would recognize her anywhere. That walk, slow and deliberate, part sway, part slouch, pants bagging in bright neon gold, topped with a tight T-shirt in black, colors that screamed to the world—or to that part of the world that mattered—her allegiance to the Latin Kings. As I pulled up alongside her, Droopy started, backing away from the car, a scared animal; her mouth sprang open in surprise, then twisted into menace, until she realized who I was. At last her face relaxed back into its natural sixteen-year-old prettiness.

"You scared the shit out of me, bro!" Droopy climbed into the car, inviting the skinny white girl with her into the backseat. "We were jumped yesterday."

She turned to show me the bump on her forehead, the scratch marks marring her baby cheeks and button nose. Her friend, a fragile girl in a preppy blue plaid skirt, looked far worse. Blood hemorrhaged into the white of her left eye, the skin around it deep purple, almost black. Her face would have been even more of a disaster had Droopy not fought off her attackers, a group of Latin Queens, who beat her simply for hanging out with Droopy. The girl slouched in back, biting her nails. The school nurse wanted to tell her mother that she needed X rays, but the girl begged her not to, worried her mother would yank her out of school and transfer her to the suburbs, away from "my man and my friends." She could deal with the pain, but not with being alone.

Protective of her unlikely companion, Droopy's anger over the fight surged until, by the time we reached the Burger King a block away, she almost gagged on it. She stalked into the restaurant, waving her arms, heaving, spitting, ranting at passersby. Ordering a grape soda, she mad-dogged the cashier, eyes narrowing in ugly challenge. "I want to fight!" she shouted as we sat down. "I need to work off steam." Behind her some girls laughed. "Shut up, girl!" Droopy yelled, not turning around. "Bitch, please, I got my own shit."

She sucked some soda through her straw, then threw her head back, spilling it down her shirt. "*Shit*, I'm gonna go to the bank and hit up some old lady."

I was used to this. Droopy was always promising to rob old ladies, but so far had jacked only a pizza delivery man with her ex-boyfriend, a Latin King. All her other attacks were unplanned, spontaneous sparks of explosive rage. Five times in the past year she'd been thrown into detention or various group homes. During one arrest, she bit a cop, leaving teeth marks on his ankle. Two schools expelled her for fighting, the last time for calling a teacher "a fucking bitch," who'd retorted, "It takes one to know one!" just before Droopy hauled off and smacked her.

Later, after we dropped off her friend, we drove to Droopy's house through Latin King territory, marked by their sign, the crown and pitchfork, splashed across small grocery stores and the sides of houses. At 12th and Mineral, the heart of the neighborhood, police towered over two manacled teenagers in gold sweatpants, spread-eagled on the sidewalk. "They got Al," Droopy said, guessing that this display had to do with the murder of a fifteen-year-old boy a few days earlier. Latin Kings were the main suspects. "Fuck you," she hissed out the window at the cops, then slumped down so that they couldn't see her.

I joked that she'd better not get us in trouble, because I couldn't run and I couldn't fight.

She sat up in her seat, suddenly serious. "Get out of here!"

"I wouldn't know what to do if someone hit me."

Confusion spread across her features. "Well . . ." She hesitated. "What do you do when someone comes up and hits you?"

Nobody ever had, I told her.

"For real?" She turned her expectant brown eyes upon me. "For real?"

By some people's definition, Droopy was a wanna-be—a girl associated with gangs through a boyfriend, family members, or best friends. Some gang counselors dismissed them, while others believed they had the most to gain if society focused on them and the most to lose if neglected. Cops often viewed wanna-bes with a mix of pity and contempt. A Puerto Rican girl from Milwaukee's South Side, Droopy was identified as "gang-affiliated" by her teachers and the police who arrested her. Her fingers were tattooed ALKN, a letter on each digit, for "Almighty Latin King Nation." But she could not call herself a Latin King and hadn't joined its sister organization, the Latin Queens. She knew of only one clique that called itself Queens. Instead Droopy hung around SOS, "Sisters of the Struggle," a neighborhood posse run by a family of seven sisters, branching out to include cousins and friends. Less a menace than a menace in the making, they drank, club hopped, slept over at each other houses, dated King men, and occasionally threw bricks through windows of girls they didn't like or struck at them with bats or padlocks swung from key chains. Adults, dealing with boys who carried high-powered guns, tended to shrug off such female violence as cat fights, though the victims of their assaults probably took it less lightly.

Girls were reluctant to label themselves Queens because the current generation of Latin Kings didn't want them. "In the early eighties, the girls' leaders would meet with our leaders and give us a report, like a board of directors of a bank," a Latin King told me. "But in time they either had babies or got strung out on drugs and we had no use for them." A few women in their late twenties still claimed the title of Queen, hiding guns for Kings who were their cousins or uncles or, if married to a dealer, counting money and steering business phone calls from their homes while their children played at their feet. "To me a Queen is someone waiting for her man, to treat him like a King. If she has a kid, to take care of her kid. A Queen's job isn't to be out banging, it's to stay home and keep the house the way it was taught historically in the Latin race. There's no place for a girl in this. My Nation's business is none of her concern."

A few Milwaukee girls had paid the price for knowing too much. A Cobralette was shot in the head while sitting in her car at a gas station. A girl who flipped between the Latin Kings and the Spanish Cobras was murdered, as well—word on the street had it she was set to testify about Cobra activity.

BEHIND BARS

What was the fate of a wanna-be? "Milwaukee girls?" Sad Eyes pursed her lips distastefully. "The girls didn't know how to fight, didn't know shit about gangs, gang violations, what to do to get money. When I came here from Chicago, these bitches weren't nothing but punks."

I visited the Women's Correctional Center in Milwaukee each Saturday throughout much of the summer of 1994. Most of the 45 women were here for drug-related offenses, retail theft, forgery, or battery, such as beating an older woman or kids for their clothes, something that can be unloaded for fast cash. I'd befriended one of the few inmates considered "gang-affiliated," Sad Eyes, a twenty-one-year-old mother of three, serving the last two months of a three-year sentence for assault of a minor. Her release was contingent on completing a drug treatment program; she had been an alcoholic since the age of eight. Prison was the only therapy she had received in a life marked by perverse violence and humiliation, a life she at times described with forced breeziness. At other moments her nightmare world would suddenly snap into terribly clear focus and she'd flee inward, angry at my intrusion.

Her family had moved often, trying to escape their neighborhood's brutality, from Chicago to California and back, until finally settling on Milwaukee's South Side near Droopy's neighborhood. Everywhere she went, Sad Eyes managed to slip by or rebuff social workers and teachers, each failing to stem her destructive course. It was a tragedy I had seen repeated dozens of times. Sad Eyes had ended up in prison. I looked to her for insight into what might become of Droopy.

I'd wait for her in the library, a humid, claustrophobic room filled with an eclectic mix of donated books: *Charlotte's Web*, *The Meat and Potatoes Cookbook*, the diaries of Anais Nin and Virginia Woolf, *Fatal Vision* by Joe McGinnis, romance novels and mysteries, an Encyclopaedia Britannica from 1974. The single barred window overlooked the back lot of a warehouse strewn with rubber tubing and rusted machinery.

Sad Eyes would show up, brown hair in a topknot, usually wearing a sleeveless shirt exposing the large LQ, for "Latin Queens," branded on her tricep. Her eyes were black, her skin white as milk; her mother, she said, was Puerto Rican, her father Mexican. She took her nickname from the teardrop tattooed beneath her eye, a symbol that Sad Eyes liked to keep mysterious; maybe it meant she killed someone, maybe not. She grew up in Chicago. "My mother was a Lady Unknown, my father was a chief of the Unknowns. She sold women, he was a pimp. I saw my dad beat up on his women. He didn't live with us—out shooting dope, I guess. He'd just come and spend the night. When my ma was pregnant with me, she told me he threw the dining room table on her stomach."

Her earliest memories were of seeing a neighbor woman's ear shot off and of her brother running into the house, his hand ripped apart from a shotgun that backfired. When she was nine, she cradled a boy shot on her front lawn one night, her pink pajamas soaking up his dark blood, its rank odor hanging in the air like spilled beer.

To numb themselves from the carnage, she and her brothers sniffed glue, gasoline, lighter fluid, paint thinner, hair spray, nail polish remover, anything to make them feel better. Sad Eyes would prop herself on the seat of a neighbor's motorcycle, inhaling the escaping fumes from the open gas tank. At times her mother, finding her brother flying from spray, handcuffed the boy to the bed and beat him.

Their uncle introduced the kids to drinking, giving them shots before he himself passed out. "All us girls on the block were drinking, smoking cigarettes, doing speed. My ma knew I was taking speed because I'd bring black beauties to pop with her. Matter of fact, I turned her on to black beauties."

I shook my head, incredulous that adults shared drugs with children. Sad Eyes let out a dismissive laugh. That was nothing to be surprised about, she informed me; a lot of adults gave little kids drugs so that they wouldn't have to get high alone. Her ten-year-old nephew, tattoos covering his hairless body, drank and smoked weed with his mother, his dad, with everybody. Perhaps it was inevitable that Sad Eyes sought another family. "My mom was everybody else's mother, so I just clicked on to all these older Queen women and said, 'Well, these are gonna be my moms. This is who I'm gonna look up to.' My family was disappointed I didn't join the Unknowns. But I wanted my own thing."

At first the girls just let her tag along. Then one afternoon a group of Kings and Queens took her to an old el track overpass. The trains took the route to the stockyards, via a corridor of small factories and warehouses at roof level. Kids, including Sad Eyes' two brothers before her, were dared to scale the tracks, then leap through the sky to the roof of an abandoned building. Not every one made it. One girl ended up in a cast to her waist. Two boys died when they were hit by trains. But if you didn't jump, the kids believed, you'd be fired upon by railroad men for trespassing on the tracks. During her turn, afraid to look down, Sad Eyes stood on the rails between two older girls, clenching her hands tightly, all three sufficiently drunk for the occasion; finally she shut her eyes and took a running jump. "Stretch your legs!" one cried. "Like you're running on air!" She didn't open her eyes again until she felt her feet crash upon the tar roof.

Sad Eyes, who prided herself on her defiance against her mother, teachers, anyone in a position of authority, let other kids tell her what to do. "Well, 'cause I looked up to them and I knew I had to go through that if I wanted to get on top. 'Cause you know you're gonna be on top one day, but with a parent or teacher you're never gonna be on top of them. Everybody goes through it; even the person who is telling you what to do has been in your shoes. Being on top, it's like the goal you go for. That's what has always been in my mind.

"I was a peewee, then juniors and seniors, and then—boom—you're there, you Ladies. I jumped through a couple of ranks so fast by going on missions." Because she was pretty, Sad Eyes was used for missions to set up rival gang members. The setup required you to face the enemy. The drive-by was faceless—maybe you knew who you were shooting at, maybe you didn't, either way you never saw the blood you spilled—but the setup forced you to charm your foe before luring him to his death. Seen in the flesh, the enemy, the physical embodiment of everything you feared and hated, turned out to be just another scared teenager, like yourself.

Teenage boys lived in terror of being set up, and though they themselves slept with rival girls for information, it was girls who were known to kiss and kill. On a balmy summer evening, Sad Eyes and Suzy Q disguised themselves in Cobra colors of black-and-green, showing up uninvited at a Cobra block party. The girls lurked on the fringes of the crowd to avoid drawing attention, scanning the partygoers. The mark had to be someone naive or too drunk or high to realize what was going on—too many gang bangers kept their antennae up for trouble, even when relaxing with their own. They picked out a tall lanky teenager known as Slim and his friend, a short kid with a crew cut. They chatted for a few minutes before Sad Eyes suggested that the four of them break away from the party and take a walk. The two guys needed no persuading. They strolled through a backyard and down an alley, leaving the sounds of music and party conversation behind them. In the alley Sad Eyes began nuzzling against Slim, glancing sideways at the Nova with tinted windows parked in the shadows, before stretching up to kiss him. Then she heard the roar of the engine and jerked free of Slim's embrace. The smile faded from his face as he turned just in time to see the car speed toward him. The short boy, realizing his fate, screamed, "You bitch!"

"Someone in the car yelled, 'Now!' and they just opened fire," Sad Eyes said. "The guys fell on the ground. Suzy Q spit on one of them.

Someone grabbed me and threw me inside the car. I looked back and that boy was still kind of kicking, but Slim didn't move. Not at all."

How had she felt talking to the boy, knowing that she was leading him to possible death? She made a face. "I was scared to death. Ain't no shame in my game. I was thinking I was gonna get killed. And I thought I had something to be angry about. The Cobras shot at us, too. To me, it's power to see someone get killed or having a gun in my hand, it's a natural high. It was having power over a person." The key, she thought, was not to allow yourself to think. "If I think about it, now that you asked, it was kind of nice talking to Slim, he had a good conversation. Most of them are like, 'Bitch, give up that pussy,' and try to get you in a corner and fuck you. He had more of a gentleman way about him. But I kept telling myself he had to go, and you know when you tell yourself something, your mind is set and you don't care."

But she was not a hardened criminal at this stage; she was still a child. The process of befriending the enemy, methodically setting him up for pain or death, required a steel coldness she had yet to develop. She ended up having her first crush on someone her gang and her brothers would have shot on sight. He was a Latin Lover, and he discovered early on she was a Queen, yet continued to see her. In a perverse *West Side Story*, Sad Eyes sometimes carried a gun when they met, in case he turned on her. One night he risked going into her neighborhood to see her. Sad Eyes' brothers set upon him with bricks and bats. She screamed at them to stop, but they struck him again and again, breaking his skull. Afterward, he lay in the hospital, steel pins in his head, for four months.

"I don't know how he thought he could visit me and not get caught. We guarded our neighborhood. When you think we are sleeping, three, four o'clock in the morning, we are up in the trees. When you think we're not around, that's when we'll be around. We are like ghosts. Our shadows, always watching."

The ghosts had turned on her.

Weeks later she woke up in the middle of the night with excruciating cramps. She curled up into a ball, her hands tucked between her legs. Her thighs felt wet and, turning on the light, she saw in ugly panic that it was blood. She knew that it wasn't time for her period—which she'd started at age nine. The next day her cousin took her to the hospital. She had miscarried the enemy's baby at ten years of age.

Whenever I listened to Sad Eyes, I felt gripped by the feeling that her story was a kind of road map of Droopy's fate. Unless someone intervened to help her control the rage inside her, Droopy could end up charged with battery herself, bound for a long term of imprisonment. When I told Droopy about Sad Eyes, she cut me off, dismissing the older woman as a no-name has-been. She leaned against her porch railing, her five-year-old sister Tina snuggling against her. "My mom loves to see me fight," Droopy boasted. "She'll sit there and cheer me on. To me, mothers should understand. An ordinary mother wouldn't want gang members in the house. But my mom understands that's what's in the street."

At her feet her ten-year-old brother Juan listened, watching the stream of cars pass by on their way to nowhere. I asked Droopy whether the little kids should hear this.

"They know all about gangs. He's on the street twenty-four/seven. And her"—she toyed with her little sister's thick hair—"if she gets involved with gangs, I'll fuck her up. I mean, I'll smoke dope with her—"

"At five?"

Droopy laughed. "Not at five, but at ten. I don't want her to be no little punk bitch. When I call her a bitch, I want her to talk shit back. If I slap her, I want her to slap me back. That's the way I see it." She prodded her brother's back with her sneaker. "I beat the fuck out of him every motherfucking day when we were young. Sometimes to get my frustration out, sometimes 'cause I wanted him to hit me back. To this day he has not hit me back. So when I fight him, I beat the fuck out of him. It just makes him stronger and harder, he knows how to take pain. I don't want him to get jumped, but it's going to happen sooner or later. He lives in a fucked-up world."

She knew that it was only a matter of time before Juan would join the Latin Kings. Children as young as eight or nine hung on corners with their hats turned to the left, showing loyalty to the Kings or the Vice Lords, or to the right, for the Spanish Cobras and the Gangster Disciples.

Later, at dinner, Juan transformed from a shy youngster into the man of the household. He sat at the head of the table, a place normally reserved for Droopy's sister's boyfriend, who was driving another Latin King down South on the lam for a murder. On one side of the room the Puerto Rican flag hung next to a painting Droopy made of a rose beneath the words I LOVE MOM, the same sentiment sloppily tattooed on her upper thigh. Her mother now staggered to the dinner table, mumbling in Spanish. Droopy rolled her eyes and nudged me. "She says you're a cop." I complimented the meal of yellow rice, hamburger, and mushrooms and once more the woman spoke in Spanish, though she knew English. "She says you just like it 'cause you're hungry," Droopy said. "She's real high."

"Yeah, she lit up a joint an hour ago and she's still flying." Juan studied the latest manifestation of his mother's transient hair color; yesterday's persimmon red was now saffron yellow, matching the rice. "That's the best dye job yet," he asserted between mouthfuls. "She's tried blonde before and it came out white. Looked weird."

Droopy thought her little sister Tina had the best hair in the family. "When she was two, she had hair down to her butt. But she got lice and we cut it off to the middle of her back. That didn't help, so we cut it off until her shoulders. The bugs were still in there, so we shaved her whole head. We all had lice 'cause of this girl, who if I see I'm gonna kick her ass. She slept over and after that, 'cause I sleep with my whole family, everyone got it."

"Except my mom," Juan pointed out, "because of her hair dye. She sprayed all our heads with Raid and put on shower caps. That finally killed them."

After eating, the family moved to the living room. I noticed on top of a glass coffee table a ceramic menagerie made up of pairs of lions, parakeets, and elephants that hadn't been there the day before. "My mom, she steals," Droopy offered, though I hadn't asked. "She stole those today, along with her hair dye." On cue her mother reappeared; her large kohl-rimmed black eyes bore a glittery, unfocused cast. She sprawled out on the plush black couch, which, like the TV and the CD player, looked expensive, her thighs bulging through the thin polyester of her pedal pushers. When we first met, I assumed that Droopy's mother was in her fifties—she was a grandmother—but Droopy told me she was thirty-one.

"Light one up, bro!" Droopy shouted to her.

Her mother watched TV.

"Fucking light one up!" Droopy hollered, laughing. Her mother laughed, too, as Droopy's demands grew more theatrical. The other children sat on the floor, playing with a deck of cards, oblivious to the din. Finally her mother passed her a joint and Droopy quieted down.

Later in the evening, little Tina, hiding behind an armchair next to me, stuck out a blonde-haired doll. "My name's Tina," she squeaked, using the doll as a puppet. "Please tell my teacher that I don't have any friends at school. They call me 'devil.'"

Droopy glared at her. "She's a liar. She's a little fucking bitch. She doesn't share her toys, then gets mad when the other kids don't share theirs."

Tina crawled out from behind the chair, looking wide-eyed at her sister. "They do call me 'devil.' They call me bad words."

"Fucking bitch," Droopy muttered.

"They give me the finger"—Tina held up her index finger instead of the middle one—"under the desk."

"Liar. You're just stupid." Droopy folded her arms around herself, scowling. I asked her if she had any homework and she groaned. Then to my surprise she retrieved her backpack and pulled out a textbook on citizenship. "I have to"—she read aloud from the book—" 'make a family tree or interview a relative or neighbor who's an immigrant—' " She tossed the book on the couch. "I can't do this."

I assured her that the assignment would be relatively easy, since her mother was an immigrant. Once I'd finished explaining a family tree, she said, "I don't even know what you're talking about." Her seventeen-year-old sister looked up from playing with her infant son. "I don't know what you're talking about, either."

Though she had managed to stay in school, Droopy had no confidence in her ability. Just as she called her little sister Tina stupid, she referred to herself in kind. She *was* provincial, displaying an astonishing ignorance of geography—she thought New York was down South and was unaware she lived in the state of Wisconsin, so focused was she on surviving in her twenty or so blocks of neighborhood—but she possessed a natural curiosity, bombarding me with questions about where I lived in Brooklyn and the cities I'd seen. Her teachers, she believed, viewed her as a delinquent or a loser and she used this as an excuse to shrink from challenge. (Two years later the Milwaukee public school system would take the unheard of step of trying to close the school Droopy attended, citing substandard performance and out-of-control violence. Soon after the announcement, a kid caused the death of another student during an argument over thirty-five cents.) She fell onto the couch, wrapped her arm around her knees, then toyed with a cigarette lighter, stealing glances at Tina, who cuddled next to me as I helped her with her alphabet. "She looks just like her damn father."

"Which one's hers again?" Juan looked up from his playing cards. "Joseph."

Juan pointed to his four-year-old brother. "And what about his?"

"Larry. He's the only Mexican in the family."

" 'Hey, *vato!* Hey, *Ese! La Prima* lives!' " Juan broke into a Mexican homeboy accent, quoting the last line of *American Me*, a film about the Mexican Mafia, referring to the moment when a little boy sticks a gun out a car window to blast his enemy. The four-year-old giggled with delight as Juan trailed behind him, cussing in Spanish.

Droopy scooted over to rest her head on her older sister's shoulder. The girls were a year apart and a pretty contrast, Droopy tall and fair-skinned, her sister petite and brown. "I love my older sister, she's so cute! Tina I love, but she gets on my nerves. She's so spoiled. I can't wait till my mother goes to Chicago so I can beat her ass."

Her mother raised an eyebrow at Droopy, then turned back to the TV. Bored, Droopy channel-surfed until she found a movie about teenage gangs. "This is good, bro." She'd seen it before. "Look at that baby Uzi."

"That's a TEC-9." Her older sister sniffed. "A 'baby Uzi!' "

"Fuck you, bitch. I think it is." For the next half hour, the movie captured Droopy's attention. The plot involved a teenage boy who goes to live with his aunt after his prostitute mother is raped and killed. He begins to sell drugs on the street. One night his aunt, a young, worried woman, comes to his room, telling him how much she loves him and pleading with him to confide in her. Droopy was spellbound.

"The problem is," she said softly, "in the real world there are no aunts like that."

In the real world Sad Eyes said there were men who paid little girls to stand in front of their car while they ejaculated on the driver's-side window. Having molded her into a willing participant (though Sad Eyes could never force herself to look at him and would watch the sky for birds), the strange man cruised her neighborhood for three years, on and off, to whisper obscene talk and stare at her young body.

Today was Saturday, the day children visited their imprisoned mothers, but for the third weekend in a row, Sad Eyes' mother had failed to bring Sad Eyes' three kids. Sad Eyes would glance into the visiting room, just some chairs and a Coke machine with toddlers running around, and the weight of her day bore down.

We returned to the prison's stifling library, its single window closed tight, a wheezing fan blowing hot air on the sweat sticking to our bodies as Sad Eyes recalled the theft of her childhood. When she was twelve, the stranger in the car took her to a motel, where they had sex and she urinated on him. The amounts she remembered he paid, upward of $500, I was sure she inflated wildly, perhaps to lessen her shame or to revisit the memory with herself in control. Because Sad Eyes told lies, to herself as well as me, the girl she wanted to be constantly struggling with the girl she was.

She never painted herself as a victim, but blamed herself for being a rebellious girl, racing to be older than her years. Though now puffy and pale from prison food and lack of sunlight, she had been an exceptionally pretty child and beauty took a high toll on the streets. There had been the man who approached her and her aunt while they were waiting for a bus to inquire about Sad Eyes modeling for photographs. Her body was so beautiful for a girl only twelve, he told them. Eventually her mother agreed. After a few sessions, during which they smoked weed and drank wine coolers, he wanted Sad Eyes to take off her clothes. She didn't want to. She was uncomfortable with her body, but she was angry with her boyfriend. So she did.

The photographer began having sex with her, hoping to film it. She agreed to let him videotape her performing oral sex, but then changed her mind. "So I never made it to the big time. You should see the pictures of me. I got a lot of respect. I really miss that."

By thirteen she was dancing in a Chicago strip joint with her mother's permission. "But then men I knew started coming, gang members, and I wasn't comfortable with that. Strangers I didn't mind. But this was my neighborhood."

One time I asked Sad Eyes what she would have done if someone in her childhood had actually treated her as a child. Instantly her voice softened. "I'd have been pissed off, but I probably would've been happier. No, I would've loved it. You know what? I'm gonna tell you something. This is straight up, I don't know why I felt this way. I used to party with this man, Joe. We used to drink and get high together. One day Joe and his fourteen-year-old son were hanging around with my brothers and I wanted to be a little kid. I wanted to swing on the swings. So I went to the swings with Joe's son and I don't know why, but I said to him, 'I'm only eleven years old. I'm just like you.' He said, 'Why are you telling me this? You're much older.' He called me a liar. I tried my hardest to make him see that I was just this little girl, that I was only eleven years old, and I would like to swing on the swings with him. But this boy wouldn't believe me for shit." She sighed. Voices of children drifted in from the visiting room. "It hurt me that a little boy my age didn't believe that I was eleven years old. I didn't know how I acted different. What am I doing wrong? Then I realized I had a can of beer in my hand and a cigarette in my mouth. Who is going to believe you when you act so mature? Nobody believed I was a kid."

"**How** old were you when you lost your virginity?" Droopy wrote "14" on the questionnaire.

"Do you think it is important to be sexually active?" Droopy checked "Not important."

"Do you think it's important for a girl to remain a virgin?" "Very important," she wrote.

Droopy had filled out a survey on female gang members for a graduate student, who showed me her answers with Droopy's permission. I brought it up one hot afternoon while Droopy and I sat on a mattress on the floor of her mother's bedroom, she lazily dragging on a cigarette, watching the blue smoke hang above our heads in the heat. Droopy hated her own room; her mother sold her bedroom set the last time Droopy was arrested because she didn't think her daughter was coming back anytime soon, and the empty room only confirmed Droopy's loneliness.

I asked Droopy why she thought it was important to remain a virgin, even though she herself had not. She leaned up against the wall, eyes on the cigarette in her lap. She didn't really like sex all that much, she said.

"To me, I was a virgin till I was fourteen."

"Meaning, you're not counting something else?"

"Nope. 'Cause I didn't give it up. They took it."

"Who did? When?"

"When I was eleven."

"You were raped?"

She let out a long breath. "Not raped. I didn't say anything. I was too scared. I should have tried to stop him." She pointed the cigarette's orange burning tip toward her wrist, then pulled it away. "That's why I hate my little sister so much."

"Tina? Why?" I stopped. Tina's father had been Droopy's first partner. "Oh."

She looked up and smiled sadly. "Understand now?"

The phone rang and she rose to answer it. I watched her in the kitchen, talking on a phone shaped like a red high heel. She returned a minute later and settled in next to me. In response to a survey question asking if anyone in the family had made sexual advances, Droopy answered yes, four times, by four different men—Tina's father, along with a mix of uncles and her mother's boyfriends.

"That's a picture of the last one right there"—she indicated a snapshot taped to her mother's mirror on top of a wooden box serving as a makeshift bureau—"the man in the middle, hugging my sister and brother. The first time he told me to look in the bathroom on the floor. My underwear was there with some stuff in it. I sent my brother in. He checked it out and yeah—you know, he came all over my underwear."

Later she would awake to find him leaning over her, breathing jaggedly, his penis in her hand. Once, watching TV, he had turned to her, his blunt face expressionless, and opened his palm to show her a knife. "This is for you one day, bitch," he said flatly. When she could take him no longer, she ran away. She was caught and placed in detention at first, then in a group home. Although he was arrested and Droopy testified against him in court, passing a lie detector test, in the end nothing happened. Before she was released from the group home, he was already freed. "I came home, there he was. My mom finally believed me and threw him out, but he still calls. That was him on the phone just now."

I remembered the last thing she said before she hung up: "I love you, too."

"It's like, I love him, 'cause he's been in my life since I was little. He brought me up to the way I am now. And I thank him for that. 'Cause if he wouldn't have brought me up, who would have? Once upon a time I used to call him Poppy—like my dad or something. For my birthday he gave me $300 out of nowhere. I mean, he was really being like my father and actually caring. And as soon as he did that weird stuff, I didn't care for him no more. I care, but I won't let myself grow so close to him. He's become crazy. You read in the paper about a nutty man who ran naked down the street? That was him. He does his mistakes 'cause he's crazy. But that's not an excuse for him to do some stupid shit to me like that."

She spoke in halting speech, staring straight ahead. Her eyes started to water, but she was unwilling or unable to cry. Then she asked, "Do people ever tell you illegal things?"

I told her they had.

"I mean, really illegal things—like killing people?"

"People have told me that," I replied.

"Well, I should tell you. I'm wanted. I was arrested again after I was molested. I ran away from my group home."

She equated her running away with killing people. Imprisonment drove Droopy crazy. In the group home some girls attacked another, holding her down while taking turns urinating on her face and hair. A friend of Droopy's tried to hang herself with her socks, becoming the target of ridicule for the feebleness of her attempt. Detention was worse because Droopy couldn't talk to her mother on the phone. She wrote to her almost daily for three months. She presumed she was being punished, torn away from her mother, because a man she trusted had molested her. Such patent unfairness bred a lingering bitterness. Not even a month after she had returned to her home, she was fighting wildly on the streets. She liked fighting; it gave her a chance to take her anger out on someone else. When she and some friends learned that a girl was preparing to testify against a Latin King for car-jacking an elderly woman at gunpoint, Droopy couldn't contain her zeal for retaliation. Four girls set upon the traitor's house. She answered the door, her belly beneath her T-shirt swollen with her child. As soon as their victim saw the girls, all in baggy gold pants and black shirts, she knew what was in store and frantically scrambled back upstairs. Droopy looked toward her leader, who nodded, then bounded up the steps, seizing the girl's hair, punching her in the face and the back of the head countless times. Even in her fury she knew not to hit her in the stomach because of the baby, but police charged her with attempted murder. After a month in detention, she escaped from the group home before her trial. To keep Droopy hidden, her mother moved the family to a new house. Droopy cried every night for her friends and the dozen or so stray cats she used to feed from her window.

Before I left, she said, "If I ever have a baby, I sure hope it's not a girl."

At the door she asked, in the softest of tones, if I would come back tomorrow to see her. "It's okay if you're busy," she quickly added, her cheeks now wet with tears.

CALIFORNIA DREAMING

Sad Eyes showed up at the library in a foul mood from an abscessed tooth. A week before she had to be driven twenty-two miles away to a men's facility in Racine, as the Women's Correctional Center had no dentist. Her cheek looked as if she'd stuffed a sock in her mouth and her eyelid fluttered involuntarily, though she tried to hide the fact that she was in pain. She wanted to know if I'd be in Milwaukee when she was released a month and a half later, hoping she and I would go on a road trip to Chicago to meet her old Queens.

We spoke this afternoon of how her mother had moved the family overnight from Chicago to save her brother Meany after his gang had put out a hit on his best friend. As a test of his loyalty, the gang ordered Meany to eliminate a boy he had known all his life and he could not go through with it. "My aunt said to go to Watts, that it was really pretty. But it wasn't pretty. Not at all."

They moved to Grape Street and 103rd, a stone's throw from three of L.A.'s largest and poorest housing projects and smack in the middle of the turf belonging to the Grape Street Watts Crips, in the early eighties, as the Crips and the Bloods began littering the streets with teenage corpses. Her brother's parole officer suggested—in so many words—that the blond-haired blue-eyed boy arm himself with something when he walked the streets. He chose a machete.

Frantic to save her son's life, her mother did not always notice the escalating loss of childhood that her daughter was experiencing. On the morning of her twelfth birthday, Sad Eyes had awakened to no present, no party, no card; no one said anything. Her family had forgotten. That morning she ran away to the house of two sisters, a pair of Bloods. Sometime while Sad Eyes hid out there, the girls' older brother appeared in their bedroom. Sad Eyes knew him, he used to call her "white girl" in Spanish. But now he seemed spaced out, wild-eyed, like he'd been shooting dope. "He told me he wanted some pussy. He never talked to me like this. I told him to get away. That's when he started hitting me. The next thing I knew, and it's a little blurry in my mind, he dragged me outside and threw me over this fence with spikes and it pierced my back."

He pulled her down off the fence, kicking her in the lower spine with combat boots, screaming, "Bitch, you're gonna die!" Then, hoisting her up by the arm, he told her that he wanted her brothers to see her because he planned to kill them, too. He dragged her six blocks to her mother's house, beating her all the way. Sad Eyes remembered people coming onto their front yards to watch, all members of the Bloods. "Nobody did a damn thing. They just stood there. Girls were yelling, 'Kick the bitch's ass!' My insides felt like they were coming out. He beat me so severe that my head, my stomach, my back was all cut open."

In front of her house he ordered Sad Eyes to call her brothers, but no one answered. An eviction notice hung on the door. Sad Eyes' family had moved out without her. A neighbor man at last came to her rescue and called an ambulance. In the hospital the police informed her that they couldn't locate her family. She was released from the hospital to a foster home.

She stayed there for a month, then ran away. "They treated me like I was different." Sad Eyes said. "I *was* different." She found herself in an unknown neighborhood—she later learned it was Orange County—and began hitchhiking, frantic to return home. The first man who picked her up scared her and at a gas station she escaped from him, begging a couple for help. They took the lost child back to Watts, driving her around familiar streets until at last they found someone who knew that her mother had moved to Compton.

"As I was walking up, my ma got up and she freaked. Everybody freaked; it was like they had seen a ghost. I was so skinny and shit. They were like, 'Sad Eyes?' My ma, when I got in her arms, just melted, like she was gonna fall to her knees and pass out. My heart was pounding, it was going a hundred and ten miles per hour. I didn't know how to feel. It was like my ma didn't care for me, 'cause she wasn't there when I was getting beat up, so I was kind of scared." Sad Eyes stopped suddenly. "I want to cry. I hate getting into these damn parts that really fuck with my head."

It was a terrible understatement. After a moment, she spoke again, with great intensity, her face betraying an expression of bewilderment and urgency. "I couldn't look at her 'cause I hated her. I was like, 'How could you do this to me? I almost got killed!' My family begged me to forgive them and told me they were sorry and this good bullshit. They wanted to take me out for ice cream. I asked them, 'Why you trying to buy my love?' just like the foster parents did, buying me clothes. 'I don't need that. I need your love'—and my mom couldn't give that to me. She said she could, but she had my two brothers to look after."

She turned away from me. "I've always been just the girl. The guys can do whatever they want, they can relapse fifty million times, that's still her son, he's a man. When they got in trouble, Ma would always baby them. But when I got in trouble, it would be like, 'She's a girl. This is a disgrace to the family. How could she be doing this?' I told them, 'Well, y'all be wondering about why I fuck around with all these men and trying to get this love that I'm missing? They make me feel *good*.'

"There were times that I thought, 'Why didn't my ma say something?' " She laughed bitterly. "But my ma couldn't have been hard with me 'cause I was a hardheaded child. I'd be like, 'Shut up. You don't know shit.' But there were times I wished I had my old mother, like when I was a baby. When I got older, it was like she wasn't around. She was there, but she was just invisible. She was nothing that I wanted."

Yet, when the social workers showed up in Compton to take Sad Eyes away, she clung to her mother. At night the family fled by bus back to Chicago. When she finished speaking, I said, more to myself than to her, "My God, you've lived twelve lifetimes."

Sad Eyes shot me a fiery look. Immediately she changed her rhythm of speech, sealing herself off from me. "Please don't even tell me that. I don't like hearing that about my own life. It's just the shit that goes on."

"**WHEN** we came back from California, my mother's life, it was over— we kids just kept gang banging, and Mom started staying away from the gangs, although they still hung around our house," Sad Eyes told me one Saturday in the library, June sunlight pushing through the barred window. "She changed her life as my brother got older and started beating her ass. She just didn't do what she used to do with selling the whores. My dad was gone. She came up to Milwaukee and ended up being a grandmother. That was it."

Intent on changing her children's circumstances, Sad Eyes' mother lured her daughter into the car one afternoon, promising a trip to the bakery. Instead they took Highway 94 out of Chicago toward what their mother hoped would be a better life. An hour or so later they arrived in front of a two-story house on Milwaukee's South Side. Here white, Latino, and Asian working-class families lived in gable-roofed houses along tree-lined streets—a real neighborhood—but they didn't know what the charmed look hid. In a fifty-block radius thirty homes peddled drugs, four taverns sold cocaine regularly, three other business establishments doubled as drug fronts, and hustlers on six street corners provided dope to passersby, the University of Wisconsin–Milwaukee's urban research center learned when it surveyed the area in the fall of 1993. Gangs were involved in only half of the drug business; neighbors who weren't in gangs made up the other half. Their new hometown struggled with a soaring child poverty rate and scarce jobs for its inner-city dwellers.

So in the end, no matter where Sad Eyes' family moved, poverty always brought them up against the same ruthless forces they faced in Chicago. The two main gangs in their new neighborhood were the Latin Kings and their rivals, the Spanish Cobras, both built on extended family ties to Chicago, with relatives moving back and forth between the two cities. Sad Eyes' brothers hoped to launch the Unknowns, a group loosely aligned with the Latin Kings under the People Nation. The block where her family settled, however, was smack in the middle of Spanish Cobra turf. When they learned a clan of Unknowns had moved into their fiefdom, the Cobras welcomed them with a barrage of gunfire. Sad Eyes' family barricaded themselves in their home in a fierce shooting war until squadrons of police moved in, surrounding the house. Her mother and her brothers refused to come out, frantically dumping bullets into the toilet, trying to hide evidence. Cops rounded everyone up in a paddy wagon, including thirteen-year-old Sad Eyes, swearing at reporters, and her mother, cradling a baby.

For her brothers the shoot-out served as a dramatic entry into Milwaukee gangs. For Sad Eyes, the Kings gave her respect because of her Chicago roots and because of her brothers. But the Queens were nothing like those in Chicago. She had no time to stake a reputation among them, though, because she was pregnant. She was thirteen; the father, who came with the family from Chicago, was six years older. "My mother didn't think that I would have any babies 'cause I was wild. I was a strip dancer, I was a gang banger," Sad Eyes waxed nostalgically. "She just couldn't believe it. Here I was, this young girl who had so much going for me. She didn't think I was going to be tied down. I still gang banged while I was pregnant. I got kicked in the stomach and stabbed in my leg and had to go to the hospital." Sad Eyes stopped. Her bottom lip slid slowly to cover the top. "I guess I just let my whole childhood go."

Her first years in Milwaukee were a full-force disaster. She skipped school daily until her mother and the principal gave up on her, and she dropped out in seventh grade to become a full-time mother. By sixteen she had a second child with another man. Her memories of this second lover were of mutually maddening obsession. His jealousy of other men grew like a disease; he exploded if she even talked to her brother. She thought he was the best thing that ever happened to her. At least, she could tell herself, he cared. When he was angry, he would stare at her while he cleaned a shotgun, held between his knees. "He'd tell me if I ever left him he'd hunt me down and kill me." Finally her boyfriend shot a man during an argument that started when the man called Sad Eyes "baby."

He was sent to prison for life. Sad Eyes was seventeen, pregnant with her third child. "My whole world ended after that. I used to go out in the street and do shit, then pray to God I'd go to jail. I thought I would be closer to him. When he was getting sentenced, I made a plan that me and him were going to kill ourselves in the courtroom by grabbing the guns from the bailiffs. If my daughter hadn't been there, I probably would have."

Without her boyfriend's jealousy to rein her in, she spent her nights in the streets in free fall. Although Kings and Queens bylaws forbid drug use, Sad Eyes now snorted cocaine whenever she could. She started up her own gang of females to do her bidding. "Two were black, one was Indian, and the rest were white. The girls didn't know how to box, they weren't down. They were Milwaukee dumb asses and I didn't know how to act toward them.

"I jumped them in when I was pregnant with my son, big as a beach ball. I know it had an effect on my son. To this day, he's real mean. This is crazy, but my little boy, from being inside me and dealing with my bullshit, acts just like those girls. I was always arguing with my Queens. They'd get on my nerves and then just laugh, 'Shit, that's Mom for you'—'cause they used to call me Mom. And that's what my son does, when he gets on my nerves, it's like looking at those girls.

"Back then, I couldn't stand nobody, except my mother. I was always drunk and angry. I would get drunk, drunker than a motherfucker, and beat those girls' ass for no reason. I used to feel bad afterward, 'cause I used to beat them up so bad. Girl, they used to cry. But it was something I had to do. I was robbing their childhood."

Little more than a child herself, she grew to resent her own children. With money from dealing weed and a car she stole from the mother of one of her Queens, she escaped with some of her girls to Chicago. There she introduced them to other Queens and to her father, who impressed them with his dope-dealing skills. She set them up in motels, buying drugs, liquor, and food. In a month they had crashed the car and squandered the cash. A King moved them into a vacant house where Sad Eyes reigned over a litter of pizza boxes and McDonald's trash, terrorized by rats that leaped at them for scraps. After a week, the King suggested to Sad Eyes that if she wanted money, he could introduce her to some men who would pay for sex. She refused, but made plans to sell her friends.

That night two men turned up. Sad Eyes told the girls that they were there to party, but once the men had arrived, she negotiated the price of a girl with one of them. "He wanted to have sex, then a blow job. I thought about it, told him how much I wanted, and that's exactly what he gave me. In Chicago there are a lot of Spanish and Arabian dudes and they want little girls. They don't want those old women. She was young, she was fresh meat to him."

She chose the youngest of her friends, a fifteen-year-old girl. "She looked at me like, 'Why are you doing this?' I said, ' 'Cause we need money. How the fuck else we gonna live, if you don't do this?' I was talking to her real snotty like, 'Either you do this or we're gonna sleep on the streets.' And she said, 'Okay, okay. Mom, don't get mad. Let's go.' "

Sad Eyes watched TV, occasionally glancing into a wall mirror to monitor the girl as she traded sex for cash in the back of an empty room lit only by the flickering set. "She didn't like it. She was shaking and kept spitting and brushed her teeth twice. I didn't care how she felt. I was drunk and wanted my money. But after that, she got used to it. I sold the others, too. I could get them to do whatever I wanted. See, they might have a mother that's strict, or a dope fiend, or a mother that had them at a young age and doesn't want them. I get hold of them and just take control."

For a few weeks Sad Eyes sold the girls and, on occasion, herself. Her teenage prostitution ring was neither typical gang activity nor an anomaly. In San Antonio boys had sold girls, as did boys in Milwaukee. The difference was Sad Eyes, a female, was in charge. The whole time she despised the men she sold to, even while she boasted that they were successful businessmen, with wives and kids. Once I asked her if she had such contempt for her clients, how did she manage not to hate herself. "Oh," she said softly, knowingly, " 'cause I was the one behind the money." Her voice dropped so low that I could hardly hear her. "I was the one that had power. When you're drunk, and I was never not drunk, all I thought about was money and power over these girls, making them do what I wanted. And I'm a girl myself, who's got all these Unknowns and Kings talking about me. I was getting known. It was an image I was building or something."

During a fit of rage one evening, Sad Eyes smashed in one of her Queens' face, breaking her jaw. The injured girl stole out of the house and phoned her mother in Milwaukee for help, crying uncontrollably that she was being held against her will. The police tore apart Sad Eyes' father's house, searching for her. Soon afterward Sad Eyes' mother came down to Chicago and found her daughter in hiding. She told Sad Eyes that Social Services in Milwaukee had taken away her three children.

Sad Eyes headed back to Milwaukee to fight for her children's return. On the morning of her court date, she failed to appear. Two days earlier she had beaten a girl who had accused Sad Eyes' brother of raping her. Just as she had been dragged and beaten years earlier in Watts, Sad Eyes dragged the girl to her house, locking her in an upstairs bedroom. After a few phone calls, she had a buyer. The transaction, though, never went through. One of the Queens staying there let the girl out of the room, perhaps out of pity. Police arrested Sad Eyes a day later. The fourteen-year-old girl she'd attacked was placed in the hospital, where doctors found festering cigarette burns on her body. Now eighteen, Sad Eyes was treated as an adult and sentenced to three years in prison for assault of a minor. "I can't say I'm sorry for what I did. The whole time I was doing it I saw myself as a kid."

DROOPY'S childhood, too, was slipping away.

She stared angrily at her face in the bathroom mirror and tried again to line her huge brown eyes with kohl pencil. *"Shit!"* she yelled for the third time about some invisible flaw, her voice echoing through the upstairs hallway. Little Tina's face ducked out from a doorway, then retreated. She knew to stay out of her older sister's path. I followed Tina into her bedroom, offering to read a book I'd given her weeks earlier, but she looked up at me blankly. She didn't have it anymore. "They," Tina said, meaning someone in her family, "got mad and threw it in the garbage."

Down the hall Droopy stomped into her room. This afternoon she was a fury, cursing and smoking and acting nasty. Tina stole her lipstick, her older sister was an asshole, the shorts she wanted to wear faded in the wash and now they sucked. Somewhere in the course of this tirade I learned the reason for it. Her mother's old boyfriend, one of the gang of four who'd molested Droopy, was downstairs visiting and Droopy's old terror was seeping out. The night before she'd slept with a girlfriend and her brother Juan, so scared was Droopy to be alone, the three of them huddled together sideways in a twin bed, their legs hanging onto the floor. She hated the world now and in this state of mind was in the perfect mood to pick a fight. She sat on the floor, sifting through a pile of letters strewn on her bedroom floor from a girlfriend at Lincoln Hills. "She's so lonely up there. I write her all the time, but I know they aren't showing them to her 'cause she keeps asking why I don't write her. Probably 'cause they think I'm gang-related."

I brought up the man downstairs. "I was thinking it might help if you were counseled by someone who deals with sex abuse."

"No," she replied, not looking up. She viewed everyone's efforts to help her with anger or an air of indifference as if humoring the last attempt by society to save her from her inevitable tragedy. "They tried counseling me at the group home. I never told anybody my problems. I would go crazy if I talked to anyone like that. I cannot talk to a lady. If she sits down and tries to make me look wrong, then right away, I'll get mad and I'll get up and fight her. I don't care."

She made a little sniffing sound, but I couldn't tell if she were crying.

"I wouldn't tell anybody nothing about me. Nothing. Nobody really knows anything about me. They just know who I am and my age."

As she grew more comfortable with me, Sad Eyes made requests during my prison visits. Quarters for the candy machine. A six-pack of Pepsi. A carton of Newports. When it became apparent that I would soon return to New York, she asked me to take her and another inmate, Candy, a Vice Lord, out to dinner. "Ask the superintendent," she told me. To my surprise, permission was granted. It would be the first time Sad Eyes was out on her own in two and a half years.

The women were giddy when I picked them up. Sad Eyes wanted to go to a South Side McDonald's to eat—she hadn't had a Big Mac in more than two years. Candy hoped to use her food money on three roses for an inmate who had comforted her earlier that day while she cried for her mother who lay dying of cancer in the hospital. There was nowhere to park outside the florist, so I told Candy I'd drive around the block and pick her up. Over her shoulder Sad Eyes watched her friend go into a store by herself and grew emotional. "It's really important to us that you trust us. I really appreciate this. I really do. I'm going to be a counselor 'cause of you."

She seemed to be rehearsing her future role. As we rolled down an alley, two little boys on tricycles peddled next to the car. "You should go home to your mommies. It isn't safe here," she called out. Then she turned to me expectantly. "Listen, can I ask you a favor?" The counselor bit had lasted maybe three minutes. I waited for the request for cash to buy weed. Instead she asked if we could visit her mom. She knew the address, although she'd never seen the house; her mother had moved during her incarceration. After I picked up Candy, I headed toward the street address.

A large blonde woman, seated on the porch, chin resting on the railing, straightened at the sight of Sad Eyes, who spotted her mother out the car window before she read the house number. "Oh my God!" her mother wailed to no one. "Sad Eyes is on the run!"

"No! No! It's okay." Rushing to reassure her mother, Sad Eyes flew up the porch steps and collapsed in her arms. A little boy with her brown eyes stared at Sad Eyes silently. Brushing away tears, she reached out to stroke the long braid down his back. "This is Pete, and this is Lily—" She stretched her arm toward a tiny girl with chestnut skin and hair who emerged from the house, smiling shyly. Sad Eyes looked down at her daughter's dress and frowned. "*Damn.* What's wrong with you? Why you so dirty!" She glanced around the porch, at the loose stairs, the couch spewing foam stuffing. "Look at this house!"

Her mother shrugged. "It's a ghetto house."

"What you doing here!" a man with the same brilliant blonde hair as her mother cried out; it was her brother Meany. Soon the porch was crowded with tattooed men and little children and Fat Fred, a potbellied hillbilly-looking gangster who Sad Eyes' mother kept around for a bodyguard.

Mrs. Rodriguez stared at Sad Eyes as though if she looked away, her daughter would disappear. "Two and a half years," she said to no one in particular, eyes shining with the threat of tears. "And just for fighting with that little girl." She wiped at her face. "My God, it's been hard, raising three children."

Sad Eyes would be out in forty-nine days, I remarked.

"It will still be hard. The police harass them. The police know all my children by name."

A wasted-looking Unknown dragged his eyes over Candy, who stood off by herself in the front yard. "You got a nice-assed body."

Meany asked Candy what she was in for.

"Possession of a gauge. A felony."

Meany nodded. "Yeah, that's what they're charging me with."

Candy wandered back to the car, where she sat sideways in the passenger seat with the door opened. I followed to ask if she were okay. "Yeah. I just been crying all day. And now, seeing Sad Eyes, I miss my family."

Ten minutes later Sad Eyes slowly made her way back to the car. Her children scattered. She called out to her oldest girl, Cici, who looked about eight. "You keep away from those alleys and you quit going down the block! You-all don't know when I'm coming by! I'll catch you doing something and you'll get this!" She smacked her hands together, but the child, busy chattering to her friend, wasn't listening. "My family's crazy." Sad Eyes rolled up the window. "Just straight-up ghetto. But you know what? When I get out, I'm gonna take my mama with me. And my kids."

Candy nodded thoughtfully. "That'd be nice."

"I'm gonna take my mama and my kids to a quiet neighborhood. I know it's not gonna be *quiet* quiet. But mellow. I don't want all those gang members going in and out of my house. It feels good that people miss me, but I'm not being missed that much."

None of them, she said wistfully, visited her in prison. "Hasn't been a damn soul ever been there for me since I been locked up three years, not one them bitches except one girl I used to sell and a little Latin Queen who lives upstairs from my mom. Only one of the King brothers came through; he brought me money and looked out for me. We just broke up. I told him, seeing that I was getting out, I don't want a relationship now. I don't want a man. I don't want a woman. I don't want nobody in my life right now but my kids. I want my life back."

A week later I returned alone to Sad Eyes' house. Peering through the screen door, I could see Mrs. Rodriguez in the back, bent over a dryer, one hand on her knee to steady herself, the other clutching a child's pink shirt. Her feet disappeared among a sea of kid's clothes that covered the floor.

She rose with a groan when I called to her, telling me to come around to the back porch, she'd be out in a few minutes. There in the yard a pair of cats, one snow white, the other calico, wandered around Sad Eyes' two youngest children. The cats were the cleanest of the four. A dirt mustache caked Peter's upper lip, his hands and feet were filthy; it crossed my mind that he might have lice.

The back door opened. Mrs. Rodriguez lumbered out and, wincing, lowered herself into a chair, letting out a long breath. As she spoke, her pale blue eyes welled up with tears. "If only you could have known Tama when she was growing up," she said, calling Sad Eyes by her real name. "Oh, she was a beautiful person, absolutely beautiful! There was nothing tarnishable on her. She was very affectionate and kind." She paused to admonish Peter, who scaled the next-door neighbor's stairway. "But see, I kind of pampered her. She never had to do housework when she was little. I was very fast and always going. I had twelve, thirteen neighbor kids at one time, taking care of them in the afternoons. They called me Nina's Day Nursery, there in Chicago. No, I was never afraid of children."

She wiped the sweat from her face on her shoulder. Her stomach hung low, almost between her thighs, the skin on her bare arms sagged, but if you looked at her face long enough—brightened by freckles and sky-blue eyes—she was quite pretty. She did not look Puerto Rican, as Sad Eyes had said, and when I asked if she were, she eyed me strangely. She was a Russian Jew. "Evidently Tama is ashamed of her nationality. Her father is Mexican, but he's never been in the picture." She sighed deeply. "We had terrible fights. I told him I'd give him a year, and that if things were not straightened up, I was leaving, and he'd never see our kids again. Well, nothing changed. He was nice and decent for a while, and then one day, they cut our gas off. When he came home from work, he threw a big baby cream jar and hit me in the head, and I was feeding Tama on my breast. It cut my head wide open. Then he passed out on the couch.

"I asked my oldest son—he was only five years old, he remembers it to this day—'You want to leave now or stay? 'Cause if you want to stay, I'll stay. I will put up with it, but if you want to leave, let's go now, 'cause I can't take no more.' He said, 'Let's leave.'"

I brought up the Unknowns, how Sad Eyes had told me that her mother and father were members. Mrs. Rodriguez squinted at me. "Oh no. I didn't know anything about that. What happened was the leader of the Unknowns sucked me in 'cause he was such a nice neighbor. See, I had a terrible time with my sons. This man told me, 'You know what? I'm gonna make them feel very important. We're gonna try them out.'" She leaned back and shrugged. "What that meant I didn't know. He guaranteed me that within a week my sons wouldn't be sniffing glue. He was such a nice man, I didn't expect anything bad. He dealt with a lot of little kids, taking them to softball, forming a basketball league. I didn't know that they were Unknowns."

As for her youngest daughter, she couldn't recall exactly when she joined the Queens. "Well, I was a very naive person when it came to gangs." Her face grew rueful. "I was just trying to hold things together. But this one night Tama walked in acting strange. I said, 'What in the name of God is wrong with you?' She went, 'Mom, I had to drink so I wouldn't feel it,' and she shows me this 'LQ' on her arm. I was like, 'What does it mean?' I thought maybe love, or something. She said, 'Latin Queen.' I got sick to my stomach. The guy that did it to her, I tried to shoot. He was real old, twenty-five or twenty-six. She was, I don't really know, between eleven and thirteen. I had a fit, but what could I do? Anytime I ever said anything to Tama, she'd tell me I'd never see or hear from her again. Simple as that. I figured she'd run away with the

Queens." She looked down at her red hands and rubbed her knee. "She was always a real good girl—until she started drinking."

Increasingly, though, Mrs. Rodriguez grew more preoccupied with her sons' behavior. With her mother overlooking her pain, Sad Eyes' attempts to gain her attention escalated. I mentioned the birthday in Watts when she ran away. "We didn't know what the hell happened to her," Mrs. Rodriguez said. "Come to find out she'd been in the hospital, she had been beaten up and raped—"

Sad Eyes had not told me about the rape. When I told Mrs. Rodriguez about this omission, she seemed shocked. "He raped her, hell yes! I guess he held her for a couple of days. And his sisters knew about it! She begged them to help her and they wouldn't. After that, she was a lot different. She was still a nice person, but she was very frightened of men. Frightened of a lot of things."

Her mother's account of Sad Eyes' life diverged from her own in other ways. Mrs. Rodriguez admitted knowing that Sad Eyes performed in a strip club at thirteen, snorting coke to work up her nerve, but she denied vigorously that she had provided her signature on a legal contract allowing her daughter to pose for nude photos. "I was the last one to know anything. Like when I found out she was pregnant at thirteen? Of course, I told her she couldn't go with the guy. She said she'd leave. I couldn't take that, so I said, 'We'll work it out. Everything will be okay.' And it never was. It never, never was."

Later in the afternoon Sad Eyes' oldest child Cici returned from school and immediately began to do her homework at the kitchen table. As her grandmother spoke about her mother, the girl pressed her hands against her temples like blinders, but I sensed she took in everything. When she was finished, she handed her grandmother her homework. Mrs. Rodriguez studied it, nodding approvingly, while Cici waited in my lap.

Cici was eight—a year younger than her mother was when she first began having sex. Her grandmother had raised her since she was five, after Sad Eyes ran away to Chicago to start a prostitution ring. When she talked about Sad Eyes' selling young girls, Mrs. Rodriguez cast about, as if looking for somewhere to dislodge something distasteful from her mouth. "She said she was going to Chicago to get a job and asked would I please take care of the kids for the weekend? I said sure. I felt like Milwaukee's not the proper place to raise children, 'cause of all the child molestation here. But she didn't come back. In the meantime, my land-lord came out and seen me with her three children in a one-bedroom apartment and told me I had to get out. I had to go to Chicago to find her. It was chaos. I went through so much hell."

She looked at me with red and watery eyes. "And then, after she got arrested for assaulting that girl?" Her voice faltered and she hit the porch railing with her hand. "That girl was *just* like Tama, a runaway, sleeping with all the guys over here. The judge said he was going to make an example of Tama because she was out of control. Well, maybe, but because she beat the shit out of a girl that put herself on the line? She smacked Tama first. Someone knocks you on your ass, you're gonna get up and knock them back, right? Well, I would think so, or they're gonna call you the biggest sissy in the world. Or the biggest asshole, and I wouldn't be called that. No way.

"But the judge said Tama had no parents—and I was sitting right there in the courtroom! I wouldn't stand up and say he was wrong; he was a judge and I wasn't going to get taken in for something bad, so I just kept my mouth shut. He said she got pregnant—like it was my fault. So I just sat there. And my daughter went to prison."

With Sad Eyes away, Mrs. Rodriguez enrolled in parenting classes to become her grandchildren's foster mother. She also took in her son Meany and his older brother, who was dying of liver cancer, all on a yearly income from Social Security and AFDC of $12,000. She viewed her life as an ongoing struggle; sometimes she fell, her family drifting in and out of illegal behavior, and had to pick herself up and start again. Struggle was all anyone could claim in an environment that showed her few options. Her situation was not one of either/or. The key word was "and." It was possible to be a bad mother at times *and* love your children *and* feel guilty. "Tama thinks I lowered myself by moving here. That this is a ghetto. I'm sure you've heard her say that she wants to move me out of this place. She worries about her brothers being hooked on dope. She wants to change her lifestyle. Tama's changed an awful lot. She claims they've taken the power out of her. Well, now, she's coming home to a big job. I'm here for her. I'll help her. I know sooner or later she's going to be a good mother, too."

I asked Cici, still seated on my lap, if other kids asked her about her mother. The little girl pulled absently at a strand of hair. "I just tell them she's moved away."

. . .

SAD Eyes didn't come home as planned. Months later I found out that she had neglected to tell me that the trip we'd made to visit her mother was prohibited without advance permission. The superintendent learned about it from the photos I'd mailed to Sad Eyes. She was thrown in lockdown and lost her place in the drug treatment program, postponing her release until another opened up and she could complete her stint.

She wasn't expecting me when I went to see her in the fall. Down the hall she argued with someone, demanding to know why she was being sent to the superintendent's office. The muscles in her cheeks tightened when she saw me waiting, but she only said listlessly, "Oh, it's you."

We hadn't spoken since our outing, but her mother told her that I'd gone to see her on my own. This visit obsessed Sad Eyes. "She's not giving me all the details my whole life," she said angrily after she sat down. "Here I've been thinking I was Puerto Rican, I never knew she was white. And Jewish! 'Cause all she talks is Spanish around me. She told me all this other bullshit, that I have stepsisters. My dad has a lot of other kids, 'cause he was a ho. My ma started crying, saying she didn't know how to tell me."

I acknowledged that her stories and her mother's didn't jibe, like how her mother denied belonging to the Unknowns. Sad Eyes flinched as if I'd spit on her. "They used to call her Mama Unknown!" she snapped. "She threw meetings in the house all the time for the Lady Unknowns in Chicago. Whenever the Cobras would come past—she got shot, she tell you that? She got skimmed in the back of the leg, standing outside on the porch."

Disgust and pain crossed her face. She sat silently for a moment, biting her lower lip. "Well, this is bullshit," she said at last. "Now she's fat and just sits in the house and takes care of my kids like she's trying to repay me for all the times that she fucked up my life. Well, she didn't fuck it up, I fucked it up, but she ain't coming out with the truth."

This mess that was her life all boiled down to, Sad Eyes believed, not having a father in the house. She craved a father who would have disciplined her, who cared enough about her to yell at her, and brothers who respected her. "I was being told the wrong things. That's how I grew up so fast." She rubbed her eyes. "I can't deal with all this. I'm tired. I work in the kitchen and do everybody else's work, so I am exhausted."

I started to say something, but she held her hand up. "Don't tell me not to be mad at my ma. I am pissed off at her. And my brothers are nothing but dope fiends. If my ma ever kicks out my older brother, he's gonna come back. I'm tired of it, he done put us through enough pain, why make my mother keep on suffering—lay down and die. I mean, I'm pissed off, but I love her to death, and I would die for her."

There were those who would have Sad Eyes die for them. The superintendent told me that Sad Eyes received death threats from the outside, from Latin Kings who took an unkindly view of certain of her actions, mainly talking to me. She had revealed nothing of the Kings' affairs, yet she was clearly frightened. The superintendent recalled Sad Eyes coming back from a prison excursion, crying violently, unable to be comforted. She had seen a Latin King on the street, and the look he gave her terrified her. "When I was in lockdown, I had a dream I was getting shot," she said now. "Three dreams in a row. The next day I called my house 'cause I was scared that something was going to happen. My cousin told me the niggers were talking shit. He said, 'You know you're going to take it from the head.' 'From the head' means getting taken out in a body bag. I said, 'Yo, I'm not taking no blow to the head. Y'all can't fit in the casket with me.' He wasn't gonna do shit to me 'cause I'm his cousin, but he knows they want to kill me 'cause I want to get out."

Her voice was quiet, but it was not calm. "I want out," she said again. Her fingers found the tattoo below her eye. "I'm tired of people looking at this teardrop and telling me it means something. Yeah, this means something. I'm sick of that old me. When I went to my ma's, I was happy I went with you 'cause I seen something I didn't want to be like."

She met my gaze, her voice a mix of bad feelings: despair, remorse, a deep biting resentment at the culmination of her years. "They're talking shit, saying, 'You giving info.' Yeah, I am. That's my past life and I'm going to give it to whoever I can to make them look at it."

She turned her face to the window. "Let them see what the hell it's about. It ain't all that funny."

WHEN I returned to Milwaukee that fall, the police had finally caught up with Droopy. She pleaded guilty to the assault of the pregnant girl, but just as she had predicted, the fact she'd remained in school while dodging the law had sat well with the judge—appearances are everything in juvenile court—and she received a year's probation. She asked if I would drive her to her first meeting with her probation officer, insisting the bus took five hours. As soon as I pulled up, I spotted her watching for me out the front window, her face looking as though it could break. "I figured you weren't coming," she said in the car. I was three minutes late.

"Ye of little faith."

She smiled without mirth. "I have no faith."

Neither Droopy nor her mother knew the way because ordinarily they rode the bus, nor had they bothered to get directions. I stopped to ask strangers, got on and off wrong highways, which struck Droopy's mother as funny. She asked if I were nervous. I responded that I was afraid I'd make them late. She laughed again, reassuring me that they'd just make another appointment.

About fifteen minutes after Droopy's scheduled time, we pulled off the freeway, heading up a green embankment pruned to golf course perfection toward the impressive yellow-stone structure that housed Milwaukee's Children's Court Center. Next door was the group home Droopy had fled, a modern one-story building overlooking the rolling lawn. But Droopy scoffed at the view. "You hardly ever go outside."

Droopy's probation officer was leaving as we entered the double doors and I rushed to explain why we were late. The three abandoned me to the waiting area. There a teenage boy loped down the majestic wooden staircase to the bottom, where he gripped hands with another boy so that their index fingers pointed up, the Folks' handshake, oblivious to their surroundings. They slid into chairs beneath a poster depicting a group of teenagers casting sinister shadows; the Grim Reaper stood behind a girl, a rat behind one of the boys, next to the warning STREET GANGS: TAKE A CLOSE LOOK AT YOUR FRIENDS. The boys chatted about an old lady who'd been shot in the head and someone who "got sixty years for something he didn't do." Nearby sat a girl, around fifteen, and her mother, the two almost identical, except that the daughter's face was still fresh and hopeful, while her mother's had worn thin, perhaps a sad omen of her daughter's fate.

An hour later Droopy reappeared, lips locked tight, eyes dark. I hoped we could make it to the car without an outburst. The probation officer thanked me for bringing them, then made stabs at small talk, commenting on the weather.

"Fuck you, bitch," Droopy said under her breath, but loud enough that the woman probably heard.

Inside the car, she went off. "The bitch didn't ask me a motherfucking question, just told me to get here by four o' clock! I get out of school at three. We don't have a car. You can't get here all the way from the South Side by four o'clock!" She punched the car door. Droopy knew if she failed to make it on time her probation officer would have already left and Droopy would be blamed for violating court orders. "She read my record and thinks I'm fucked up. She made me seem like I'm whoring the fucking streets. She wants me to fuck up, she don't care."

I suggested Droopy telephone the woman before she boarded the bus so that she realized she was on her way.

"I ain't gonna wait at no fucking bus stop for an hour! All those maniacs be out there and shit. Then I gotta go by the Cobra hood. Do you know how crazy that shit is? I'll be riding back at nine o'clock at night with this—" She waved her tattooed hand. There was no way the trip back would take that long, but the distance provided Droopy with a built-in incentive not to show up.

"I got mad at the way she talked to Droopy," her mother said meekly from the backseat.

"She asked if my ma and me were doing okay. Bitch, it's none of your fucking business! At times we do okay and at times we get into arguments. She don't even know who I am and she acts like I'm an evil-ass person. I done my mistakes and you know that bitch done hers when she was young." She looked out the window at the Milwaukee River. "I may move. Get the fuck out of Milwaukee. My ma says you should take me to Manhattan."

She closed her eyes tightly, then opened them. "This bitch was talking about calling my school every fucking day, like I was some demon. She says if I don't come on time, I'll get locked up again. She doesn't care. She'll put me right back in detention and I swear to God I'm gonna beat the fuck out of her. I don't give a fuck. If I go back in, I'm kicking her ass before I do."

I took Droopy's ranting seriously. For all her fury, she perched on the verge of childish, helpless tears. Droopy, a wounded girl, easily threatened by the slightest feint of hand, was terrified of going back to detention and I believed that she would beat anyone who tried to send her there.

Soon afterward I left her life, uncertain how her story would turn out. I thought of Droopy as I last saw her, angry and scared, and how her future depended on her ability to transcend the model her mother and neighborhood had set for her. Back in New York, I wrote her to learn if she had made it through her probation, but she did not answer my cards. The tinny voice of the computer informed me that the telephone number had been changed to an unpublished number when I called months later. I have not heard from her since.

PART IV
L.A. Redux

HANGING ON THE EDGE

Gangs dropped out of the headlines in L.A. during August 1994. Although kids still killed each other, the action slowed down, the truce between the Crips and the Bloods held in Watts, the city's overall crime rate fell, and O. J. Simpson became the most famous resident of the L.A. County Jail. While away from L.A., I'd spoken to Coco often. Each time her ambivalence about gang life, her relationship with Bird, her poverty reverberated over the line. She viewed impoverishment and Bird as intertwined and continually contemplated leaving him. Roylene offered to fix her up with another ex-gang member, but Coco scoffed, saying she didn't need someone with tattoos all over, she wanted a businessman with money. She'd enrolled in a community college to study child development, leaving Bird to watch the kids while she attended class. When I talked with Bird, he mentioned that he still stopped by the Victory Outreach church occasionally. Reeling from his ex-wife's attempts to wrest his daughter Tasha away from him, he'd begun to rethink his life.

As Coco and Bird grew out of their gangs, her teenage nieces Jade and Wanda immersed themselves even further. One broiling Wednesday I arranged to pick up Wanda at a middle school's cafeteria, where she served lunch to summer school students. The city buses were on strike, an action affecting only those rare Angelenos without cars—primarily blacks and Latinos and poor whites—and she needed a ride home. She hopped off a wall in front of the school, trudging to my car with a slight limp, the lingering reminder of an encounter three months earlier with some Bloods. A gang of fourteen-year-old boys stole the car she was riding in after pulling Wanda out and pistol-whipping her across the face. As she lay unconscious in the street, they drove over her leg. She awoke in the hospital, her face the color of smashed eggplant and her leg in a cast.

None of that mattered now. Tomorrow she would turn seventeen and she pondered what to buy herself. The occasion required a new tattoo, of what, though, or on which part of her anatomy she didn't know—except that it couldn't be anyplace too conspicuous. "For jobs, you know?" She checked her pockets. She had three dollars to her name, four short of the price of a tattoo. Though Wanda also worked part-time at Coca-Cola, both jobs paid minimum wage. The tattoo would have to wait.

We headed back to her house, taking Central Avenue past the corner where Wanda, her sister Jade, and their homeboys usually hung out. This afternoon the small parking lot next to a cinder-block wall spray-painted CRIPS was deserted. Wanda explained that a homeboy had been killed. "He was sixteen years old, his birthday was Friday, and we're supposed to be giving a party, but instead we had a funeral." The Crips' absence was not due to mourning, however, but because they feared that the cops were out to pin the kid's murder on anybody, even his own gang. "First person the police see standing out here wearing blue is going to jail. We got to wait until like September, when it's cooled out. This area is patrolled by a crooked bitch. She plants guns on people. Everybody in jail, it's because of her." Wanda evoked the name of the neighborhood's local gang cop, chasing it with a string of expletives.

At home Jade rested on the porch, G'd-up in Crip-blue shorts and a baggy navy T-shirt. Inside the living room, the curtains were parted to allow a crack of sunlight so that I could make out Wanda and Jade's three-year-old niece seated on the couch next to a round woman with chocolate-hued skin and an alert expression. "This is my sister," their mother told me, beaming. "Next week she'll be *Doctor* Franklin." The young woman smiled shyly as Mrs. Franklin proudly rattled off her sister's accomplishments. After she left, Mrs. Franklin turned to assess her daughters as they traipsed into the room. Jade disappeared into the back. Wanda sat down on the couch. "Jade and Wanda, they are doing fine. I teach my children that they have a choice. It just depends on what choice they make. They ain't no rowdy kids—Jade got a friend sixteen years old who's in prison until she's twenty-five 'cause she robbed a bank! She saw some boys with a Jaguar and wanted to be like them. I told my kids, 'You can have a Volkswagen or a Rolls-Royce. Both of them are going to get you to the same damn place.'"

Wanda laughed nervously, indulging her mother, but footsteps on the porch distracted her and she disappeared out the door. Mrs. Franklin grew quiet, eavesdropping on her daughter's conversation with a young man outside. "That's Wanda's boyfriend, G-Money," she uttered under her breath. The little girl jumped off the couch to spy through the screen door.

G-Money was Crip from his fashionably shaved and shiny head to his telltale blue Pumas with blue shoelaces. Mrs. Franklin leaned on her elbow on the couch, straining to hear. "I don't like him. We were taught to respect black women in my family. He's always talking about bitches and hos." She pulled her tiny granddaughter away from the door. "This little one don't like him either. She scared of him. Wanda!" she bellowed abruptly in response to some remark from the porch. "What'd you say?" She stood up, her neck jutting out in Wanda's direction, the muscles taunt. "You feel that way, you can walk to work tomorrow!"

Apparently Wanda had criticized the ride her mother had found to take her to work during the bus strike. Wanda stepped back inside, smiling sheepishly. G-Money followed. Anxious to calm his girlfriend's mother, he sidled up to Mrs. Franklin. "I can see how you feel, Ma—"

"How would *you* know anything?" Mrs. Franklin cut him off. "You don't know me. You're not my people."

Mrs. Franklin stormed out, leaving G-Money staring slack-mouthed at Wanda, shoulders hunched, palms opened in perplexity. After a few moments, he recovered by conjuring a glittering gold chain from his pocket, which he draped over Wanda's neck. "Happy Birthday." He kissed her and they talked quietly. She told him that she wanted a tattoo to celebrate. G-Money rubbed his bald crown. "I want to tattoo the hood on my head, the way the Mexicans do."

"I want a tattoo," shouted the little girl from her corner, "on my neck!"

The screen door opened and in strode Jade's tall and lanky boyfriend, Ice Capone. At the sound of his voice, Jade appeared in the living room. The two guys launched into paeans to the criminal virtues of their girlfriends. "Wanda and Jade, they gangsters! They more down than some niggers from the hood!" Ice Capone waxed. "I tell you, you do not play with this gang banging. It ain't no joke. Just as you are hard, there's another one who's just as hard as you that'll kill you in a second. *Yeeeah!*" Ice Capone stretched lazily, reaching out to touch Jade's hair. "They gangstas! They can't hide it." His voice dropped. "Their mama didn't raise them like that, so you know they must got it in them."

The little girl grabbed her jump rope, holding it up in the center of the room. "Look at me! Look at!"

G-Money leaned forward, stroking his chin. "I think if I wasn't no Crip, I'd still be shooting and all because it's *in* me. I'm a gangster. Period. Being a man is being a man."

As he said this, Mrs. Franklin came in through the kitchen, causing both young men to visibly straighten. "We're breaking it down for the writer about gang banging," G-Money rushed to inform her. "Some people think we're just killers, but"—he grinned broadly, exposing a shiny gold tooth—"we are intelligent black organized crime."

Mrs. Franklin, a hand on her hip, stared at him, one eyebrow rising dangerously. "If you-all gonna start telling me you represent a street that you don't own—"

Wanda read the look on her mother's face and her foot began moving up and down in frantic meter. "Please, G-Money, do not get my mother started."

But it was too late. Mrs. Franklin's eyes flickered from G-Money to Wanda and back again. G-Money stammered, "Uh, I figure it's 'cause since I was six, my mama been smoking that cocaine. Uh, it's just in me."

Jade slapped the arm of her chair. "Once a robber, always a robber!"

"It's not in you!" Mrs. Franklin yelled, frozen in her position in the center of the room.

The force behind her words shocked the teenagers into silence. Seizing the opportunity, the little girl frantically jumped rope. "Look at me! Look at!"

Mrs. Franklin boomed, "You got a *choice*! You can take the good choice or the bad choice."

"Sometimes you make the good choice and things still don't turn out the way they should go," Ice Capone protested. "The police came to my door and took me to jail for nothing! Twice!" He raised his long arms above his head in mock resignation as Jade popped up to mime frisking him. "Search me all over. Get it over with." Ice Capone grabbed his crotch. "Officer, you missed the best part."

Mrs. Franklin ignored their antics. "When the cops picked you up, they didn't come out of the blue. They knew you from an earlier charge. If you had never been hanging out, they wouldn't have never known you. You *allow* them to know you. Wanda!" Mrs. Franklin shouted, and her daughter jumped. "Who's that lady cop you hate? If you weren't hanging out on 42nd and came home minding your business, she wouldn't bother you."

"Well, yeah." Wanda capitulated. "But some police harass us 'cause they know the way we walk, talk, move, the way we dress. They don't have to know you to harass you."

"Look at me! Look at!" The little girl twirled in circles in her jump rope.

"If they don't have any evidence or reason to come around messing with us, it's not fair." G-Money struggled cautiously with his own logic. "We don't have nothing to do with it. We trying to get our money and have a little fun. We in the ghetto, we're stuck—"

Mrs. Franklin's mouth dropped open. Impossibly, her voice grew louder. "You're not stuck in the ghetto!"

To G-Money, poverty required an imaginative response and he raced on. "My mind is one-track. Get my money. 'Cause I been on the streets all my life."

Wanda dived in to rescue him. "When you been on the streets, I ain't saying you can't change, but he's been doing it all his life. For him to say, 'I ain't gonna rob this man, I ain't gonna sell dope,' he's gonna need some type of help. He got a problem, don't he?"

"Sure he does," Mrs. Franklin snapped, "because he wants something that belongs to somebody else! Don't say that you can't change over-night. It can be done. It can be something that happened to you that night."

G-Money was pleading now. "I ain't seen my mama in nine years. I been in foster homes twelve years. I was eleven years old and left to sleep in empty cars. Selling dope. I was crying and wanted my mama. I had to get a beer and hold that can and cry to myself."

"You constantly using this as an excuse." Mrs. Franklin waved him away. 'I didn't have this in my life—' "

Wanda stopped her. "Think about it, Mommy. If you didn't have no family, what would you do? Would you keep to yourself your whole life? You got to find somebody."

Mrs. Franklin wasn't having it. "Well, Wanda, you fail to understand there's a lot of people in the world who live without their parents."

"Those are people already grown." G-Money plowed on. "Don't you think that makes a nigger just want to go crazy? You need somebody on your side. *I* need somebody. All I *got* is my homeys." He gestured around the room. "Wanda, Jade, Ice are my family. I know, Ma, if I go to your home, you ain't gonna let somebody beat the shit out of me in front of your yard."

Wanda grew excited. "Yeah! You ain't gonna let the slobs"—she used the derogatory word for Bloods—"just come over here and beat him up!" She raised an imaginary gun. "You gonna come out firing your Beretta!"

Mrs. Franklin held her ground. "I'll call 911."

The thought of relying on the police to save them from Bloods made Ice Capone burst out laughing. "I'll be telling you to go get your gun. Give it to me!" He craned his neck to check out the Blood neighborhood outside. "If I go to jail and get life, I can't blame it on nobody. I gangbang 'cause this is what I chose to do. I'm gonna tell you what my grandmother told me when I was just a little buck. She said, 'Boy, you gang banging. I ain't mad at you. If that's what you gonna do, you be the best, whatever you do. Be serious about it. If you want to go to school, get you a job, you can do that, too.' My grandma already know what time it was. She knew she couldn't stop me."

"Yeah," Wanda said, "just think if me and Jade were boys—"

"If you were all boys, it wouldn't make no difference! I'm constantly barking at you 'cause if I was a parent who didn't really care, you-all would be considered alley cats." Mrs. Franklin swirled around toward Ice Capone, wagging her finger in his face. "Your grandma should want a better life for you! You should want a better life for yourself!"

Capone looked confused. "But see—where is the better life coming from?"

"This isn't about gangs, Mama," Wanda stepped in. "It's about people—Ice Capone, G-Money, Jade—we just love everybody from the hood. You can take the gangs away, it's still gonna be niggers representing each other—" She slammed her fist into her palm. "Jade representing me. She's my homegirl, my sister—"

Mrs. Franklin had enough. "You representing your damn self." Her voice tightened like a stuck door. The little girl, now completely wrapped in her jump rope, seized the moment to beseech everyone once more to please look at her. But the teenagers were glued to Mrs. Franklin. "Wanda, you're gonna be in your room!" she shouted suddenly. "Jade and Wanda know that when I get started, it's *on*."

Throughout this encounter I'd said nothing. Now Wanda looked to me for an out. She suggested that we go to the tattoo parlor, leaving Jade with the boys to face her mother's wrath. "My ma's got a split personality," she fumed in the car. Her mother, she thought, was harder on her than she was on Jade. "Mama likes Ice Capone. He only been in jail one time, but G-Money got like seven felonies."

As we drove through her hood, she scanned a back alley, where a crowd of Crips lounged on someone's lawn. Wanda zoomed in on a scrawny girl about thirteen. "That little girl's scared of me 'cause she's messing with G-Money." Wanda waved me on; the girl wasn't worth the trouble. "G-Money is a ho." She stated this without emotion. Though G-Money was her main boyfriend, he was only one of several. "You got to have more than one guy, it ain't cool to have just one. I know he ain't got just one."

She directed me to a bank machine with instructions to watch her back and yell if I noticed anybody suspicious. Cash in hand, Wanda wanted to go to the Slauson swap meet. Located in the middle of Blood territory, the indoor flea market stretches for miles, chockablock with black hair products, makeup, and cheap clothing, along with fashions aimed at the neighborhood's gangs, from the sports jackets and sneakers they favor to solid-gold charms of TEC-9s and marijuana leafs. Nearly all the merchants are Korean-American, a sore issue for some in the community. Activists accuse Korean proprietors of pandering to the neighborhood's worse elements, pointing out that there are more beer, wine, and liquor stores in poor black and Latino neighborhoods than state policy should allow, many Korean-owned. Some stores carried kits of Brillo pads and baking powder, paraphernalia used in cooking crack. Since the 1992 uprising, liquor stores had to meet tough new state requirements, including graffiti cleanup, full-time security, and limits on business hours, and the relations between merchants and customers remained sometimes tense.

At one of the ubiquitous jewelry counters a young chubby-cheeked Korean man in a baseball cap smiled pleasantly at Wanda. She asked to see a large Mickey Mouse charm. The clerk weighed the gold piece, quoting her $250. After a pause, Wanda pulled out the chain G-Money gave her for her birthday, explaining she needed it shortened. "It will look proper when I'm finished, homegirl," the clerk assured her, talking homeboy slang with a thick Korean accent.

Wanda ran her finger along the counter, then asked if he'd give her a good price on a charm—on account of tomorrow was her birthday. She selected a small gold G.

"Proper!" the store clerk repeated. "What's your name, homegirl?" He held out his hand. "South Central Cool B."

The charm cost $17, he said, but for Wanda, he'd charge $14. They shook hands again. "The Koreans are a lot nicer since the riots," Wanda said as we walked away. "They're afraid of us."

On the way out, a truckload of boys cruised by us. Wanda's smile caused the truck to back up, and a lanky guy jumped out. In a minute they'd exchanged numbers.

Wanda tore up the piece of paper in the car. "At that swap meet all those motherfuckers do is collect numbers. That's why I'm glad that I got a pager, so if you really want me, page me, and I might call you back. I just do it to get G-Money jealous when they call." I asked her if she eventually wanted to marry G-Money. "Hell no!" she exclaimed. "The reason I like him is he is like me. He think he's the shit, I know I'm the shit, it's like that."

Finally we arrived at the tattoo "parlor," a small stucco house where life-size cutouts of Superman and Mickey Mouse kept watch over a barren brown yard. A barefoot child with dirt at the corners of his mouth opened a cast-iron gate that hung precariously from a piece of electrical wire and extended a grimy palm, smiling at the quarter I placed there.

Wanda headed around the side of the house, stepping over a dog napping in the shadow of a rusted low-rider, to a yellow cement shack. A Mexican man in a sleeveless T-shirt recognized her, waving us inside. Mariachi marionettes dangled from the ceiling, comic book characters flew along the wall over portraits of the little boy begging at the gate drawn as a superhero and a Budweiser map of Mexico. Wanda spotted a hand-painted T-shirt advertising the name of her hood, above a gun and an eye with a skull for the pupil. "I got to have me that. How come it's not finished, Manny?"

Manny took out a needle, letting Wanda see that it was new. "No one paid for it."

Wanda agreed to pay the outstanding bill for the T-shirt, instructing him to write across the back: GANGSTERS MOVING/CRAZY WANDA. She flipped through a notebook of Manny's tattoo designs. Suddenly she wrote something on a pad: G-MONEY.

I looked at her. "You sure you want his name on you permanently when you just told me you have no plans to marry?"

"I just covered up Wanda's old boyfriend's name," Manny assured me. "People do it all the time."

It was decided that G-Money would reign above her left breast. Five minutes later Manny rubbed Vaseline over the design, handed Wanda a tissue, and collected his seven dollars.

Back at home, Jade raced to the car to see her sister's latest branding. Wanda turned strangely shy, refusing to show her. In the living room the guys looked up from a pizza carton on the floor as Wanda entered, clutching her blouse. Jade announced that Wanda was acting coy and they surrounded her on the couch, holding her down while G-Money unfastened the top button of Wanda's shirt. When he saw his name, his face fell. "What's the point of putting it there?" He jerked away to cross the room, slumping in a chair. "Girl puts a tattoo where no one can see it."

Ice chuckled. "Like hiding your hood's tattoo. That's why Jade and I got them on our arms." Jade raised her fist in the air, displaying CRIPS on her forearm, then slapped Ice Capone's palm. "If we broke up, Jade still be my homegirl!" he hollered. "The bond can't be broke. Even if we don't kiss or nothing no more, that's Jade from the hood."

I wondered if this meant she shared equal status with male Crips and asked Ice Capone if he'd trust Jade to cover his back.

He slid back on the floor, resting against Jade's easy chair, the girl's slender brown legs flanking his shoulders. "Say someone try to rob me? Jade would help. If I got my gun in the car, Jade's supposed to get it. But I try to keep her out of danger. I couldn't come tell her mama. With a boy it's different. We men. Regardless of how big her heart is, she can never be more of a man or gangster than me. Hey!" He tilted back his head and glanced up at her. "Bring me a soda?"

"No."

"Bring it. Say we both get caught. If I go to jail, I expect to call her. 'Bring me this, bring me that.' If she in jail with me, she can't do it." He took the Coke Jade fetched from the kitchen. "So I'm not gonna put her in a risky situation." He looked at his homeboy sulking in the corner. "G-Money feels the same way."

When I saw Wanda a few days later, the gold birthday necklace that G-Money had given her was gone, replaced by a string of bruises around her throat. The night before, she said, Easy Boy, another boyfriend, had stopped by to visit. She told him that G-Money was on his way, but hours passed and he hadn't shown up. At midnight G-Money appeared with his little brother in tow, eager to introduce him to Wanda, when he spotted Easy Boy on the porch. G-Money lurched toward Wanda, shoving her against the house. Wanda was his girl, his bitch, he screamed, his ho. He left before Easy Boy and he fought, but not before he damaged Wanda.

She told me that he'd gone easy on her. Once, when they were watching TV, he'd put a gun to her temple and threatened to blow her head off if he caught her cheating. "My mama don't understand. Him being abandoned by his family made G-Money crazy. But he wouldn't act so jealous if he didn't care for me."

On Friday I pulled up at Coco and Bird's new house, a one-story bungalow with a neatly trimmed yard, just as the couple returned home from the grocery store. Coco looked lean and muscular, wearing a jean skirt and matching halter, her white platforms in her hand, which she handed to Philip to put in the bedroom. She called over her shoulder at him to unload the groceries, but the boy had already started.

I followed Bird, who was carrying his infant son Li'l Chick inside. Though sparsely furnished, the living room was huge, with carpeting the color of AstroTurf, leading into an airy, open kitchen with a built-in table and benches. Philip, Tasha, and Sheba led me to their bedroom, where I doled out comic books. Philip studied the back of his *Spider-Man* comic. YOU CAN EARN THESE PRIZES! the headline screamed above pictures of bicycles, video games, and Barbie dolls. At the bottom faces of white boys and girls grinned out at him beneath copy listing the wonderful prizes they'd earned as the top salespeople. Philip's eyes eagerly jumped from one object to the next. "I'm gonna buy this for me"—he pointed to a toy Jaguar—"and this Barbie for my sister." Trotting out to the living room, he returned with a cordless phone, Coco behind him. "It's okay," she told him. "It'd be good for you to earn your own money." I read the small print, explaining to Philip that he'd have to sell a lot of stationery and gift wrap before he would receive any prizes. Though he asked what stationery was, he was not dissuaded, and at his urging I called the company, who informed me that his sales kit would arrive in three weeks.

Bird later showed me out back to a small house, painted with images of dancing island people, that the previous tenant had used as a bar. Bird planned to convert it into a kids' playhouse. "Did you know I was in jail?" he asked suddenly. "For a month. Domestic abuse." His tone betrayed neither embarrassment nor remorse. "My ex-wife Janet said I hit her. Gini, I haven't seen her since you were here last January. I don't hit women." The D.A. hoped to prosecute him under the three strikes law but dropped the charges when Janet failed to show up in court.

Bird still hustled food stamps at the corner of Manchester and Broadway on Tuesday mornings. The rest of the week he hawked PRAY FOR O.J. and FREE O.J. T-shirts in his old neighborhood in Long Beach, where his gang the Rollin' Twenties and their enemies the Insanes had established a truce. With entrepreneurial flair, he had the shirts printed in their respective colors: yellow-and-black for the Rollin' Twenties, gray-and-black for Insanes. He didn't gang-bang anymore. "I leave that for the teenagers."

Tonight, however, was his twenty-fifth birthday party and he wanted to celebrate big, putting good intentions on hold. Everyone was invited: Coco's relatives, Roylene, the crackheads Bird hired for five bucks to help sell O.J. shirts, and as many Rollin' Twenties as he could pack into the van he'd rented to transport his old friends to South Central. I left him and Coco decorating the backyard with yellow and black streamers.

When I returned for the party that evening, two large teenage girls were screaming obscenities at one another in the living room, ready to pounce. Coco shoved between them, ordering both out of the house if they planned to fight. They retreated, bristling. One of the girls, Tracy, a sixteen-year-old with hair in two ratty pigtails, was a foster child who recently moved in with Coco and for whom Coco received a check from Children's Services in exchange for her care. The other teenager was one of an assortment of runaway, homeless, or otherwise unwanted girls either not yet in, or escaped from, the state's foster system. Coco let them hang around to help with her kids, in turn providing a place to sleep, food, the occasional new outfit, and pocket cash. Such girls were never hard to find. Now that Coco was studying child development, she harbored a dream of opening a foster home as a business.

As I sat in the living room, a dark face peered furtively at me from the doorway, the deep mahogany skin surrounded by a massive halo of wild frizzy hair, then vanished. A moment later she reappeared, rushing barefoot into the room, arms and legs flailing, as she playfully struck Philip on the back, then darted for cover. I could see her in the bedroom, still eyeing me like a skittish animal. This was Scat.

I'd seen her once before at Coco's, mistaking her for one of Bird's crackhead T-shirt sales force. She never spoke to me, just stared, as if not comprehending my questions. I guessed her to be in her early twenties, but Coco told me she was thirteen, her mental facilities damaged from a life on the streets. Scat and her mother were homeless. Nightly her mother roamed barefoot and wild-eyed down Figueroa, trading her body for crack. Sometimes they slept on bus benches. Sometimes men took them home, where Scat lay awake, listening, as the sound of her mother's desperate sex drifted through the wall. Sometimes the men came into Scat's room.

Now she crept out of the children's bedroom to perch on the arm of my chair, stroking my hair as the room filled with partygoers. Most were women. Coco's homegirl Q-Mac was there, talking about the Four Trey picnic in the park that weekend. Bird's old girlfriend Roylene was also on hand. She'd been pregnant the last time I saw her six months ago, but did not look so now. When we found a chance to talk, she confided that she had miscarried. "It happened while my neighborhood was at war. They were shooting day and night, it didn't matter. I was tense and worried. My son and I didn't go out of the house for a week. We kept the doors locked and the shades pulled. When we heard gunfire, we'd hit the floor. My boy asked me if they were going to shoot him. Instead I lost his little sister."

As she spoke, I became aware that a woman with a single curl plastered in the center of her forehead like a 1920s flapper was watching me from across the room. Roylene followed my gaze to the woman, who must have been five-feet-ten and hippy, wearing tiny denim shorts cut high on her protruding rump. Another of Roylene's dancer friends. Roylene winked. "Lots of strippers like women." Roylene had arranged for the woman and another stripper to perform at Bird's party, whittling them down from $100 to $75 plus tips to dance for three songs.

About an hour later Bird's van pulled up, and some two dozen young men spilled onto the AstroTurf carpet in their black-and-gold Steelers jackets, like a football team on a steroid overdose. A little girl about three wandered through their legs wearing a T-shirt advertising BENSON & HEDGES 100'S. Some were baldheaded, a couple were pigtailed or corn-rowed, all wore low-riding Levi's with blue bandannas peeking out of their pockets. The older ones loomed on the edges of the room, silently sipping beers, eyes running over the crowd like minesweepers. The younger ones noisily clapped shoulders or hugged each other in viselike embraces. A fast-talking, wisecracking Twenty called Baby Crazy lurched toward the stereo, twisting the knobs until Ice T's voice roared into the room:

"She got wild in the backstage bathroom,
sucked my dick like a muthafuckin'
vacuum, said, 'I love you, but my daddy don't play,
he's the fuckin' Grand Wizard of the KKK.'"

Coco's son Philip and Roylene's five-year-old boy excitedly took the floor, grabbing their crotches and pumping against the carpet to the stereo's pounding bass, which rattled the bottles of booze on the kitchen table. The room swelled with heat and life and color, like blood rushing to the brain. Scat abandoned her post at the arm of my chair and disappeared into the party. In the midst of this chaos, Coco's baby Li'l Chick crawled across the floor, tugged at my leg, then curled up in my lap, promptly falling asleep.

After a couple hours, I pressed through the throng, heading for the cool of the porch. Outside a young man in a blue-and-white-striped T-shirt, probably about twenty, glanced at me, his face registering recognition. He said he'd heard I'd been pulled over by the police while hanging out with Bird and the Rollin' Twenties last winter. A small smile crossed his lips. He was glad it happened so that I could understand what it was like to be harassed. Above us a helicopter hung in the sky, but he barely noticed the white blaze of its searchlights burning circles in the yard.

Curious, a few minutes later I climbed into my car to trail the helicopter. Police had blocked off the next street with flares, as more helicopters crisscrossed the sky. A shooting had occurred just behind Coco's house.

While I was gone, I missed the depraved main event of the night, which began once the strippers performed. Sometime around eleven, the big woman with the flapper's curl shimmied out of her shorts down to a red G-string, gyrating in the men's faces. Unlike the men I'd seen at Roylene's strip party, who'd watched passively, impotently, the boys from Long Beach whooped and howled. Despite their enthusiasm, the boys either knew no better or simply refused to tip. After the third song and still no bills, the dancers picked up their clothes and beat a hasty exit. Scat, who throughout the night had stolen sips of alcohol, became overexcited by the music, the boys' leers, their approving hoots. She and another teenage girl popped out of the bedroom wearing only swimsuits, hungry for attention. The other girl danced as she'd seen the professionals, slapping away the boys' hands, demanding money. But Scat mimicked Philip and Roylene's little boy, wildly tugging at her crotch and thrusting her pelvis. Someone grabbed her arm, wrestling her onto the carpet on her back. Quickly he straddled her and pretended to hump her.

A cheer went up in the room. "Go for it!" someone yelled.

Then others piled on top of her until she disappeared, only her bare feet visible, waving in the air. Some of the women left for the kitchen, but others watched, expressionless or laughing. Coco checked the bedroom to make sure the kids stayed inside. In the living room Baby Crazy came up from the heap, his finger raised in the air, then turned to the onlookers and stuck his finger inside his mouth with an exaggerated expression of satisfaction. Another boy made his way around the circle, commanding boys to sniff his hand.

Abruptly the music stopped. "That's enough!" Bird charged through the crowd, pulling homeboys off Scat. "What you think you're doing? Go to the motel with that." He announced that it was time to cut the birthday cake, after which everyone had to go home; Coco and the kids were ready to go to sleep. Most of the boys hopped up, a few grumbling, and followed Bird into the backyard. Abandoned on the floor, Scat looked dazed and a little frightened, but she told the nearly empty room that she had fun.

A little while later Q-Mac and Coco came in from outside and heard a high-pitched voice from behind the bathroom door, crying, "It hurts!" They pounded on the door until it opened and a stocky young man sauntered out, tugging up his jeans as he brushed past the women. Behind him trailed Scat, sheepishly avoiding their eyes.

Scat ducked into the children's bedroom—the kids were all outside—and stayed there for a long time with the lights off. Q-Mac knocked on the door, softly asking why she wasn't eating cake, but Scat replied only that she didn't want to go. "I said, 'You feel stupid, huh?'" Q-Mac recalled. "She just looked at me, she don't have everything that belongs to her. I asked why she let that guy in the bathroom do that to her. She kept saying she didn't know. I asked, 'Did he ejaculate in you?' 'Yeah.' 'Did he wear a rubber?' 'No.' 'What if he gave you a disease, what you gonna do?' 'I don't know.' 'What if you're pregnant?' I told her she needed to sit down and talk to her mother about what she did and have her take her to the doctor the next day or whatever. 'Cause she's thirteen years old, just a baby still. She don't need to experience nothing like that."

A few days after the party, Scat went back to her mother.

AFTER that night, Coco cut all ties to gangs. Though she viewed Scat's experience as a sorry episode, it was not the deciding event. She had simply outgrown the chaos. Bird drifted back into hanging out with friends, street hustling remaining his sole means of support. Coco possessed no moral qualms about accepting money from the illicit sales, but the threat of the police taking Bird away from the family hovered over her like a vulture.

One evening, long after I'd returned to New York, she called to tell me of new plans that would finally change her life. She'd met someone at college. "He's a churchgoing man. He talks white, just like you, Gini. I don't want him to know all the stuff I did; he's always saying how awful gang bangers are." Breathless, she bubbled on: he ran the catering truck on campus, he earned $30,000 a year, he had a contract with a well-known singer and was going to Texas to perform. He'd asked her to come with him, where he'd buy a house for her and the kids. Cuffing the receiver, she lowered her voice. "He even told me I could take Tasha with us. If we took Bird to court and I told them I'm going to college, they'd give me that child quick. Bird just wants that check. Tasha should be mine. By the time he finds out, I'll be gone."

Whatever I'd seen of Bird, his love for his kids, especially Tasha, remained constant and I couldn't hide my surprise. "Bird hasn't done right by me," Coco responded. "First, cheating with Roylene. Now some girl has been calling me, saying things." She sighed softly. "I really don't care what he does with women. At least he watches the kids while I'm at school.

"I'm going to college. I don't need no more stress on me," she said. "I prayed and asked the Lord to deliver me. If Bird don't get it together, it's time to raise my kids right and walk away. I mean that from the bottom of my heart. Whether I have another man in my life or not, I need education and money. I do not plan to be on AFDC all my life. Women get wiser much quicker than a man. A man will take his time. If a woman ain't strong enough to say, 'That's enough,' she's gonna fall, too."

In the background I heard a small familiar voice, and Coco put Philip on the phone. It was a weekday and I asked why he wasn't in class. He'd been out for a week, he said, because he wanted to change schools. "There's too many gang bangers, sixth-grade boys. They been writing on the wall and peeing on the floor. They pick on people. Call the girls sluts."

When she came back on the phone, Coco told me that she was pregnant. "I'm not having it, Gini. I don't want to stop school for nothin'. Bird's mad 'cause it might be a boy. We had a long talk. I don't want anyone to discourage me. I'm gonna work to get my kids out of here. I got too many kids. I'm caught up in poverty. I made up my mind this year's gonna be different."

FALLING

The year was different, but not in the way Coco hoped. One day in March 1995, while she was at class, a grease fire ignited on the stove. Tracy, the foster girl who baby-sat, threw water on the fire and the shooting flames torched the ceiling. Philip broke down the bedroom door to rescue Li'l Chick, who was locked inside. The boy staggered outside, cradling his baby brother, his eyes red and teary, and paramedics rushed him to the hospital for smoke inhalation. Coco arrived home to find nothing but the smoldering foundation, her children nowhere in sight.

For seven months she went from shelters to family members to friends, wearing down their support with her erratic behavior. I called Coco's mother, who didn't know where she was. "She had to drop out of college. Isn't that a shame? She had gone so far." She broke up with Bird and moved in with the new man she'd told me about, but in time he'd asked her to leave after his ex-wife threatened him with a custody suit for his daughter.

I returned once more to Los Angeles to look for Coco. Wanda called one night to say that she'd run into her and arranged to have us meet at the Franklins' house the next morning. As I pulled up, Wanda came out, looking as athletic as ever in a blue T-shirt and sweat pants. Immediately she raised her pant leg to reveal her new tattoo: WANDA. The G-MONEY above her breast had been skillfully transformed into an abstract geometrical design. G-Money was in prison for eight years for drug sales. Her other suitor Easy Boy was in jail for a credit union robbery, although the charges weren't expected to stick. Wanda stayed away from her hood for now after a homeboy beat her up because his girlfriend claimed that Wanda spread rumors about her. She pointed to her ivory Chevy. The back tires were slashed, the handiwork of her homeboy. Wanda shrugged. She didn't have time to hang out anymore, not when she was holding down two jobs and in September would be back in school.

Wanda still had her hustles—the Chevy Capri was one of four cars Wanda was working on. I wondered how she managed to buy a fleet of used cars on the salary she made at Coca-Cola part-time and she described a system she'd developed that involved stealing cars, then stripping them down and reselling the parts for quick cash. With the money she bought old cheap cars, spending her weekends hunting for parts at the U Pick U Save lot, crawling under junk cars in the hot sun. "See, you buy a car for $200, put $200 worth of work in, then sell it for $700. You keep doing this, that's how you make your money. I want to be a mechanic."

Inside Jade sat in the dark living room with Mrs. Franklin. Something seemed different. Then I figured it out, Jade had traded in her usual Crip-blue uniform for a white T-shirt and shorts in a bright summer print that showed off her coltish legs. She'd broken up with Ice Capone and to everyone's surprise—except her mother's—had quit gang banging. I mentioned a rumor I'd heard that she was pregnant. Jade made a face. "Naah. See, I been a tomboy all my life. I wasn't even thinking about sex. I was fighting, gang banging. I waited until seventeen. I didn't want to be pressured, didn't want to rush into it. You know, you got to love a person, trust a person."

"Are you calming down now?"

She stretched her long legs in front of her. "Of course. As you get older, you get more mature. You ain't like you used to be. Like right now I ain't really into school. But I know if I want to graduate and better my education, I've got to go to school and do better. It's like when you a teenager, you think you know everything. Can't nobody tell you nothing. You think you a woman."

I thought back to the night Mrs. Franklin browbeat her children in the living room. Now the woman sat quietly, listening to her daughter explain gang banging as a teenage phase, something Mrs. Franklin had once said to me. "I used to be into track, basketball, cheerleading. I don't even know how I got to this. I wouldn't have lost no friends." Jade gently smoothed down her ponytail with her hand. "But since I been gang banging, I done lost a few friends. You be like, 'Damn! That nigger was supposed to live till he was like twenty-something.' "

WANDA peeked behind the curtain through the front window. "Coco's comin'."

Mrs. Franklin glanced sideways out the screen door and whispered. "Coco is a mess. A real mess. It's sad."

One by one Coco's ragtag family drifted in the room. Philip came first, in a dusty striped T-shirt, the waistband of dingy gray boxer shorts peeking over the top of worn jeans too big to belong to him. He struggled with a large duffel bag and the strap broke, spilling its contents on the floor: a first-aid box filled with football trading cards, a water gun, some empty video cases. This sad collection was what remained of his possessions after the fire. I moved to hug him, but he pulled away with a vacant look.

Coco trailed behind him. Her hair, which she always took pains to style, was haphazardly pulled up in a wild topknot. Her blunt, expressionless face was ashen and broken out; the whites of her eyes bore a yellow cast. Like her son, she seemed distracted. I asked where she was staying. Before she could answer, Philip responded listlessly, "In the car."

She shot him a look, but there it was, in the open for all her relations to hear. "I ran out of money. A hotel's forty-five dollars a night. That goes fast."

Outside on the porch someone stumbled, then Sheba appeared at the door in tears. A large scratch ran across the toddler's forehead and there was a nasty bruise over one eye. Coco explained that her cousin had hit her.

Next came Coco's foster child Tracy, carrying another infant I didn't recognize at first but who turned out to be Li'l Chick. Coco had given birth to Sheba and her baby brother so close together that they were now both two years old and looked like identical twins. I bent down to pick him up, but Sheba, fiercely possessive of her brother, brushed away my hand, burying her tear-stained face in his chubby neck.

Tasha, though, failed to appear and I asked after her.

"Tasha!" Sheba yelled out, fleetingly happy, then confusion took over her tiny face. "Gone."

"She's with Bird," Coco said shortly. She talked with her relatives and the kids wandered back outside. I followed them, finding Philip straddling the porch railing. "Gini, I hate L.A." Head bent down, he pondered a ragged shoelace. "I want to move away. But my mom, she don't listen."

"Where do you want to move to?"

"I don't know. Anywhere. I want to see snow. I hate L.A." Behind him was Coco's battered blue station wagon, where Philip said they'd spent the last three evenings. Nightmares plagued him nightly. "People come in there and rape you while you sleep." I rested my hand on the railing and he reached over and touched it lightly, a sparrow's foot resting on a vine. "How come you're not in New York?"

"I'm just visiting. Visiting you."

"I wanna go to New York. Will you take me?"

Coco and I had once discussed the possibility of Philip visiting me out there. Back then I had the feeling that she and Bird weren't sold on the idea. Now it crossed my mind that she might have prodded him to ask me. "Can my mom come, too?" he added. Through the screen Coco started tidying the Franklins' living room, her habit when she felt tense. I called to her, asking if she could sleep at her mother's. "My mother threw me and my kids out. I'm never talking to her again. And Bird threw his kids out. I'm not talking to him." Mrs. Franklin caught my eye, then looked away.

Coco wanted me to follow her to her old landlord's, who she hoped would let her keep some clothes at his office. She ran to her station wagon and hauled out a television from the pile of green Hefty bags holding the last of their belongings, carrying it inside the Franklins' for safekeeping. Then Wanda, Jade, and the kids piled into my rented Toyota for the trip to the landlord. Crunched against the window, Wanda made some crack about the cramped car.

Philip's expression turned ugly. "You do anything to Gini's car, I'll pull out a gun and shoot you."

Wanda glanced down at him, her mouth slowly twisting into a smirk. "Spell 'gun.'"

Philip, who at seven didn't yet read, suddenly seemed flushed and shy, looking away in humiliation.

In the lot where Coco's house once stood work crews erected a new frame. Coco behaved as though the house were hers, marching through the rooms, pointing out where the stove would be, the layout of the bathroom, the color of the children's room, even though the landlord had not agreed to rent to her again. Afterward she left the station wagon parked in front and I drove them to the food stamps office on Manchester and Broadway. Bird loitered outside with a group of men, a couple I recognized from their Steelers gear as Rollin' Twenties. Coco ducked into the office, not looking at him.

Bird gave a toothy grin, hugging me hello as I joined him on the street. His hands clutched a wad of bills and food stamps. I noticed a gash on his bicep and asked who'd stabbed him. He chuckled. "Coco."

He stuck his head through my car window. "Hey, Li'l Chick, what's—" He halted at the sight of Sheba's bruised face. "What happened to her?"

Tracy mumbled something about Sheba's cousin hitting her. Bird fixed on Philip, his voice rising. "Did you jump on your cousin?"

The boy fiddled with a thread on the seat upholstery. "I hit him."

"Look at me!" Bird's voice exploded inside the tiny car. "Did you jump on him? Don't be lying to me."

"I did bust him! I don't have no reason to lie."

"You better not be. You're supposed to bust anyone who hits your sister." Bird stepped away as Coco returned from the food stamps office. In the car she pounced on Philip. "What are you doing, talking to him? Don't you *ever* talk to him! He threw you out." Coco's chest rose heavily; she was having trouble breathing. "I had them at Bird's house and wanted to take a blanket so I could sleep in the car. He didn't want to give it up. We fought and he threw the kids out. Over a blanket!"

I asked her about stabbing Bird to pull her attention away from Philip. "Is that what he said? I didn't stab him. It was a tire jack. Everything he says is to make himself look good."

Throughout the morning we took care of errands. Wherever we went—the bank, the store—Coco flirted desperately with men, an act laced with pathos. In a parking lot she complimented a security guard, who stiffened, focusing on passing traffic as she swooned about his uniform and build. Meanwhile we waited inside the packed car, sweltering with the smell of stale bodies. Sheba whimpered that she had to pee. At last Tracy opened the door, I thought to find a rest room for the child, but Sheba hiked up her dress—she was naked underneath—and squatted on the curb, clearly a habit.

Finally I dropped Coco and her brood back at her station wagon with cash for a motel. "Whew, that Tracy girl was stinky!" Jade fanned her hand in front of her nose. "Worse than Sheba's pee! Coco's always got a pack of little homeless girls, like Scat."

Scat, Wanda now informed me, was working the streets. "She's a ho. I saw her standing at the corner, the light changed three or four times, the girl wasn't going anywhere." Wanda sighed. "God forgive me for saying this, but Coco could have been something if she didn't have all those kids. One right after another—Li'l Chick and his sister, both two! Men want you to have all their kids so you can't have no life."

In the next breath Wanda defended Bird. "I don't care what Coco say, she did something to Bird. There's no way that man would give up his kids over a blanket. Of the two, Coco's less stable. Where's all Coco's money going? She could get another apartment. She's still getting $700 from the county, which ain't a lot, but she gets food stamps and nobody sees the food stamps and nobody sees the money. She's always looking for a man to help her. You can't depend on a man. No man's gonna take a woman with three kids who doesn't have a job, someone who's gonna drag him down. You got to meet in the middle. Her son Philip's gonna grow up hustling dope, jacking people to get money to help his brother and sisters. He's gonna be in and out of jail. And eventually he's gonna resent Coco."

I mentioned that I was considering taking Philip with me for a trip to New York. The girls didn't say anything for a while, then Wanda spoke again. "You do that, the whole family's gonna fall apart. That little boy's the one holding it together."

THE next morning, on a hunch, I headed back to the corner of Manchester and Broadway. There was Coco, resting on top of a car hood in front of the food stamps joint, waving as I passed. I suspected that, faced with her current circumstances, she'd resorted to selling food stamps herself. Philip raced up, his curly hair tamed into two tight braids, jumping in the front seat to show me a ten-dollar bill. Breathlessly the boy told me that the night before someone stole his duffel bag of belongings from the car, but he'd hidden a box of football cards in the seat. He'd just sold them on the corner.

Coco's face appeared at my window, a big bump in the middle of her forehead. She'd fought with some teenage girls who had jumped Tracy, her foster daughter. Despite the bruise, she looked better. Her hair was combed in a pretty bun and she wore a short brown skirt and vest with matching boots. She'd spent part of the money I'd given her to wash their clothes, some $45 worth of laundry. Roylene let them spend the night, lying to social workers looking for Tracy that she and Coco's family lived with her. Given the choice between roaming the street with Coco or returning to the custody of the state and the tidal flow of human tragedy that made up California's foster care system, Tracy would take her chances on the street.

After collecting Tracy and the two toddlers at the corner, I took them to Sizzler. Coco herded the toddlers to the salad bar, piling their bowls high with orange slices, peaches, watermelon, pineapples. Philip circled the banquet of food, plate positioned, shoveling on macaroni and cheese, beef enchiladas, luncheon meats, baked zucchini, baked beans, and carrots. He ate three servings, then headed to the dessert table, returning with two heaping bowls of red Jell-O and whipped cream. Coco barely touched a thing, collapsing in the booth behind us, her head resting heavily against the seat back.

Once the children finished gorging themselves, Coco, desperate for sleep, wanted to use the rest of her money for a motel. She directed me to one on Florence and Vernon, a beige two-story stucco building that actually looked all right. A woman with a stroller and a toddler stood in the parking lot with a couple of men, sipping beers. There was no office, just a booth where the clerk sat behind scratched bulletproof glass. I started to follow Coco to the window, but Philip stopped me. "Just wait, Gini. This might cost too much money."

Coco argued with the woman. She returned, asking for $10 more. Ordinarily a room was $32, but the woman upped the price when she saw the carload of kids. I only had $4 left. "She'll have to take this," Coco said. "I'll give her the rest later."

Room 19 was a drab box with a small double bed and no towels, but not the flophouse I'd feared. As soon as he was in the door, Philip pulled out the TV from the wall, sliding his ten-dollar bill behind the set. The rest of the children piled on the bed and fell asleep almost instantly, the teenager Tracy among them, collapsed in a fetal position, sucking her thumb.

Coco embarked on her story of troubles as she alienated one friend or relative after another. Money went fast on the street; they ate their meals out, slept in motels, had to replace their destroyed clothes. "I beat a Mexican man recently, robbed him 'cause I was so angry. I needed to put a roof on my head. Bird will tell you how the police were chasing me. I regret jacking people for money." She briefly looked lost, as though she'd forgotten who and where she was. "I thought I was over that."

An hour later the kids began stirring. Li'l Chick was smelling pretty badly. Coco removed his soiled diaper, though she didn't have a fresh one. Tracy woke up with her cheek stained with bright tears. No one asked why.

THE last time I saw Coco she'd called me at the apartment where I was staying. Sick in bed with the flu, I hadn't gone out in a week and was leaving the next day. I listened to her on the answering machine, to the sugary tones she adopted when she wanted something, reluctant to call her back. Like her relatives, I was running out of patience, aware she manipulated me. Once on the phone, she excitedly asked me to meet her. Her car had broken down. "Bird won't give me any money. I saw him driving around with a woman and I flagged him down. He drove away." Overnight her indignation with Bird dissipated, and she humbled herself, begging him for money in front of another woman. He'd agreed to take Sheba and Li'l Chick to his relatives whom Coco had fought with last year. She then called Roylene, who told her that she was busy, and Mrs. Franklin, who said that Jade and Wanda weren't home. She was left with Philip and Tracy, wandering the sidewalks in the unforgiving August heat. I explained that I was too sick to meet her.

But falling back asleep was impossible as I played the phone call over in my head: Philip's small drained voice whining into the phone that he was hungry. Maybe Coco put him up to it, but that didn't really matter. I paged her. She whispered that she couldn't talk, the people who owned the phone were growing annoyed and she was still trying to find somewhere to sleep. I said I'd give her money for a motel, agreeing to meet her at 73rd and Broadway.

She flagged me down and led me to a back alley behind a mean, rundown apartment building. A guy in a knit cap, sagging khakis, and a blue sweatshirt trudged over to check me out. Behind him limped a young man with a cane and a lazy eye. Coco introduced them as her homeys from Grape Street Watts Crips. No one looked like they were doing very well. Philip came out bare-chested, wrestling with yet another dusty black bag he'd found somewhere, but this one was nearly empty, his belongings having dwindled away, left behind in hotels, forgotten on street corners. His feet hurt, he complained. "Philip, I can't do anything about it," Coco muttered as she and Tracy crawled in. As the car crept down the alley, a homeless man with eyes the colors of egg yolks, pushing a shopping cart, yelled at me to blow him.

I dropped her off in the parking lot. One year out of gangs, Coco was worn down by motherhood, ruined hopes, and bad luck that followed her like an unwanted dog. Gang life had distracted her from the hardships of poverty and invested her with a sense of invincibility, but the longer she lingered in the straight world, the more elusive the feeling grew—and she feared failure. I handed her enough cash for a night in the motel. Coco wadded it up, not looking at me. "I'm gonna get my life together," she promised—to me, more than to herself—her gaze sinking into some bleak interior landscape. Then she gathered the remainder of her family behind her and they trudged through the lot, the California sunset sky deepening to indigo. "We're just going through some bad times."

CONGRATULATIONS, IT'S A GIRL

TJ cried the morning of her first wedding anniversary, a day that served merely as a marker in her solitude. The young disguise artist from Lennox-13 stood in the doorway of her apartment, blinking at me in the white sunlight, wearing an ankle-length dress in navy with tiny white flowers. The golden hair was gone and her own chestnut mane flowed over her shoulders, framing pale sullen features.

She let me in the living room, where her chubby-cheeked infant daughter cheerfully swatted at the grunting pro wrestlers on the TV set. TJ met the child's father through the mail while he was incarcerated, the cell mate of a homeboy who told her that the new inmate had no friends. TJ, who was nothing if not loyal, wrote to him out of pity. Upon his release, she moved in with him and soon became pregnant. Later they married and as her husband adjusted to life on the outside as an ex-con, she struggled to accept the passivity and limitations she felt as a new wife and mother. They moved out of Lennox to escape its dangers and lures, fleeing to an identical city of strip malls and modest pastel stucco apartments just south, off the San Diego Freeway. TJ took care of the baby and grew up fast; her husband, who had no such requirement, often stayed out till 3 A.M.

A month earlier, on the fourth of July, he had declared his independence. Since then he'd stayed in East L.A., getting high with his friends. She'd called him one day to let him know that his daughter, while looking at his picture, had blurted out, "Daddy," her first word, and he'd left an excited message on her machine but never came by. "I don't think he'd ever have left me if she were a boy."

TJ's mother crouched in front of the fireplace, scissors in one hand, the Sunday paper in another. Her body looked heavy and shapeless beneath her T-shirt, but her face was smooth, with blue eyes, like a doll's. "Hello," she muttered, lips pressed tight on a cigarette, not glancing up, before attacking a coupon with the scissors. Still not looking up, she protested as TJ started to show me around, "TJ! This place is a mess!" But it wasn't. It was a light, airy three-bedroom apartment, all blue and beige. We went into TJ's bedroom, pretty and girlish, with a nightstand draped with a pink tablecloth and a pastel quilt covering the bed, where we stretched out. "I cried in church today," she said, smiling thinly. She'd gone to a "prophecy lady," an elderly black woman in Inglewood who catered to the faithful. "She said I had a sweet heart. No one's ever called me sweet before." The church woman told TJ that she had survived her gang days because God protected her on the street and her ex-husband would be safe there, too, because he had a sanctified wife. But she warned TJ that if she fell, he'd fall harder, dumping one more burden onto the young woman's shoulders.

Her little daughter followed us in, busying herself dropping TJ's hairbrush on the floor, then reached for a paycheck on the nightstand. TJ snatched it from her. She'd lost her job designing children's books when she and her husband moved from Lennox and she now worked in a factory, painting ceramic animals for $4.50 an hour. To apply for the job, she'd tried to remove her tattoos, slicing the ones off her fingers with a scalpel, although she'd mangled one on her leg and half still remained. This week she'd filled in for a supervisor. GREAT JOB! her boss had written on the pay stub. With overtime she managed to pay $600 in rent. TJ lived with her mother, not, as I thought, because she needed financial help, but because her mother couldn't make her own rent of $825 each month. TJ's mother was among thousands of California employees abandoned by the aerospace industry. Since she was laid off in 1991, she could find only part-time work as a security guard.

Despite TJ's own meager salary, and with no support from her husband, TJ had taken herself off welfare. "I no longer need cash assistance," she'd written AFDC. "I have been working (and reporting it) and my job is now permanent. I will not cash this check." But she had no health insurance and wanted to maintain her Medicaid benefits.

Later in the afternoon, after she'd put her daughter to sleep, she talked about her old life when she disguised herself as a man to carry out a payback shooting. The muscles in her throat tightened visibly. "My old life—it's like a movie. Do I feel regret? Regret? What is it? What can I do with that? I'm not sure. But I can talk to another person or kids at church. I know the score. If you go to a rich counselor or psychologist, they haven't walked the walk.

"I see the future as hard. It's gonna be grim. I can't protect my daughter from that. But I'll teach her about the Bible. Education is the only answer. Can you cook better with a good cookbook or without? I'm gonna have to give her a good cookbook. I'm gonna teach her how to be life-smart and make wise decisions. When I was growing up, I didn't know right from wrong. I didn't have guilt. I was street-smart and book-smart, but I didn't know nothing about life choices. I went to mass and went to confession, but I didn't know it was a sin to do tattoos. I didn't know it was a sin to lose my virginity. I didn't know it was a precious thing to give away; no one told me that. I know my mom didn't.

"I didn't want to end up like my mom, raising a kid on my own." She chuckled wryly. "My mom can't stand my husband, says he's just like my father. Now I see myself working my whole life, breaking my back. Alone."

Near the bedroom door hung a pencil drawing of a nude man and woman locked in an embrace. She noticed me looking at it and said she'd drawn it for her husband as a gift. She wanted him back, not just as a father for their child, but for the companionship. "I don't know if I'm just weak with guys. I was suicidal a few months ago. He was gone, I was working all the time, I thought maybe I should give my child away." She put her head down a moment, then raised it and the words came rushing out. "It sounds awful, but I regret having her. I didn't want this responsibility so young. I'm twenty-two years old. I miss freedom. I want to have fun. I want to go scuba diving, bungee jumping, horseback riding. I never had fun in Lennox when I was in a gang. Hitting up walls, tagging my name, that was fun because I could do it well. There was nothing else to do. I guess that's why you resort to stealing. I don't want to blame anybody. But there's no horses, no farms. Just concrete to play ghetto ball. And that gets boring. If it weren't for the church, I'd be dead or in jail. If I hadn't had someone to listen to me, show me something outside existed. Otherwise you are enclosed in four invisible walls."

She stood up and went into the kitchen to prepare a bottle for her daughter. Her mother called the two of us into the living room to take our photograph, then TJ walked me out to my car. "What pisses me off is that my husband has his freedom. I'm the one who's trapped." And she with so much more potential than he, I thought to myself. "At least I gave my marriage my best shot. And I needed welfare to survive," she said, sighing, making a truce with her circumstances.

Then I was on the highway, leaving TJ to her daughter and her mother and the approaching night, fraught with missing promise.

COMING OF AGE IN AMERICA

Back in TJ's old turf of Lennox the scene was a hotbed of gunfire that summer. The Mexican Mafia's imposed truce, fragile from the start, was crumbling and four boys had died. Among the reasons for the breakdown were packs of graffiti artists called "taggers" who had pushed into the neighborhood. Like gang bangers, taggers dressed in hip-hop clothes, their weapon a can of spray paint used in the artistic rendering of their name, or "tag." Unlike gangs, who paint graffiti to mark their boundaries, taggers at first pledged loyalty only to their individual talent, but in the last year rivalries had ignited into fights and shootings, leading to the moniker "tag bangers." Lennox-13 greeted the newcomers with a show of force. Its leaders put out the word that the taggers either join one of the Lennox cliques or risk being killed.

This placed Shygirl in the awkward position of defending her cousin Annie, whose best friend was a tagger. Shygirl liked Annie's friend all right, but she didn't respect him, and her protective side feared for his safety. He begged to be jumped in to Shygirl's clique, and despite lingering doubts that he possessed the guts, she put him through the ritual beating herself, one-on-one. But once a member of Lennox-13, the boy continued to hang out with taggers, in direct violation of the mandate. Finally a group of Lennox renegades shot up his house, in effect creating the crisis situation of a gang turning against its own members. For her role in the matter, Shygirl lost rank within Lennox, a devastating blow.

Her disappointment was deep. She and some others jumped the boy out of Lennox and this time she released her fury upon him, kicking him in the head while he lay writhing on the ground, leaving her boot print on his face. But afterward, instead of towing the line, Shygirl's cousin Annie grew even more committed to her tagging crew. Police arrested her and another girl for attacking a rival tagger with a billiard ball hidden in a sock; they'd hit him full-force in the face, shattering his nose. Again and again Annie brashly challenged Shygirl's authority, forcing her to choose between her cousin and her gang.

Shygirl's attempts to go back to school failed, too. It'd been the same old story. The moment she entered a classroom the teacher saw her LENNOX tattoo defiantly branded across her forehead and came down harder on Shygirl than the other students. Eventually she found it difficult to show up in the morning, and the high school kicked her out, citing bad attendance, grades, and the threat she posed by virtue of her past reputation.

Sometimes the strain showed on her face. When she became lost in thought, she'd purse her lips and clench her jaw tight, like a fist. At night she'd roll herself up into a ball in her bed, crying from pain. A close girlfriend, seeing the damage in Shygirl's dark eyes, invited her to come stay with her in Riverside, where her own parents had moved to take her away from the gangs.

Shygirl stayed away for four months and now wanted to return to Lennox to look for a job. Rachel Romero, the counselor from the middle school, volunteered to make the one-hour drive to Riverside to pick her up. She brought along a friend of Shygirl's named Flip, not only to cheer up Shygirl but to give Flip a needed break from the neighborhood as well. Flip was a fast-talking, gun-snapping tomboy, with blue eyes—one slightly cocked—dirty blonde hair, and bad skin. Well-versed in Lennox lore, she was never jumped in, believing that gang life was purchased at the price of one's soul. "If they come to you at three o'clock in the morning and say, 'You have to do this,' there's no way of backing down. I don't want no one owning me. 'Cause you can't get out of it. Shygirl's cousin Annie didn't understand the ban on taggers, she said it wasn't fair. Shygirl even knew it wasn't fair, but you've got to understand it's not about being fair, it's about what the homeboys do. You've got to back up what the homeboys do, whether it's fair or not."

Instead of gang banging, Flip had become a tattoo artist, trying to make a name for herself. A few days earlier she'd tattooed her brother's name on her ankle. "Only one more tat," Flip said, "but I'm saving my back."

"You're saving your back?" Romero sounded incredulous. "For what?"

"For my dead homeboys."

Romero exhaled. "Putting a roll call of dead homeboys on your back . . ."

"If I'd already tattooed the name of every boy who died in eleventh grade, I wouldn't have a spot left."

"It's already been done. Ask TJ. She tattooed a whole roster on this homegirl's back. Next to each one it says 'Rest In Peace.' She has some twenty names. You're not supposed to do that to your body." She shot a glance at Flip. "The dead don't see it."

Flip and Romero disagreed on much, Romero always allowing the girl to express herself, then gently trying to show her another side. Romero encouraged her to experience the world outside of Lennox, but Flip didn't see the point. "It's all good in the hood," she repeated like a mantra. "If the rest of the world blew up, you could find everything you need in Lennox. They got a supermarket. They got a Pizza Loca. They got love. They got hate."

"They don't have a city hall."

"Build one!"

"They don't have a disco."

"Just put on some tapes. *Whew!*" The stench of a cattle ranch or slaughterhouse distracted Flip. "Must be some 18th Street girls down here!" She laughed at her own swipe at a Lennox enemy. "Damn! I didn't know there were cows like this in California!" She thrust her head out the window, her hair whipping about her face. "Where the hell are we? I've never seen so many trees in one place!" She rolled up the window. "Oh, poor Shygirl!"

Romero exited the freeway, making a series of turns until we came upon a two-lane residential road where local stores displayed Western fronts with names like the Cowgirl Café and the Saloon. "Are you serious?" Flip asked. "Shygirl's living *here?*"

Romero pulled up in front of a small house, where Shygirl and her girlfriend waited outside. Shygirl looked conspicuously out of place in this rural setting, wearing a baggy T-shirt, shorts, and a baseball cap that she raised in greeting, revealing a newly shaven head that rendered her bald and virtually unrecognizable as a female. The two girls led us behind the house, where the family raised hens and roosters. Shygirl loved fighting roosters, taking four-hour trips to bet on cockfights. Flip was going crazy from the dog barking, the smell of manure. Tiptoeing through mud, she crept up to the solitary cow as Shygirl dashed to the house for a camera.

Everyone headed inside and plopped down on an overstuffed couch. A *trompe l'oeil* of a rain forest covered one entire wall, dominating the living room. After some excited small talk, Romero turned serious.

"Have you gone to the hospital?"

Shygirl studied her fingernails. "What?" Clearly she heard the question.

"You haven't, have you."

"I'm gonna go. I'm gonna go Sunday." Shygirl said, then giggled.

Romero didn't laugh, sticking her face close to Shygirl's to look her in the eyes. "You broke your appointment today. I want you to make a new one. When was the last time you had a headache?"

"She had one at the West Side party," Flip offered. "That was supposed to be her excuse for having an attitude with everybody."

Shygirl's other friend looked somber. "She had one Sunday, too. She cried all day. She's had two since she's been here."

"The doctor gave me pills," Shygirl said weakly, searching for an out.

"What kind of pills?" Romero asked.

"What is this, a quiz? It was Motrin, but with codeine in it."

Shygirl, I learned, had suffered severe headaches during the past months. The girls thought maybe her cousin Annie's betrayal and her loss of rank caused too much stress and hoped the move to Riverside would relieve it. But a few weeks earlier Shygirl had blacked out. Frantic, her mother's friend placed alcohol beneath her nose, but it did nothing. Minutes passed. When she did come to, she refused to go to a hospital. Then last week, after much prodding, she went to a doctor. Preliminary tests suggested a brain tumor.

She was to go back for more tests, but so far had put it off. The main reason Romero was taking Shygirl back to Lennox was so that she could monitor the girl's doctor visits. In the car on the way home, she tried to talk with Shygirl about her cousin, urging her to let it go. But Shygirl seethed.

"It's a difficult time for Annie," Romero said evenly. "She's feeling ostracized. She just turned eighteen and graduated, too. It's scary to be eighteen and out there. The taggers have become some support. You wouldn't want to beat her up, beat her into reality, if she didn't mean the world to you guys. One thing she's confident about is that she's still got your love—"

Flip snapped, "She ain't gonna have no love if Shygirl's motherfuck-ing head busts open!"

Romero didn't flinch. "That's not a reality to her. You will work things out. People come around. Patience is necessary. It's like when I'm trying to help a kid who keeps pushing me away. You have to be strong enough to say, 'I'll let you go and do it on your own and when the time comes that you're ready for me to be there to help you, I'll come running.'"

Shygirl was quiet for a long time. When she finally spoke, her voice was steely. "You know what, Miss Romero? Fuck that." She turned away from the older woman to look out the window, but it was dark now and she stared into the eyes of her own reflection. "She's pushed me too far. I'm gonna beat her ass when I get back to Lennox."

ROMERO won in the end. Not long after Shygirl returned to Lennox, the gang unit hauled her in on a weapon possession charge, carrying her .380 in her underwear again. The Lennox sheriff's department, long an admirer of the middle school's ongoing struggle to help kids in gangs, made a deal with Romero. If Shygirl stayed in school and kept out of trouble for a year, they'd drop the charge.

A year later, when I returned to L.A., I didn't see Shygirl. She was too busy working at a Toys "R" Us, an unpaid internship, part of an alterna-tive high school's curriculum. Instead Romero and I met at Jim's, a hamburger stand at 111th and Lennox, the heart of the neighborhood. As we ate chorizo and eggs, kids marched by the window, knocking on the glass to wave to Romero and trade private jokes in Spanish. After a medical exam failed to show a tumor, Romero believed that Shygirl's headaches weren't physical but repressed anger. As her accomplishments increased, they came less frequently. Romero raved about Shygirl's prog-ress. Shygirl received her driver's license so that she could drive to work, no small feat in a neighborhood where kids pile up too many arrests to qualify for a license or are too poor to own a car. "My assistant said the driving instructor took one look at the tattoo on her forehead and really put Shygirl through the ringer, gave her the longest test. My assistant was furious, but Shygirl shrugged it off.

"She is trying so hard, it would bring tears to your eyes. Sometimes when she's at work she's been covering the tattoo with makeup. She's talking about going to the high school prom. She doesn't know I'm aware of this, but at school she bumped into a rival girl. For a moment they stared at each other, then both smiled. It just wasn't a priority anymore."

Romero waited to see how Lennox-13 would react to Shygirl's new role. "It's very difficult to get out. She played an important part in her gang. But she's smart. She trained someone to take her place, advises him and gives him direction, so her absence isn't as great a shock. They know her heart is there for them, but she's paid her dues. She doesn't go places that might be dangerous for her. In this area she will always be known."

Another kid stopped at the table to tease the counselor. Her energy for the kids seemed boundless. She kept a pager with her at all times; I'd seen her race out of a restaurant or suddenly stop her truck to return a phone call from a kid in need. In her early thirties, she had few romantic relationships because of the energy she poured into girls like Shygirl. "A lot of kids say to me, 'I'm really glad you're not married and don't have kids.' I say, 'God, why?' They answer because they wouldn't be able to spend as much time with me. But if I got married, the kids would probably wind up at my house anyway, to baby-sit or hang out. I've had dreams like that. But it's a rare man who would take the kind of life that I lead."

Her relationship with gang girls constituted a courtship. It took time to gain their trust. Ironically one of the hardest girls I had met, the one most people would have given up on, represented one of Romero's greatest successes. "I love Shygirl," she said without embarrassment. "She touches a place in my heart I haven't been to in a while. I don't know why her. It's the same as asking why you fall in love with one person and not another. There's not one factor. I think I love her for her potential, for her capacity to love others, and for the amount of pain she has gone through to still make it."

Romero told Shygirl that she could retire from counseling if she knew there was someone to replace her who would love the kids the way she loved them. She arranged for Shygirl to meet with the Lennox Middle School principal, who promised if she completed high school or took the GED test, he would guarantee her a job at the middle school. "He wasn't judging her exterior, he was judging what he sees every day, the amount of love she has for this community and how he might redirect that energy. Because if he could take the energy she puts into the neighborhood and put it into the school, she could do some amazing things. If they trust you're taking them in the right direction, they're willing to give up everything to follow you. These kids have already risked death. Once you've got their loyalty, it's a to-the-death type of loyalty. People have just got to see that."

Epilogue

Once more TJ carefully dressed for what lay ahead. Black hat pulled low, proclaiming LENNOX in large letters, baggy pants, the forty-inch waist hanging from her twenty-eight-inch frame, plaid flannel shirt fit for a lumberjack. Fully G'd-up. She sauntered through the round tables of businessmen and women, the successful citizens of her community, tax-paying, law-abiding churchgoers, the white and upper-middle-class. A few quickly looked down at their plates as she passed, embarrassed. Others tensed apprehensively. When they learned that TJ had been invited to speak at their Kiwanis' Good Friday brunch, a few protested, demanding to know why she, a gang banger, was addressing them.

TJ took the stage, meeting their wary stares. Although she didn't look it, she felt jittery. She'd never backed down on the street, but there she was among equals, and a gun always helped. Here she was alone, with nothing to rely on but her wits. The wrong move and she risked public humiliation.

"All of you have a preconceived notion of me," she said in a strong, even voice, which sounded fiercely nonchalant to some in the audience. "Some of you are probably afraid when you see me, some of you are probably saddened. At one time you had a right to be." In one hand she clutched a ragged roll of paper that she now held up, letting it unscroll almost to the floor. Her arrest record. She recited the charges, none of which ever made it into court, a litany of auto theft, drunk driving, kidnapping, and vandalism. Ignoring shocked expressions in the audience, TJ kept going, detailing past horrors. Suddenly her voice softened.

She described how she found refuge in the church. As she spoke, she bent down and untied her shoes, stepping out of her sneakers into a pair of high heels.

"Don't think you cannot make a difference in someone's life," she went on, unbuttoning the plaid shirt. "The person who helped change my life was not Hispanic, he was not a gang banger, he was just an old bearded guy." She threw a smile at the pastor of her church as she snatched off the Lennox cap, freeing hair that fell past her shoulders.

"I'm here to tell you not to judge a book by its cover." TJ stepped out of the huge baggy trousers to reveal the burgundy dress pants and suit jacket underneath. She paused to allow the crowd a long look at the strong, clear-eyed young woman in front of them. "Just as I changed in front of you now is how someone's heart can change if you show them how."

Around the room TJ spotted a few approving nods. "When you see a kid like me, don't judge her by her clothes. There may be a child of God underneath."

The room echoed with applause.

Afterword

Shortly before I left San Antonio, I went to a party thrown by an all-girl gang called the Bad Girls, a band of tough fighters who had earned the respect of the local male gangs. Now in their late teens or early twenties, most of the members had given up fighting, but tonight they swapped war stories—the time a bullet reduced the macho father of one girl's baby to a paraplegic, or the night a B-Girl was attacked by eleven Queens and survived. I sat at the kitchen table with a young couple, Mary and Charlie. Mary, pretty with an olive complexion, green eyes, and a lovely smile, had left the Bad Girls to raise her infant son. Her boyfriend Charlie, though not the baby's father, was helping her care for the child. Charlie had been a hard-core gang banger himself. He grew up in East Oakland, California, where he stole his first car and made his first drug deal at the age of twelve. When his family moved to San Antonio, he joined the Ghetto Boys. While he was locked up in juvenile jail, Charlie's mother helped to run the gang, holding meetings and stockpiling guns at her house. "I'd do drive-bys, shoot people, break in houses. I figured if I got busted, that's the way it goes," Charlie said flatly. "Until I met Mary. Then everything changed. She calmed me down."

While the other teenagers partied, Mary and Charlie talked with me throughout the evening. Charlie wanted to make sure I told the public what was going on. What impressed me was that this couple had changed their lives without any external help or support, but sheerly through their own willpower. Mary, during a moment alone with me, admitted that it had taken time to come this far. Charlie once had been possessive and abusive, but she was proud that they'd worked things out. "He's learning because of my little boy."

A week later I got a phone call. "Remember me?" Mary asked in a hushed voice. A few nights after we'd met she, Charlie and some of his friends sat on her porch, playing with a .22 revolver. Mary begged them to put the gun away, but Charlie grinned and assured her they were just kidding around. He smacked the chamber against his palm, checking for bullets, then stuck the barrel to his temple in a mock gesture of Russian roulette. But he'd made a mistake. When he pulled the trigger, it fired.

She stayed with him in the hospital until the next afternoon. When she returned, Charlie's angry mother barred her from his room, believing her son had shot himself because Mary had fought with him. The TV news reported that Charlie's gun accidentally went off during an argument with his girlfriend; a rumor spread among his old gang that there'd been a setup and Mary was somehow responsible. Someone called her house, threatening her. The day before she called me Charlie had died.

On the phone, Mary politely asked me for a donation toward the funeral. "We have no money to pay for a coffin," she said softly. "If the insurance company rules it was suicide, it won't pay anything."

During the course of writing this book, none of the girls I met were killed. They simply do not die at the same rate as the boys. Instead, like Mary, they are left behind to pick up the pieces, to scrape together money for all the funerals, to raise their children without fathers. When society gives up on such young women, it abandons the next generation of children they are raising as well.

In ten years the number of teenagers in the United States is predicted to increase 22 percent. The Juvenile Justice Department anticipates that by the year 2010, violent crime will double and the number of juvenile arrests for murder will jump 145 percent. If they remain overlooked, young girls will be among these new criminals.

I am not a sociologist or politician. I approached this book as a journalist. In immersing myself in the lives of these girls, however, I have come to some conclusions. The first and foremost is that I believe society has an obligation to save its children, simply because they are children.

In these political times, society has become obsessed with punishment, rallying for an end to efforts to rehabilitate criminals. There are few funds for youth programs; Democrats and Republicans pour money into prisons, demanding that states lengthen sentences and cut amenities, and make younger and younger children eligible to be tried as adults. In Wisconsin the age requirement has dropped to as low as ten years of age. It costs $30,000 to $40,000 in Wisconsin to imprison a person for a year. California, with the highest juvenile incarceration rate in the United States—twice the national average—spends $32,000 a year on each adolescent inmate at the California Youth Authority, the country's largest juvenile prison system. Yet the state doles out roughly only $4,000 yearly to educate one child in a school system that suffers from the most crowded classrooms in the nation.

As I write this, the likelihood is there will be no rehabilitative programs, education, or jobs for troubled youth in the foreseeable future. It's simply not on either party's agenda. Instead the gang girls who manage to go straight through their own personal strength will most likely face careers of unsatisfying minimum-wage work, without benefits or opportunity for advancement for themselves or their children. It is no wonder that many children today are given to the very unchildish apprehension that life is a dead end. For them, there's little reason to adhere to the sustaining tenet of the American dream: that the way to happiness is through hard work and sacrifice. "The collective 'we' has failed," says Father Greg Boyle, of Dolores Mission Parish in L.A., a man known as the "gang priest." "There has always been a ghetto, but in the sixties there were social programs, and while they didn't benefit most residents, they did put some brakes on the deterioration and provide some hope. In the past, the kids got into gangs before they really began life. Now they're never going to begin life."

The fact that gangs are increasingly violent is a barometer of the state of childhood itself. The message our kids are sending is chillingly clear: society has failed to provide nurturing, attention, safety, discipline, and positive role models. We've left behind a generation of children to choose from a set of increasingly bleak options.

▮ found these thoughts in a notebook scrawled in a weak moment after a long night in San Antonio:

It's like everyone told me, You can't trust these kids. They'll manipulate you and turn on you for no reason at all . . . They're hopeless.

But we can't give up hope. Three years ago I attended a conference on youth violence, where New York senator Daniel Patrick Moynihan, a lifetime student of social welfare policy, decreed that we had simply lost the next two generations of children to crime. Holding up a graph illustrating how the same disaster occurred in the 1850s when German and Irish immigrant kids ran wild in the streets, he attributed the problem to unwed mothers and the perils of illegitimacy and said, essentially, that we would have to forget these children's potential and write them out of our future.

Yet they are in our future, whether as partners in the rebuilding of a damaged society or as casualties and perpetrators of that damage. The feeling of futility is one we can't afford.

I began my story about violent girls in fear, but I end it with a note of hope. As often as not, kids like TJ will turn away from crime—choose not to become criminals—if given another option. Not because they are compelled to do so, but because it makes sense to them. In TJ's case the church made the difference. Shygirl made the change with a supportive school counselor. Alicia turned the corner with the arrival of a baby, struggling to become a good mother, even with little means of support. None remained the remorseless monsters of newspapers and talk shows. We need to get to know these girls. Once we see them as individuals, we might become more determined to find the money, time, and people to help them. If we want to save them, we must be willing to pay the cost of education and prevention and intervention programs for kids who are hard to reach. But first we have to listen.

Author's Note and Acknowledgments

Because most of the gang girls were minors, and because I believed many of them would outgrow their lifestyle and, therefore, should not be stigmatized as adults, the names of the girls and young women in gangs have been altered, along with some identifying traits. Similarly family members, friends', and boyfriends' names have also been changed. None, however, is a composite character. True names have been used for all other adults, except when noted in the text.

I witnessed the majority of scenes described in this book, except in those cases in which a person remembered a past event. I note in the text when a scene is being recalled by a participant. In those instances where dialogue is recreated, it was based on the memory of one participant, and in some cases, two or three.

Because this book involves gang children, who may exaggerate a story to inflate their importance, I tried to verify such memories with at least two other sources, including other children, parents, or police. This was not always possible, yet I was able to double-check the majority of accounts.

I did not pay anyone for cooperating with me, and everyone who spoke with me did so without the promise of any remuneration, but there were times I helped out the girls financially in small ways. I paid for meals at McDonald's or for rides at a carnival. When Coco, for example, needed money for a lawyer, I gave her $100 toward the fee; later I paid for two nights in a motel after she had become homeless. The women and girls repaid me in priceless ways with their time and candor.

• • •

WRITING is often described as solitary work, but I could not have completed this book without the generous help of many friends and strangers. From the start my editor Roger Scholl shared my interest in and sympathy for these neglected girls. Much, much thanks for his belief in this book and the intelligence and acuity of his editing for improving it. Thanks to my agents Laurie Fox and Linda Chester, who spurred me on to write this in the first place, and, in the same office, to the very able Joanna Pulcini.

I owe a world of gratitude to L. Suzanne Stockman, researcher extraordinaire, for her tireless energy and invaluable help in all stages of preparation of the manuscript; also to Staci Bonner, Debi Taffet, and Jeryl Brunner for additional research. Diane Croland and Lynn Simmons put in countless hours transcribing tapes recorded under the most inaudible circumstances.

I'm grateful to the talented magazine editors who assigned me to write about gangs: Diane Cardwell, Phil Sudo, and Steve Manning.

In each city I visited, strangers reached out to me, offering their expertise and hospitality. A few of them appear in the pages of this book, but there were many others. In Los Angeles, thanks to members of the L.A. County sheriff's department for their time and experience: Wes McBride, Toni Martinez, Ralph Ruedas, Herb Giron, Holly Perez; at the LAPD: Kraig M. Seltzer, John Radtke, Chris Amador, Roylene Saulsberry. Also thanks to Irene Davila, and especially Socorro Aguilar, of the Los Angeles County Probation Office, for many hours of help; Father Greg Boyle, Marianne Diaz-Parton, Pastor Mark Garcia, Mike Rayo, Dan Jurenka, and Dr. Amondo Morales.

In San Antonio, I am indebted to the Good Samaritan Center and members of its dedicated and intrepid staff (Mingo Bueno, Joe Gallegos, Roy Valdez, Andy Hernandez) and the Downtown Youth Drop-In Center; other counselors on the front lines: Cynthia Test, Serafin Sanchez, Lanny Schooley, Jimmy Ybarra, Arturo Chavez, Reverend Michael Harrington, Reverend Ann Helmke, and Johnny Zamarippa; Kyle Coleman and Jeff Colunga of the sheriff's gang unit; Raul Flores and Reuben Frausto of the San Antonio Independent School District Police; those officers in the San Antonio police department who spoke with me despite an official refusal on the part of the department to do so; Mike

Martinez of the juvenile probation department; also Tanji Patton, Sister Mildred Truchard, Julio Chaperon, and Carlie Estefan.

One young woman in San Antonio deserves particular mention, especially since, much to my regret, I could not find room for her in this book. I met Jennifer Ontiveros at the city's gang summit, where she spoke out against her old gang even as she received death threats. But she would not be silenced. In the spring of 1994 she was invited to Washington, D.C., to talk at President Clinton's conference on urban violence. She is now enrolled in college, working toward her education degree and achieving her goal of teaching at-risk kids and providing female models for young Latinas. She was a constant source of inspiration.

In Milwaukee: Gary Graika, Lisa McElwee, and Anthony Adams of the Social Development Commission; Jose Flores of Milwaukee County Fighting Back; James E. Causey, Tom Held, and Jesse Garza at the *Milwaukee Journal Sentinel*; Rocio delCarmen Medico, Nestor Figueroa, John Holmes, Shari Greske of Career Youth Development, and the members of the Milwaukee police department who spoke with me, also despite an official refusal on the part of the department.

Other experts around the country who helped me include Dick Busha, Diane Crucius, Pat James, and Terry Timm of Lincoln Hills School; Duane "Duke" Voltmer, Carl Upchurch, George Kalergios, John Galea, Marc Bullaro, William Cahn, Loren Evenrud, and especially Sandy Hahn. I am indebted to the work of Anne Campbell, John Hagedorn, Joan Moore, Mike Davis, Luis Rodriguez, James Diego Vigil, and Léon Bing.

For friends and family who fed and sheltered me during my reporting: my cousins Tommy and Greg Kepner, my fearless aunt Charlotte Von Rosenberg, my grandmother Virgie Kryshak for her prayers, and my brother and sister-in-law Rex and Carolyn Sikes, who not only put me up but helped in the research. My mother and father, Rex and Mary Sikes, offered me tremendous support and fifty-seven videotapes of every television show that had the remotest connection to gangs.

Several writing teachers offered invaluable advice: Bruce Porter, Joyce Johnson, Carole Klein. In addition a number of friends read this manuscript, or portions of it, and gave me their encouragement and advice. Special thanks to: Tina Ruyter, Nina Malkin, Robin Glenn, Ken Miller, Julie Ries, Stephen Williams, Betsy Israel, Ellen Welty, Judy Meyers, Val

Van Galder, Adrienne Rich, Josh Weinstien, Richard Swearinger, Maria Duryeé, Cynthia Webb, and The Writers Room. Thanks also to Shane Stevenson for the lesson in firearms.

I met my soul mate David Conrad shortly before I embarked for a year of travel to do this book. He endured my absence and my tears, shared my victories, and married me when it was finished. I can't begin to thank him for all the support, intelligent advice, editorial wisdom, and spiritual uplift I receive from him.

Finally I thank the girls and young women in this book who opened their hearts and lives to me. Their decision to let me, and subsequently readers, into their world was a brave act and it was done with the hope their stories might make a difference for other girls.

—Gini Sikes
New York City
1996